# Learn Chart.js

Create interactive visualizations for the Web with Chart.js 2

**Helder da Rocha**

**BIRMINGHAM - MUMBAI**

# Learn Chart.js

**Commissioning Editor:** Kunal Chaudhari
**Content Development Editor:** Pranay Fereira
**Technical Editor:** Diksha Wakode
**Copy Editor:** Safis Editing
**Project Coordinator:** Kinjal Bari
**Proofreader:** Safis Editing
**Indexer:** Manju Arasan
**Graphics:** Alishon Mendonsa
**Production Coordinator:** Nilesh Mohite

First published: February 2019

Production reference: 1280219

Published by Packt Publishing Ltd.
Livery Place
35 Livery Street
Birmingham
B3 2PB, UK.

ISBN 978-1-78934-248-2

www.packtpub.com

`mapt.io`

Mapt is an online digital library that gives you full access to over 5,000 books and videos, as well as industry leading tools to help you plan your personal development and advance your career. For more information, please visit our website.

# Why subscribe?

- Spend less time learning and more time coding with practical eBooks and Videos from over 4,000 industry professionals

- Improve your learning with Skill Plans built especially for you

- Get a free eBook or video every month

- Mapt is fully searchable

- Copy and paste, print, and bookmark content

# Packt.com

Did you know that Packt offers eBook versions of every book published, with PDF and ePub files available? You can upgrade to the eBook version at `www.packt.com` and as a print book customer, you are entitled to a discount on the eBook copy. Get in touch with us at `customercare@packtpub.com` for more details.

At `www.packt.com`, you can also read a collection of free technical articles, sign up for a range of free newsletters, and receive exclusive discounts and offers on Packt books and eBooks.

# Contributors

## About the author

**Helder da Rocha** has taught, written, and developed applications with Java and web technologies since 1995. In 1996, he wrote one of the first books in Portuguese about HTML and JavaScript. Since then he has created hundreds of presentations, tutorials, and course materials on Java, Java EE, programming tools, patterns, techniques, methodologies, HTML, CSS, JavaScript, SVG, XML, data visualization, Arduino, and the Internet of Things. He holds a master's degree in computer science. He also has a background in the visual arts and design and has some of his artwork in permanent museum exhibits. He lives in São Paulo, Brazil, where he works as an independent consultant, developer, and instructor, and is a frequent speaker at technological events.

*I would like to thank my wife, Ana Carolina, and my daughter, Marina, for their patience and inspiration. Many examples created for this book use data from public portals and scientific publications. Thanks to the researchers for sharing it, which certainly made this book much more interesting. Finally, I must thank the creators of Chart.js 2.0, Ranner Linsley, Evert Timberg, and the GitHub community, since this book would not exist without them.*

# About the reviewer

**Bruno Joseph D'mello** is proactively working at Truckx as a full stack developer. He is a JS enthusiast and loves working with open source communities. He possesses more than 6 years' experience in web development. Bruno follows kaizen and enjoys the freedom of architecting new things at work. He is socially active via coaching web technologies or participating in other research projects and meetups. When not engaged with technology, Bruno likes to spend quality time traveling with family and friends.

*I would like to thank my family for their patience and support, especially my mom.*

# Packt is searching for authors like you

If you're interested in becoming an author for Packt, please visit `authors.packtpub.com` and apply today. We have worked with thousands of developers and tech professionals, just like you, to help them share their insight with the global tech community. You can make a general application, apply for a specific hot topic that we are recruiting an author for, or submit your own idea.

# Table of Contents

**Preface**   1

**Chapter 1: Introduction**   5
  **Data visualization**   6
    Chart types   6
    Choosing a chart   7
    Web-based visualizations   11
  **Why use a data visualization library?**   11
    Creating data visualizations for the Web   11
  **How to use this book**   15
  **Summary**   17
  **References**   18

**Chapter 2: Technology Fundamentals**   19
  **Essential JavaScript for Chart.js**   20
    Browser tools   20
    JavaScript types and variables   21
    Data structures used in charts   22
    Arrays   22
    Strings   25
    Functions   27
    Objects   28
  **Other technologies**   30
    HTML Document Object Model(DOM)   30
    Cascading Style Sheets   33
    JQuery fundamentals   36
    HTML5 Canvas   37
  **Data formats**   41
    CSV   42
    XML   43
    JSON   43
  **Loading and parsing external data files**   44
    Using a Web server   45
    Loading files using standard JavaScript   45
    Loading files using JQuery   46
    Loading files using the standard Fetch API   46
    Parsing JSON   47
    Parsing CSV   48
    Loading multiple files   48
    Displaying a map   48

**Extracting and transforming data**                       51
  Online tools                                    51
  Extracting data with XPath                      52
**Summary**                                                 55

**Chapter 3: Chart.js - Quick Start**                       57
**Introduction to Chart.js**                                58
  Installation and setup                          58
**Creating a simple bar chart**                             61
  Setting up the graphics context                 61
**Creating a bar chart**                                    63
**Configuring colors, fonts, and responsiveness**           66
  Dataset configuration for bar charts            66
**Options configuration**                                   68
  Text and fonts                                  70
**Global defaults**                                         72
**Transitions, interactions, and tooltips**                 73
  Transition duration                             73
**Updating charts**                                         73
  Tooltips                                        75
**Working with larger and multiple datasets**               76
  Loading data                                    76
**Horizontal bar chart**                                    79
  Adding extra datasets                           80
**Stacking bars**                                           83
**Summary**                                                 85
**References**                                              85

**Chapter 4: Creating Charts**                              87
**Line and area charts**                                    87
  Creating a simple line chart                    88
  Dataset configuration                           89
  Options configuration for line charts           95
  Line charts with more than one dataset          96
  Loading data from external files                99
**Stacked area charts**                                     104
**Radar charts**                                            108
**Pie and doughnut charts**                                 113
  Creating a simple pie chart                     113
  Dataset properties for pie charts               115
  Configuration options                           116
  How to show values in the slices                116
  Preparing data for pie and doughnut charts      118
  Changing the circumference                      123
  Pie and doughnut charts with multiple datasets  125

**Polar area charts** — 127

**Scatter and bubble charts** — 130
   Creating a scatter chart — 130
   Revealing correlations with scatter charts — 133
   Scatter charts with large quantities of data — 137
   Bubble charts — 139

**Summary** — 143

**References** — 143

**Chapter 5: Scales and Grid Configuration** — 145

**Configuring scales** — 145

**Cartesian configuration options** — 146

**Cartesian axes, ticks, and grid lines** — 148

**Numeric Cartesian scales** — 149
   Linear scales — 150
   Logarithmic scales — 151
   Configuring axis titles — 153
   Configuring ticks — 154
   Configuring grid lines — 158

**Category scales** — 162
   Configuring the axes — 162
   Configuring ticks — 166
   Configuring grid lines — 167

**Time scales** — 168
   Configuring the time format — 170
   Configuring the axes — 172
   Configuring ticks — 173
   Configuring grid lines — 175

**Radial scales** — 175
   Configuring point labels — 176
   Configuring ticks — 177
   Configuring grids and angle lines — 180

**Configuring advanced scales** — 181
   Multiple Cartesian axes — 182
   Callbacks — 184
   The scale service — 185

**Summary** — 186

**References** — 186

**Chapter 6: Configuring Styles and Interactivity** — 187

**Default configuration** — 187
   Global defaults — 189
   Scale defaults — 191
   Graphical elements — 192
   Chart defaults — 193

**Fonts**                                                      195
  Selecting standard fonts                           195
  Using Web fonts                                     196
**Colors, gradients, patterns, and shadows**                  198
  Configuring colors                                 198
  Color schemes and palettes                         199
**Gradients**                                                  203
**Patterns**                                                   206
**Shadows and bevels**                                         209
**Adding text elements and labels**                            210
  Legends and labels                                 211
**Titles**                                                     215
  Adding labels to lines, bars, and slices           215
  Interactions, data updates, and animations         219
  Data updates                                       220
**Events**                                                     222
  Configuring animations                             222
**Summary**                                                    226
**References**                                                 226

**Chapter 7: Advanced Chart.js**                               227
**Tooltip configuration**                                      227
**Hovering interactions**                                      232
**Scriptable properties**                                      234
  Tooltip callbacks                                  236
**Custom HTML tooltips**                                       238
  Advanced legend configuration                      241
  Generating labels                                  241
**HTML legends**                                               243
**Displaying multiple charts**                                 245
  Rendering many charts on one page                  245
**Mixed charts**                                               248
  Overlaying a canvas                                250
**Extending Chart.js**                                         254
  Prototype methods                                  254
**Creating plugins**                                           256
**Chart.js extensions**                                        262
**Summary**                                                    262
**References**                                                 262

**Other Books You May Enjoy**                                  265

**Index**                                                      269

# Preface

*Learn Chart.js* will make visualization easy and attractive for websites that are data intensive. I will explain how to make complicated data simple, accessible, and intuitive, so that your users will be able to better understand your website.

This book is a practical introduction to creating and publishing your own interactive data visualization projects on the Web.

After reading this book, you will be able to create beautiful charts for the Web with Chart.js.

## Who this book is for

The book is for designers and artists who wish to create interactive data visualizations for the Web.

Basic knowledge of HTML, CSS, and JavaScript would be of great help.

## What this book covers

Chapter 1, *Introduction*, introduces Chart.js and explains the basic concepts.

Chapter 2, *Technology Fundamentals*, explains the various fundamentals and setups needed for Chart.js

Chapter 3, *Chart.js - Quick Start*, provides a quick start to creating web-based data visualizations with Chart.js. It will show you how to set up the library and configure a basic web page on which you can place a chart. We will walk through a complete step-by-step example, describing how to create a bar chart and configure it with labels, tooltips, titles, interactions, colors, animations, and more.

Chapter 4, *Creating Charts*, covers several charts that can be created with Chart.js to efficiently communicate quantitative information and relationships. The choice of a chart depends on the type of data, how each set of values is related to one another, and what kind of relationships you want to show.

Chapter 5, *Scales and Grid Configuration*, explains how to configure the look and feel of a chart so it reflects a desired layout or style, follow good practices of chart design, and tune its interactive and responsive behavior.

Chapter 6, *Configuring Styles and Interactivity*, explores configuration topics that you won't use as frequently and that may require additional coding, extensions, and integration with other libraries, such as tooltip behavior configuration, label generation, scripting, creating mixed charts, creating plugins, using the Chart.js API, and using HTML Canvas with Chart.js.

Chapter 7, *Advanced Chart.js*, will explore fonts, padding, axes, screen resizing, and responsiveness.

# To get the most out of this book

I recommend that you read the first chapter to make sure that you are up to speed with the basic concepts and fundamentals of Chart.js. In the next chapters, we will see the setup that Chart.js needs and the various visual representation techniques this book will teach us and their uses. There will be tutorials on using the different chart types, and we will explore their interactivity.

## Download the example code files

You can download the example code files for this book from your account at www.packt.com. If you purchased this book elsewhere, you can visit www.packt.com/support and register to have the files emailed directly to you.

You can download the code files by following these steps:

1. Log in or register at www.packt.com.
2. Select the **SUPPORT** tab.
3. Click on **Code Downloads & Errata**.
4. Enter the name of the book in the **Search** box and follow the onscreen instructions.

Once the file is downloaded, please make sure that you unzip or extract the folder using the latest version of:

- WinRAR/7-Zip for Windows
- Zipeg/iZip/UnRarX for Mac
- 7-Zip/PeaZip for Linux

The code bundle for the book is also hosted on GitHub at `https://github.com/PacktPublishing/Learn-Charts.js`. In case there's an update to the code, it will be updated on the existing GitHub repository.

We also have other code bundles from our rich catalog of books and videos available at `https://github.com/PacktPublishing/`. Check them out!

# Conventions used

There are a number of text conventions used throughout this book.

`CodeInText`: Indicates code words in text, database table names, folder names, filenames, file extensions, pathnames, dummy URLs, user input, and Twitter handles. Here is an example: "This sets the color to be used in `fill()` commands."

A block of code is set as follows:

```
const chartObj = {...}; // the chart data is here
const context = canvas.getContext("2d");
new Chart(context, chartObj); // this will display the chart in the canvas
```

Any command-line input or output is written as follows:

```
npm install chart.js --save
bower install chart.js --save
```

**Bold**: Indicates a new term, an important word, or words that you see onscreen. For example, words in menus or dialog boxes appear in the text like this. Here is an example: "You just need to add the Chart.js CDN in the **Resources** tab."

Warnings or important notes appear like this.

Tips and tricks appear like this.

# Get in touch

Feedback from our readers is always welcome.

**General feedback**: If you have questions about any aspect of this book, mention the book title in the subject of your message and email us at customercare@packtpub.com.

**Errata**: Although we have taken every care to ensure the accuracy of our content, mistakes do happen. If you have found a mistake in this book, we would be grateful if you would report this to us. Please visit www.packt.com/submit-errata, selecting your book, clicking on the Errata Submission Form link, and entering the details.

**Piracy**: If you come across any illegal copies of our works in any form on the Internet, we would be grateful if you would provide us with the location address or website name. Please contact us at copyright@packt.com with a link to the material.

**If you are interested in becoming an author**: If there is a topic that you have expertise in and you are interested in either writing or contributing to a book, please visit authors.packtpub.com.

# Reviews

Please leave a review. Once you have read and used this book, why not leave a review on the site that you purchased it from? Potential readers can then see and use your unbiased opinion to make purchase decisions, we at Packt can understand what you think about our products, and our authors can see your feedback on their book. Thank you!

For more information about Packt, please visit packt.com.

# 1
# Introduction

This is a book about data visualization using JavaScript with Chart.js, one of the most popular data visualization libraries, and also one of the easiest to use. Chart.js provides ready-to-use interactive visualizations for your data with minimal coding. After loading your data into a standard JavaScript array, you can add styles and other configuration using simple object-based declarative structures. Chart.js automatically scales your data, generates ticks and grid lines, creates interactive tooltips, and fits the available space, making your chart automatically responsive. It's a great way to start creating data visualizations for the Web.

Chart.js is free, open source, and maintained by an active community of developers on GitHub. As a data visualization library, it is in second place on GitHub in terms of the number of stars it has. First place belongs to D3.js, a much larger and complex library with a steep learning curve. You still need to know JavaScript, HTML, and CSS to use Chart.js, but you don't have to be a guru. Besides JavaScript, it's also based on other Web standards, such as DOM, CSS, and Canvas. Charts are automatically rendered in Canvas and control all canvas configuration, resizing, and pixel ratios. The only thing you need to know about Canvas is how to include a `<canvas>` tag in your page and obtain a context, but Canvas knowledge can be useful in advanced charts.

This book assumes you know some JavaScript, HTML, and CSS. The next chapter provides a quick refresher on specific topics and the main technologies you are likely to encounter while learning Chart.js. You can skip it and jump straight to `Chapter 3`, *Chart.js – Quick Start*, if you wish. This chapter provides a brief introduction to data visualization and data visualization frameworks, and gives an overview of the rest of the book.

This chapter will cover the following topics:

- Data visualization
- Why use a data visualization library?
- How to use this book

# Data visualization

Visual representations provide data with contexts that stimulate the viewer's brain, revealing information that is usually not obvious from tabular data. It's normally much more natural to capture the substantive content of data using visual artifacts. Charts and maps are a powerful, clear, and effective means to tell stories through data. They can pack huge quantities of information in small spaces and make it easier to compare data, provide insights, and reveal trends, relationships, causality, and other patterns hidden in the numbers.

Charts reveal and emphasize data by attracting the viewer's attention. They can simplify complex data sets to foster discovery and comprehension, helping viewers to analyze and reason about data in different contexts. But they can also exaggerate, mislead, and even lie. A visually attractive chart is important, but designers should discover how to achieve a balance between form and function.

Data visualization is both an art and a science. A chart does not need to explain everything. It doesn't always have to be precise. It may be directed toward a specific audience, which should provide the context necessary to understand and decode it.

# Chart types

Data visualization usually refers to the visual display of quantitative information, as in statistical and information charts, plots, data maps, and so on. but it can include any kind of visual representation of data, such as mathematical graphics, path networks (subway systems, roads, electronic circuit diagrams), word clouds, musical and sound representations, timelines, geographical information systems, chemical and atomic diagrams, or any other way of coding of data using visual artifacts.

You can create any type of visualization if you use a data-driven library such as D3.js. A charting library such as Chart.js, which comes with a set of pre-configured formats, is more limited, but much easier to use.

Chart.js supports eight basic types of chart:

- Bar (horizontal and vertical)
- Line/area (including stacked)
- Radar (radial line)
- Polar area (radial bar)
- Scatter
- Bubble
- Pie
- Doughnut

It doesn't offer support for network diagrams, trees, or geographical maps, but you can create Chart.js visualizations that share data with other graphics. In Chapter 4, *Creating Charts*, we will create a bubble chart, representing populations of cities around the world, and plot them on a map with Chart.js.

# Choosing a chart

Choosing a chart requires knowing your data. Charts are a means of communication aimed at revealing information, so the main question is: what do you want to show? Once you've answered that question, you should analyze your data and discover what kind of data you have. Data values used in visualizations can usually be classified as one of these three types:

- **Quantitative**: A value that can be measured or counted (a number, a length, an area, an angle)
- **Ordinal**: A value can be ranked or compared (color saturation, area, angle, length, words)
- **Nominal:** A category (a name)

What is the purpose of you chart? Do you wish to reveal relationships, trends, or causality? What kind of relationship do you wish to emphasize? Do your variables relate to time or space?

Visualizations can be organized into categories, which make it easier to choose the kind of chart you need. Most charts and maps can be placed in one of these categories:

- *Time-series* (plots a single variable over a period of time). For example, a line chart that demonstrates a trend.
- *Temporal/linear* (categories placed in a time-line). For example, a series of events.
- *Spatial/planar/volumetric* (categories distributed in a spatial map). For example, a *cartogram* or *choropleth* with data distributed on a geographical map.
- *Comparison* (categories associated with quantities are compared and ranked during a single period). For example, a bar chart that compares values.
- *Part-to-whole* (categorical subdivisions as ratio to a whole). For example, a pie chart with slices as percentages.
- *Correlation* (comparing two or more variables). For example, a scatterplot comparing two variables, or a bubble chart comparing three.

In his classic book, *The Visual Display of Quantitative Information*, Edward Tufte defines some aspects that can be used to measure the quality and integrity of visualizations. They are the following:

- **Data-ink ratio**: The amount of ink (or pixels) dedicated to the data shown
- **Chartjunk**: Visual garbage that is irrelevant to the data shown (and that frequently get in the way)
- **Lie factor**: A number that measures the integrity of a visualization; for example, charts that lie by not representing proportions and lengths with enough precision

The data-ink ratio can be improved by removing chart-junk such as unnecessary lines and labels from charts. Sometimes the lines are important for context, but in interactive Web visualizations you can be very minimalistic. You can always provide details of demand with tooltips or other interactive resources.

Communication is deeply affected by the way humans perceive graphics, and may be improved or distorted by optical illusions. There are no charts with a lie factor of zero, but an adequate choice can improve it significantly. A bad choice increases the lie factor and can induce viewers to false perceptions.

Position and length are best for representing quantitative information. Direction and angles come next, then area, volume, curvature, and finally shadows, saturation, and color. Since lengths and positions are easier to perceive and compare than angles and areas, data in a bar chart is perceived with greater accuracy than the same data in a pie chart. Consider the following pie chart, which compares the areas of continents:

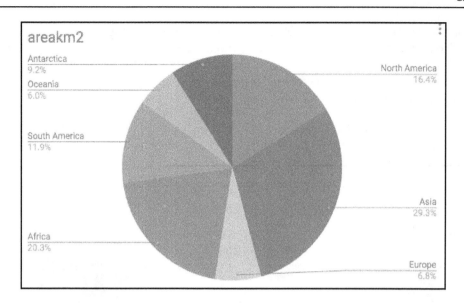

A pie chart comparing areas of continents

Now look at the exact same data represented in a bar chart:

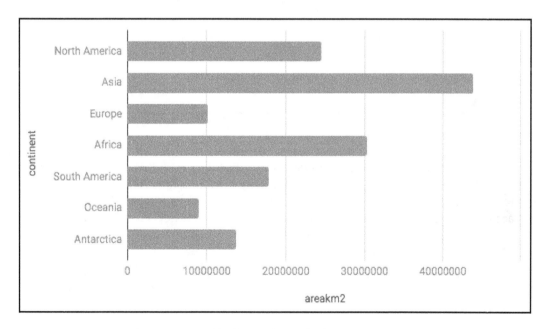

A bar chart comparing areas of continents

Which one is clearer? While the pie chart is good for showing proportions, angles are much harder to compare. Differences in length are much easier to compare and a bar chart is better in this case. But it would probably be clearer to use a pie chart to compare *two* values as *part of a whole*, such as the area of one continent compared to the remaining area, to reveal the proportion of land it occupies compared to the rest of the planet.

To have both proportions and lengths, you might be tempted to try a single stacked bar chart, but it still rates worse than the simple bar chart, since stacked bars aren't as easy to compare as when they are placed side-by-side:

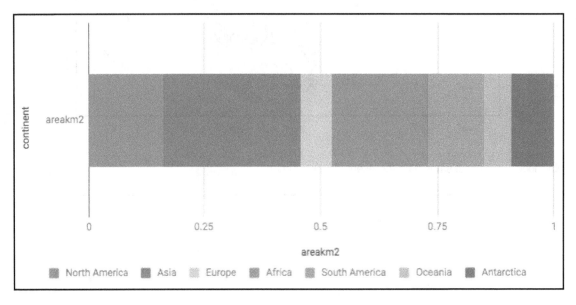

A stacked bar chart comparing areas of continents

Of course, you can choose a chart for other reasons, but it's important to know what you lose and gain in each case. Analytic and exploratory visualizations require a high degree of accuracy, but you might want to use a more attractive visualization at the price of losing some accuracy if you need to capture the attention of your audience.

# Web-based visualizations

When Edward Tufte wrote his classic books on data visualization, most of it was intended for printed media. Today, you can create visualizations that use data that can be updated in real time, with dynamic interfaces that allows interaction by the user. The design guidelines for web-based visualizations are different. They *can* and *should be* dynamic and interactive. Interactive charts can pack in much more information by hiding the details, which can be requested by the user on demand. Charts are sometimes rendered as overviews or sparklines, only revealing details through strategies such as zooming and brushing.

# Why use a data visualization library?

Actually, you don't need any coding to create fantastic and interactive visualizations for the web. You can always use a charting service. There are many; some are paid, others are free. They offer configuration screens and data transformation tools that allow you to create all kinds of beautiful charts. Popular services include *Google Charts*, *Tableau*, *Infogram*, and *Plotly*. If they fully satisfy your data visualization needs, you don't really need this book.

But if you know HTML, CSS, and JavaScript, you don't need to use these platforms. Web standards provide all the tools you need to create any sophisticated graphics, with no restrictions imposed by a platform or a plan. Using web standards also facilitates the integration of your visualizations with web applications, frontend frameworks (such as *React*, *Angular*, and *Vue*) and backend web services (such as resources and data provided by RESTful services).

But do you really need to use a library like Chart.js? Can't you just use standard JavaScript, HTML, CSS, and Canvas?

# Creating data visualizations for the Web

You don't really need any libraries or frameworks to create and display interactive and animated data visualizations on the Web. Plain standard HTML, CSS, and JavaScript already do that for you. Basic HTML provides structural elements that can be styled with CSS to display simple graphical elements such as colored rectangles. That means you can create a basic static bar chart just applying different widths in CSS to `div` elements.

Take a look at the following HTML and CSS code:

```html
<html lang="en">
<head>
    <meta charset="UTF-8">
    <title>Title</title>
    <style>
        #data {
            width: 600px;
            border: solid black 1px;
            padding: 10px;
        }
        .label {
            display: inline-block;
            width: 60px;
        }
        .bar {
            display: inline-block;
            background: red;
            margin: 2px 0;
            text-align: right;
            padding-right: 5px;
            color: white;
        }
        #data .bar1 { width: 500px; }
        #data .bar2 { width: 200px; }
        #data .bar3 { width: 300px; }

    </style>
</head>
<body>

<h1>Bar chart</h1>
<div id="data">
    <div><span class="label">Item 1</span><span class="bar
bar1">50</span></div>
    <div><span class="label">Item 2</span><span class="bar
bar2">20</span></div>
    <div><span class="label">Item 3</span><span class="bar
bar3">30</span></div>
</div>

</body>
</html>
```

If you run it in a web browser, you get the following chart:

A simple static bar chart created with just HTML and CSS

Of course, this is not the best way to draw a bar chart. The numbers were inserted somewhat arbitrarily in the HTML, and the lengths are defined by CSS width properties. You have to calculate the scales yourself. It's easy to make a mistake and reveal the wrong numbers. This is just to illustrate that all the graphical tools already exist in HTML and CSS. All we need is a library that generates that code for us.

Since the **Document Object Model** (**DOM**) allows scripting languages to access and change style attributes of an element, widths can be specified in JavaScript and can even respond to events or change with time, allowing the creation of interactive graphics with animation. Adding the following JavaScript function to the previous chart, you can the change value, length, and colors of the bars when the user clicks on the chart using standard DOM commands:

```
<div id="data" onclick="changeData()">...</div>
<script>
    function changeData() {
        let chart = document.getElementById("data");
        let elements = chart.children;
        let values = [5, 35, 15];
        for(let i = 0; i < values.length; i++) {
            let labelElement = elements[i].children[1].innerText =
            values[i];
            elements[i].children[1].style.background = "blue";
            elements[i].children[1].style.width = values[i] * 10 + "px";
        }
    }
</script>
```

The following screenshot shows the same chart as the preceding one after clicking, with new colors and values:

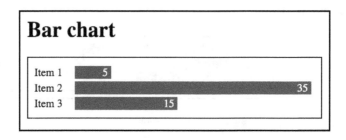

An interactive bar chart created with the standard DOM, CSS, HTML, and Javascript

But you don't have to use `div` and CSS to draw bars. Since HTML5, you can also use the Canvas API—a complete graphical library that can be used to create any kind of graphics, not just rectangles. The following example displays the same data as a pie chart using only standard HTML and no extra libraries:

```
<canvas id="chart" height="200" width="400"></canvas>

<script>
    const canvas = document.getElementById('chart');
    const ctx = canvas.getContext('2d');
    const rad = Math.min(canvas.height, canvas.width) / 2;

    const data = [100, 100, 100];
    const comp = n => Math.floor(Math.random() * 255);
    const colors = function() {
        return "rgba("+comp()+","+comp()+","+comp()+",0.5)";
    };

    let angle   = 0.0;
    let total   = data.reduce((a, b) => a + b, 0);

    for (var i = 0; i < data.length; i++) {
        ctx.fillStyle = colors();
        ctx.strokeStyle = 'white';
        ctx.lineWidth = 4;
        ctx.beginPath();
        ctx.moveTo(rad, rad);
        ctx.arc(rad, rad, rad, angle, angle +
                (Math.PI * 2 * (data[i]/total)), false);
        ctx.lineTo(rad, rad);
        ctx.fill();
        ctx.stroke();
```

```
        angle += Math.PI * 2 * (data[i] / total);
    }
</script>
```

You can download all these code examples from the GitHub repository for this chapter. See the last section for details. The result is shown as follows:

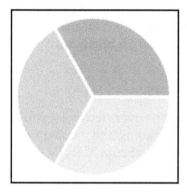

A simple pie chart created using HTML Canvas

You can make even nicer pie charts in Chart.js without writing a single line of Canvas code, and you won't have to worry about calculating angles in radians or adjusting scales to fit the page. You also get free tooltips with far fewer lines of code than we used previously. Chart.js may not satisfy all your data visualization needs, but it certainly is a great way to start. You can then apply your knowledge of HTML and JavaScript and extend it with plugins, integrate with other charting solutions, or migrate to a larger and unrestricted library such as D3.js.

# How to use this book

This book was designed as a practical hands-on guide on how to create data visualizations with Chart.js. It doesn't cover all aspects of Chart.js, but does cover most of the features you are likely to use to create visualizations. All eight Chart.js charts are covered, exploring different configurations and applications using external data obtained from public repositories.

Each chapter covers fundamental concepts. Each concept is always illustrated with a simple code example, but more complex examples that might require extra JavaScript programming are also presented in each chapter, and include solutions to real-world problems, such as downloading, parsing, and filtering a data file to convert it into a format usable by Chart.js.

Code listings are used throughout the book, but most of the time, they focus on a specific feature and show only a fragment of the full code. But you can download the full listing. All the code examples used in the book are available from a public GitHub repository located at: `https://github.com/PacktPublishing/Learn-charts.js`.

There is a folder for each chapter in the repository, named `Chapter01`, `Chapter02`, and so on. Each code listing and every image generated by code contains a relative reference to a file located in the corresponding folder for each chapter. You can try out all the code examples as you learn. You can also use it in any way you like, since it's free and open source.

Here's a brief summary of each chapter:

`Chapter 2`, *Technology Fundamentals*, covers technology fundamentals, data formats, and also explores some techniques for loading and parsing files. It gives a general background on topics used by Chart.js, such as JavaScript, CSS, DOM, and Canvas. You may skip these sections if you wish.

`Chapter 3`, *Chart.js – Quick Start*, includes a quick start and overview of several Chart.js features. It shows how to set up a web page to use Chart.js and how to create your first chart. You will learn a bit of everything Chart.js has to offer. It also introduces the bar chart type (vertical and horizontal).

`Chapter 4`, *Creating Charts*, covers all other chart types available: line/area, radar, polar area, pie, doughnut, scatter, and bubble. It also shows how to load and parse external CSV and JSON data from public data portals and use them to create real-world visualizations.

`Chapter 5`, *Scales and Grid Configuration*, focuses on configuring scales, axes, and grid lines for all charts. You will learn how to use radial grids and Cartesian grids with linear, logarithmic, category, and time axes.

`Chapter 6`, *Configuring Styles and Interactivity*, deals with configuration of several properties, for which Chart.js already provides defaults: fonts, titles, and labels. It also explores some neat labeling plugins and color schemes, which are important for accessible charts. This chapter also shows how to configure transitions, animations, and interactions.

`Chapter 7`, *Advanced Charts.js*, covers some advanced features that you will are less likely to use on a regular basis, since Chart.js already provides good defaults. These include tooltip configuration, creating custom legends, mixed charts, how to display multiple charts on a single page, overlaying Chart.js on a Canvas, and creating plugins.

I believe the book covers the most important topics in Chart.js. It leaves out some advanced programming topics, several plugins, and integration with front-end frameworks, which are also not covered.

I am not affiliated with Chart.js in any way and this book does not replace the official Chart.js documentation, which is the ultimate reference guide on the topic. The documentation is community-maintained and freely available at `www.chartjs.org/docs/latest`. There are also many samples that explore its main features that are also part of the documentation at `www.chartjs.org/samples/latest`.

When writing this book, I did my best to provide the most accurate information possible. All code listings were tested, and additional efforts were made to guarantee that all code examples are properly referenced in the book and work as expected. This book is based on Chart.js version 2.7.3. I expect that the examples should continue working with any 2.x version, but there is a small possibility that some code may not work as expected if you are using a later version.

The Chart.js community is very active on *GitHub* and *StackOverflow*. If you have any questions about Chart.js, you can submit a question on `stackoverflow.com` and you will probably have an answer within a few hours or less.

I hope you enjoy this book and have as much fun as I had when learning Chart.js.

# Summary

This chapter provided a quick introduction to data visualization topics and introduced Chart.js, the JavaScript library with which you will learn to create responsive interactive visualizations for the web. We also demonstrated how standard web technologies provide all you need to create charts for the web, and how a data visualization library such as Chart.js can be beneficial.

In the next chapter, we will cover the fundamentals of some standard technologies used by Chart.js—data formats and data manipulation techniques—but if you want to start using Chart.js right away, you can skip it and jump straight to Chapter 3, *Chart.js – Quick Start*.

# References

**Books and websites**:

- Edward R. Tufte. *The Visual Display of Quantitative Information*. Graphics Press, 1997
- Isabel Meirelles. *Design for Information*. Rockport Publishers, 2013
- Stephen Few. *Data Visualization: past, present and future*. Perceptual Edge, 2007
- David Kahneman. *Thinking Fast and Slow*. Farrar, Straus and Giroux. 2011
- Ben Bederson and Ben Schneiderman. *The Craft of Information Visualization*. 2003

# Technology Fundamentals

# 2

This book assumes that you have a working knowledge of HTML, CSS, and JavaScript, which are essential tools for creating visualizations with Chart.js. All examples in the book are written with JavaScript ES2015 or ES6. One of the goals of this chapter is to review the fundamental topics of these technologies. This includes JavaScript topics related to string, object, and array manipulation, the HTML document object model (DOM), basic JQuery, CSS selectors, and HTML canvas. You can, of course, skip these sections if you already feel comfortable with these technologies.

This chapter also describes popular data formats used in visualizations, such as CSV, XML, and JSON, and how to load, parse, and use external data files in these formats in your Web pages. You will also learn how to set up a small testing Web server to run files that load external resources.

The final section contains some tips on how to obtain and prepare data for your visualizations, how to convert HTML data into standard formats, and how to extract selected information from HTML pages.

In this chapter, you will learn about the following:

- Essential JavaScript for Chart.js
- Other technologies: DOM, CSS, JQuery, and Canvas
- Data formats
- How to load and parse external data files
- How to extract and transform data

# Essential JavaScript for Chart.js

Client-side applications, such as interactive Web graphics, depend on browser support. This book assumes that your audience uses browsers that support HTML5 Canvas and ES2015 (which include all modern browsers). All examples use ES2015 syntax, including *const* and *let* instead of *var*, arrow functions where appropriate, spread operators, maps, sets, and promises. External files are loaded using the Fetch API, which has only been supported more recently, but you can easily switch to JQuery if necessary.

Although the creation of visualizations with Chart.js is mostly a declarative process, it is still a JavaScript library and requires basic knowledge of JavaScript. To create a simple chart, you need to know how to declare constants and variables, perform basic mathematical Boolean string and attribution operations, call and create functions, manipulate objects and arrays, and instantiate the Chart.js object. A typical chart also requires enough knowledge to program control structures, write callbacks, sort and filter datasets, generate random numbers, and load external files. This section is a quick refresher on the main ES2015 topics you will need to use Chart.js.

# Browser tools

You don't need a full frontend modular Node development environment to create visualizations with Chart.js, but you still need a good debugger. Every browser comes with development tools that allow you to navigate a static page structure and generated DOM elements, and a console where you can interact in real time with the data used by the JavaScript engine.

The most important tool is the **JavaScript console**, where you will see any error messages. It's very common to get a blank page when you expected something else and not have a clue as to why your code doesn't work as expected. Sometimes, it's just a comma you forgot, or the internet is down and some file was not loaded. If you have the JavaScript console open while you run your page, it will instantly tell you what's going on. It's also a good idea to use an editor with line numbering, since most error messages inform us of the lines where the problem occurred:

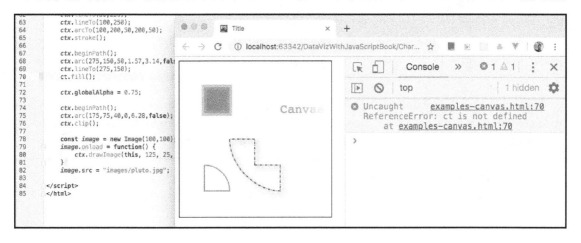

Debugging JavaScript with the JavaScript console

You can open the developer tools as a frame in your browser or as a separate window. The following are the menu paths for the JavaScript console in latest versions of the three most popular browsers:

- Chrome: **View | Developer | JavaScript Console**
- Firefox: **Tools | Web Developer | Web Console**
- Safari: **Develop | Show Error Console**

Most of the code fragments and examples in this section can be tested by typing them in the JavaScript console. It's a great way to learn JavaScript. It will also access the functions of any JavaScript library file that was loaded with the `<script>` tag, and any global variables declared in the `<script></script>` blocks.

# JavaScript types and variables

JavaScript is not a typed language, since types are not declared and variables can receive different types, but data values do have types. The main types are *Number, String, Boolean, Array, Object,* and *Function*. The first three are scalar types, and the last three are also objects. A value is treated differently in the same expression if it has one type or another. For example, in an expression such as $a = b + c$, the value of $a$ will be different if $b$ and $c$ are numbers (they will be added) or if one of them is a string (they will be concatenated).

Values can be compared, and their types are important if the comparison is *strict* (for example, using === instead of ==). But it can be confusing to rely on such conversions (0, "", null, NaN , and undefined are all considered false, but the false string converts to true, since its not an empty string).

In ES5 JavaScript, var was the only keyword for declaring a variable. It ignores block scope and is hoisted to the top of the functions. Since ES6 (ES2015), two new keywords have been introduced: const and let. They both are block-scoped and need to be assigned a value before they are used (var defaults to undefined). Declarations with const are constants and can't be reassigned. It's usually considered good practice to use const whenever possible, and only use let if you actually need to redefine a variable.

# Data structures used in charts

Data used as sources for visualizations is usually organized in some kind of structure. The most common structures are probably *lists* (arrays) and *tables* (maps), stored in some standard data format. When using data from external sources, you usually need to clean it up, removing unnecessary values, simplifying its structure, applying bounds, and so on. After that, you can parse it and finally store it locally in a JavaScript array or JavaScript object that can be used by the chart.

Once your data is stored in a JavaScript data structure, you can transform it further by applying mathematical operations on the stored values. You can change the structure, create new fields, merge, and delete data. Typical operations include pushing new values into the dataset, splicing or splitting the array, creating a subset, transforming data, and so on. JavaScript provides many native operations that make it easier to modify arrays and objects. You can also use libraries such as JQuery.

# Arrays

The main data structure you will use to store one-dimensional data is the JavaScript array. It's used as the main dataset format in most chart types in Chart.js. An array of values is all you need to make a simple bar chart. You can create an array by declaring a list of items within brackets, or simply a pair of opening-closing brackets if you want to start with an empty array:

```
const colors = ["red", "blue", "green"];
const geocoords = [27.2345, 34.9937];
const numbers = [1,2,3,4,5,6];
const empty = [];
```

You can then access the items of an array using an array index, which starts counting from zero:

```
const blue = colors[1];
const latitude = geocoords[0];
```

Each array has a length property that returns the number of elements. It's very useful to iterate using the array index:

```
for(let i = 0; i < colors.length; i++) {
    console.log(colors[i]);
}
```

You can also loop over the elements of an array using the *of* operator (introduced in ES2015) when you don't need the index:

```
for(let color of colors) {
    console.log(color);
}
```

And you can use the `forEach()` method, which runs a function for each element and also allows access to the index, item, and array inside the function:

```
colors.forEach(function(i, color, colors) {
    console.log((i+1) + ": " + color);
}
```

Multidimensional arrays are created in JavaScript as arrays of arrays:

```
const points = [[200,300], [150,100], [100,300]];
```

You can retrieve individual items like this:

```
const firstPoint = points[0];
const middleX = points[1][0];
```

JavaScript provides many ways to extract and insert data into an array. It's usually recommended to use these methods whenever possible. The following table lists useful methods you can use on arrays. Some modify the array; others return new arrays and other types. The examples provided use the `colors` and `numbers` arrays as declared previously. Try them out using your browser's JavaScript console:

| Method | Description | Example |
|---|---|---|
| push(item) | Modifies the array, adding an item to the end. | `colors.push("yellow");`<br>`/*["red", "blue", "green",`<br>`    "yellow"];*/` |

| | | |
|---|---|---|
| `pop()` | Modifies the array, removing and returning the last item. | `const green = colors.pop();`<br>`// ["red", "blue"];` |
| `unshift(item)` | Modifies the array, inserting an item at the beginning. | `colors.unshift("yellow");`<br>`/*["yellow", "red", "blue",`<br>`   "green"];*/` |
| `shift()` | Modifies the array, removing and returning the first item. | `const red = colors.shift();`<br>`// ["blue", "green"];` |
| `splice(p,n,i)` | Modifies the array, starting at position p. Can be used to delete, insert, or replace items. | `const s = numbers.splice(2,3);`<br>`// s = [3,4,5]`<br>`// numbers = [1,2,6]` |
| `reverse()` | Modifies the array, reversing its order. | `numbers.reverse();`<br>`// [6,5,4,3,2,1]` |
| `sort()` | Modifies the array, sorting by string order (if no args) or by a comparator function. | `numbers.sort((a,b) => b - a);`<br>`// numbers = [6,5,4,3,2,1]` |
| `slice(b,e)` | Returns a shallow copy of the array between b and e. | `const mid = numbers.slice(2,4)`<br>`// mid = [3,4]` |
| `filter(callback)` | Returns new array where the elements pass the test implemented by the function. | `const even = numbers.filter(n =>`<br>`n%2==0);`<br>`// [2,4,6]` |
| `find(function)` | Returns the first element that satisfies the test function. | `const two = numbers.find(n =>`<br>`n%2==0);`<br>`// 2` |
| `indexOf(item)` | Returns the index of the first occurrence of the item in the array. | `const n = numbers.indexOf(3);`<br>`// 4` |
| `includes(item)` | Returns `true` if an array contains the item among its entries. | `const n = numbers.includes(3);`<br>`// true` |
| `lastIndexOf(item)` | Returns the index of the last occurrence of the item in the array. | `const n =`<br>`colors.lastIndexOf("blue");`<br>`// 1` |
| `concat(other)` | Returns a new array that merges the current array with another. | `const eight =`<br>`numbers.concat([7,8]);`<br>`// [1,2,3,4,5,6,7,8]` |
| `join()`<br>`join(delim)` | Returns a comma-separated string of the elements in the array (an optional delimiter may be used). | `const csv = numbers.join();`<br>`// "1,2,3,4,5,6"`<br>`const conc = numbers.join("");`<br>`// "123456"` |

| `map(function)` | Returns a new array with each element modified by the function. | `const squares = numbers.map(n => n*n);`<br>`// [1,4,9,16,25,36]` |
|---|---|---|
| `reduce(function)` | Returns the result of an accumulation operation using the values in the array. | `const sum =`<br>`    numbers.reduce((a, n) => a + n);` |
| `forEach(function)` | Executes the provided function once for each element in the array. | `const squares = [];`<br>`numbers.forEach(n =>`<br>`squares.push(n*n)`<br>`// squares = [1,4,9,16,26,36]` |

JavaScript functions for array manipulation

Besides arrays, ES2015 also introduced two new data structures: Map, an associative array with key-value pairs, easier to use than simple objects, and Set, which doesn't allow repeated values. Both can be transformed to and from arrays.

# Strings

Strings are primitive types in JavaScript that can be created with single quotes or double quotes. There is no difference. It's only a matter of style. ES2015 introduced two new string features: *template literals* and *multiline strings*.

Multiline strings can be created by adding a backslash at the end of each line:

```
const line = "Multiline strings can be \
reated adding a backslash \
at the end of each line";
```

Template literals are strings created with backticks. They allow the inclusion of JavaScript expressions inside the ${} placeholders. The result is concatenated as a single string:

```
const template = `The square root of 2 is ${Math.sqrt(2)}`;
```

If you need to use a special character in a string, such as a double quote in a double-quoted string or a backslash, you need to precede it with a backslash:

```
const s = "This is a backslash \\ and this is a double quote \"";
```

There are several methods for string manipulation. They all return new strings or other types. No methods modify the original strings:

| Method | Description | Example |
|--------|-------------|---------|
| startsWith(s) | Returns true if the string starts with the string passed as a parameter. | `const s = "This is a test string"`<br>`const r = s.startsWith("This");`<br>`// true` |
| endsWith(s) | Returns true if string ends with the string passed as a parameter. | `const s = "This is a test string"`<br>`const r = s.endsWith("This");`<br>`// false` |
| substring(s,e) | Returns a substring between start (incl.) and *end* indexes (not incl.). | `const k = "Aardvark"`<br>`const ardva = k.substring(1,6);` |
| split(regx)<br>split(delim) | Splits a string by a delimiter character or a regular expression and returns an array. | `const result = s.split(" ");`<br>`// result =`<br>`//["This","is","a","test","string"]` |
| indexOf() | Returns the index of the first occurrence of a substring. | `const k = "Aardvark"`<br>`const i = k.indexOf("ar"); // i = 1` |
| lastIndexOf() | Returns the index of the last occurrence of a substring. | `const k = "Aardvark"`<br>`const i = k.lastIndexOf("ar");`<br>`// i = 5` |
| charAt(i) | Returns char at index *i*. Also supported as 'string'[i]. | `const k = "Aardvark"`<br>`const v = k.charAt(4);` |
| trim() | Removes whitespace from both ends of a string. | `const text = "    data    "`<br>`const r = data.trim();`<br>`// r = "data"` |
| match(regx) | Returns an array as the result of matching a regular expression against the string. | `const k = "Aardvark"`<br>`const v = k.match(/[a-f]/g);`<br>`// v = ["a", "d", "a"]` |
| replace(regx,r)<br>replace(s,t) | Returns a new string replacing the matching of regexp applied to the string with a replacement or all occurrences of the source string with a target string. | `const k = "Aardvark"`<br>`const a = p.replace(/a/gi, 'u')`<br>`// a = "uurdvurk"`<br>`const b = p.replace('ardv', 'ntib')`<br>`// b = "Antibark"` |

JavaScript functions for string manipulation

# Functions

Functions are typically created in JavaScript using the `function` keyword, using one of the following forms:

```
function f() {
    console.log('function1', this);
}
const g = function(name) {
    console.log('function ' + name, this);
}
f(); // calls f
g('test'); // calls g() with a parameter
```

The `this` keyword refers to the object that owns the function. If this code runs in a browser, and this is a top-level function created in the `<script>` block, the owner is the global `window` object. Any properties accessed via this refer to that object.

A function can be placed in the scope of an object, behaving as a method. The `this` reference in the following code refers to the `obj` object and can access `this.a` and `this.b`:

```
const obj = {a: 5, b: 6}
obj.method = function() {
    console.log('method', this)
}
object.method()
```

Arrow functions were introduced in ES2015. They are much more compact and can lead to cleaner code, but the scope of `this` is no longer retained by the object. In the following code, it refers to the global window object. Code that uses `this.a` and `this.b` will not find any data in the object and will return undefined:

```
obj.arrow = () => console.log('arrow', this)
object.arrow()
```

You can use arrow functions in Chart.js callbacks, but you should use regular functions instead of arrow functions if you need to access the instance of the chart, usually available using `this`.

# Objects

An object is an unordered collection of data. Values in an object are stored as key-value pairs. You can create an object by declaring a comma-separated list of *key:value* pairs within curly braces, or simply a pair of opening-closing curly braces if you want to start with an empty object:

```
const color = {name: "red", code: ff0000};
const empty = {};
```

Objects can contain other objects and arrays, which can also contain objects. They can also contain functions, which have access to local properties and behave as methods:

```
const city = {name: "Sao Paulo",
              location: {latitude: 23.555, longitude: 46.63},
              airports: ["SAO","CGH","GRU","VCP"]};
const circle = {
    x: 200,
    y: 100,
    r: 50,
    area: function() {
        return this.r * this.r * 3.14;
    }
}
```

A typical dataset used by a simple chart usually consists of an array of objects:

```
var array2 = [
    {continent: "Asia", areakm2: 43820000},
    {continent: "Europe", areakm2: 10180000},
    {continent: "Africa", areakm2: 30370000},
    {continent: "South America", areakm2: 17840000},
    {continent: "Oceania", areakm2: 9008500},
    {continent: "North America", areakm2=24490000}
];
```

You can access the properties of an object using the dot operator or brackets containing the key as a string. You can run its methods using the dot operator:

```
const latitude = city.location.latitude;
const oceania = array2[4].continent;
const code = color["code"];
circle.r = 100;
const area = circle.area();
```

You can also loop over the properties of an object:

```
for(let key in color) {
    console.log(key + ": " + color[key]);
}
```

Properties and functions can be added to objects. It's common to write code that declares an empty object in a global context so that operations in other contexts add data to it:

```
const map = {};
function getCoords(coords) {
    map.latitude = coords.lat;
    map.longitude = coords.lng;
}
```

Objects can also be created with a constructor. You can create an object that contains the current date/time using:

```
const now = new Date();
```

A Chart.js instance is created using a constructor that receives at least two parameters. The second parameter is an object with two properties, a string and another object:

```
const chart =
    new Chart("bar-chart ",{type:"bar", data:{labels:[],datasets:[]}});
```

JSON is a data format based on JavaScript objects. It has the same structure as a JavaScript object, but the property keys have to be placed within double quotes:

```
{"name": "Sao Paulo",
            "location": {"latitude": 23.555, "longitude": 46.63},
            "airports": ["SAO","CGH","GRU","VCP"]};
```

To use a JSON string in JavaScript you have to parse it.

# Other technologies

This section presents a brief summary of other technologies you should know about, covering their fundamental concepts. They include HTML DOM, JQuery, CSS, and HTML Canvas. You can skim or skip this section if you already know about and use these technologies. The next sections also provide code examples that can be downloaded from the GitHub repository for this chapter.

## HTML Document Object Model(DOM)

The structure of an HTML document is normally described with tags, but it can also be specified using JavaScript commands with a **Document Object Model (DOM)**: a language-neutral API that represents an HTML or XML document as a *tree*. Consider the following HTML document (`Examples/example-1.html`):

```
<html>
<body>
    <h1>Simple page</h1>
    <p>Simple paragraph</p>
    <div>
        <img src="pluto.jpg" width="100"/>
        <p>Click me!</p>
    </div>
</body>
</html>
```

This page builds a tree of interconnected *nodes* containing HTML elements and text. The exact same result can be obtained with the following JavaScript commands (`Examples/example-2.html`):

```
const html = document.documentElement;

const body = document.createElement("body");
html.appendChild(body);

const h1 = document.createElement("h1");
const h1Text = document.createTextNode("Simple page");
h1.appendChild(h1Text);
body.appendChild(h1);

const p = document.createElement("p");
const pText = document.createTextNode("Simple paragraph");
p.appendChild(pText);
body.appendChild(p);
```

```
const div = document.createElement("div");
const divImg = document.createElement("img");
divImg.setAttribute("src", "pluto.jpg");
divImg.setAttribute("width", "100");
div.appendChild(divImg);

const divP = document.createElement("p");
const divPText = document.createTextNode("Click me!");
divP.appendChild(divPText);
div.appendChild(divP);

body.appendChild(div);
```

Of course, it's much simpler to write tags, but JavaScript gives you the power to make the structure and content *dynamic*. Using DOM commands, you can add new elements, move them around, remove them, and change their attributes and text contents. You can also navigate the DOM tree, select or search for specific elements or data, and bind styles and event handlers to elements.

For example, if you add the following code, a new <p> containing the "New line" text will be created every time you click on the image (Examples/example-3.html):

```
div.style.cursor = "pointer";
div.addEventListener("click", function() {
    const p = document.createElement("p");
    p.innerHTML = "New line";
    this.appendChild(p);
});
```

Normally, you wouldn't write your entire document using DOM, but only the parts you wish to control dynamically. Normally, you write the static parts as HTML and use scripting only when necessary (Examples/example-4.html):

```
<html>
<body>
<h1>Simple page</h1>
<p>Simple paragraph</p>
<div id="my-section">
    <img src="pluto.jpg" width="100"/>
    <p>Click me!</p>
</div>
</body>

<script>
    const div = document.getElementById("my-section");
    div.style.cursor = "pointer";
    div.addEventListener("click", function() {
```

```
        const p = document.createElement("p");
        p.innerHTML = "New line";
        this.appendChild(p);
    });
</script>
</html>
```

For data-driven documents, you can use DOM scripting to bind data stored in arrays and objects to attributes of the elements, changing the dimensions, colors, text contents, and position. Most data visualization libraries do exactly that by providing functions that are built over the DOM, and make this task much simpler.

The following table lists the most important DOM commands:

| Method or property | Description |
|---|---|
| `createElement(tag)` | Creates an element (not connected to the node tree) and returns its reference. |
| `createTextNode(text)` | Creates a text node (not connected to the node tree) and returns its reference. |
| `appendChild(element)` | Connects the element passed as a parameter as the child of the current element. |
| `removeChild(element)` | Disconnects the child element from the current element. |
| `setAttribute(name, value)` | Sets an attribute for this element with the name and value passed as parameters. |
| `getElementById(id)` | Returns an element identified by the `id` passed as a parameter. |
| `getElementsByTagName(tag)` | Returns a `nodelist` (array) containing all the elements that match the tag name passed as a parameter. |
| `addEventListener(e, func)` | Attaches an event handler to this element. The first parameter is the event type (for example, 'click', 'key', and so on) and the second parameter is a handler function. |
| `documentElement` | This property references the element at the root of the document. For HTML and XHTML, it is the `<html>` element. |
| `children` | This property returns a node list containing the child elements of this element. |
| `innerText` | In SVG or HTML documents, this read/write property is a shortcut for creating a text node and appending it to the element. |

| | |
|---|---|
| `innerHTML` | In HTML documents, this read/write property is a shortcut for appending an entire HTML fragment as a child element. |
| `style` | In SVG or HTML documents, this property allows access to the element's CSS styles. You can use it to read and modify styles dynamically. |

A selection of properties and methods supported by HTML DOM

# Cascading Style Sheets

**Cascading Style Sheets** (CSS) is a W3C standard that specifies how HTML and XML elements are displayed on the screen. It's a declarative language where visual properties are applied to tag selectors. You can use CSS to apply properties such as colors, fonts, margins, shadows, and gradients to one or more tags, perform coordinate transformations in two and three dimensions, and set rules for transitions and animations. CSS properties and selectors are also used in JavaScript libraries, such as JQuery and D3.js.

CSS selectors are expressions used to select elements by type, class, ID, wildcards, attributes, context, state, and position. The result of a selection expression may consist of none, one, or more elements. JavaScript libraries use selectors to obtain objects that can be manipulated programmatically via DOM. A result set can be formed from a list of comma-separated selection expressions. Elements may also be selected from context with combinator selectors. The following table lists some of the main selectors and some examples:

| Selector | Syntax | Description Example (in CSS) |
|---|---|---|
| Type selector | `tagname` | Selects a set of elements of the specified type (tag name), for example `td, h1, prect { ... } /* all <rect> tags */`. |
| Class selector | `.classname` | Selects a set of elements that belongs to a specified class, for example `.selected` and `p.copy`. |
| ID selector | `#idname` | Selects one element with the specified `id` attribute, for example `#main` and `#chart`. |
| Universal selector | `*` | Selects all elements. |
| Attribute selector | `[attr]` `[attr=value]` (several other combinations) | Selects elements that contain an attribute. Selects elements that contain an attribute with a specified value. Other combinations match a string in the attribute value. |

| Descendant combinator | `ancestor selectedtag` | Selects elements nested within a specified ancestor element (may have other elements in between), for example table `td`. |
|---|---|---|
| Child combinator | `parent > selectedtag` | Selects elements nested *directly* below a specified parent element (`selectedTag` is a child of a parent), for example `table >tbody >tr >td`. |
| General sibling combinator | `preceding ~ selectedtag` | Selects elements that appear after a specified predecessor (both have the same parent), for example `h1 ~p.last`. |
| Adjacent sibling combinator | `previous + selectedtag` | Selects elements that appear *directly* after a specified sibling (both have the same parent), for example `h1 +p.first`. |
| Pseudo-classes | `tag:state` | Selects elements that are in a specified *state*, for example `a:hover, p:last-child, td:nth-of-type(2), :not(x)`. |
| Pseudo-elements | `tag::property` | Selects elements with a specified `property`, and is rarely used. |

CSS selectors

Most of the time, you will use the simplest selectors. The ID, class, and type selectors are the most common. Eventually, you might use descendant combinators or attribute selectors.

The following code uses simple selectors to change the visual appearance of an unformatted page containing three sections. The sections are stacked one on top of the other. The CSS properties and other parts were omitted, but you can see them in the full code listing (`Examples/example-5-selectors.html`):

```
<html lang="en">
<head>
    <style>
        h1 {...}
        .tab h1 {...}
        .tab p {...}
        .illustration {...}
        .tab {...}
        .tab .contents {...}
        .container {...}
        .tab:nth-child(2) h1 {...}
        .tab:nth-child(3) h1 {...}
    </style>
</head>

<body>
<h1>CSS and JQuery selectors</h1>

<div id="container">
```

```
<div class="tab first" id="section1">
    <div class="contents">
        <img class="illustration" src="jupiter.jpg" />
        <p>...</p>
    </div>
    <h1>Tab 1: Jupiter</h1>
</div>

<div class="tab" id="section2">
    <div class="contents">
        <img class="illustration" src="saturn.jpg" />
        <p>...</p>
    </div>
    <h1>Tab 2: Saturn</h1>
</div>

<div class="tab" id="section3">
    <div class="contents">
        <img class="illustration" src="pluto.jpg" />
        <p>...</p>
    </div>
    <h1>Tab 3: Pluto</h1>
</div>

</div>
</body>

</html>
```

The result is as follows:

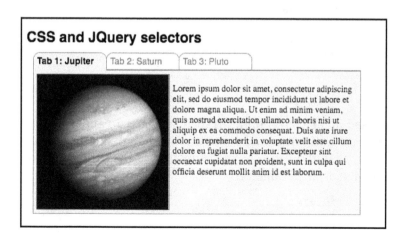

An HTML page with stacked information styled using only CSS

# JQuery fundamentals

JQuery is not a standard technology, but it's a de facto Web standard. It uses CSS selectors to locate elements in any HTML file, and provides the same power as the DOM but with a much cleaner syntax. To use *JQuery,* you first need to include its library in your HTML page using the `<script>` tag. This is easily done with a CDN URL:

```
<script src="https://code.jquery.com/jquery-3.3.1.min.js"></script>
```

The code fragment here is a page that uses *JQuery* to perform the exact same operations shown in the last DOM example. The result is much easier to understand (`Examples/example-6.html`):

```
<html>
<body>
<head>
    <style>
        #my-section {
            cursor: pointer;
        }
    </style>
</head>
<h1>Simple page</h1>
<p>Simple paragraph</p>
<div id="my-section">
    <img src="pluto.jpg" width="100"/>
    <p>Click me!</p>
</div>
</body>
<script src="https://code.jquery.com/jquery-3.3.1.min.js"></script>
<script>
    $("#my-section").on("click", function() {
        $(this).append("<p>New Line</p>");
    });
</script>
</html>
```

CSS selectors are used in JavaScript libraries such as *JQuery* to apply dynamic styles and manipulate a document's structure and contents. The main JQuery(selector) function, normally used via its alias, the `$(selector)` function, is an element selector that receives a CSS selector expression as its parameter:

```
const divSet = $("div");
const title1 = $("#section1 h1");
```

A selection can return zero, one, or a list of elements. You can test the length of a selection using the `length` attribute:

```
if($("table").length == 0) {
    console.log("there are no tables in this document")
}
```

Using *JQuery* and the code shown in the CSS example, we can make the tabs fade in and fade out as they are clicked using selectors and *JQuery* functions (`Examples/example-7-selectors.html`):

```
<script src="https://code.jquery.com/jquery-3.3.1.min.js"></script>
<script>
    $(".tab").on("click", function() {
        $(".tab h1").css("color", "gray");
        $(".tab h1").css("background", "white");
        $(".tab h1").css("font-weight", "normal");
        $(".tab h1").css("z-index", "-1");
        $("#" + $(this).attr("id") + " h1").css("color", "black");
        $("#" + $(this).attr("id") + " h1").css("background",
"whitesmoke");
        $("#" + $(this).attr("id") + " h1").css("font-weight", "bold");
        $("#" + $(this).attr("id") + " h1").css("z-index", "1");
        $(".tab .contents").fadeOut();
        $("#" + $(this).attr("id") + " .contents").fadeIn();
    });
    $("#section1").trigger("click");
</script>
```

# HTML5 Canvas

There is no way to draw circles or gradients using HTML tags, but you can use HTML Canvas: a full-featured JavaScript graphics API for 2D vector graphics. You can draw anything you wish with Canvas, and since it's JavaScript, you can make it animate and respond to events.

To draw using Canvas, you need to create a `<canvas>` element in your page. You can do that using plain HTML:

```
<body>
    <canvas id="canvas" width="300" height="300"></canvas>
</body>
```

You can also create it dynamically, using HTML DOM:

```
const canvas = document.createElement("canvas");
canvas.setAttribute("width", 300);
canvas.setAttribute("height", 300);
document.body.appendChild(canvas);
```

You can create it using *JQuery* too:

```
const canvas = $("<canvas/>",{id: "canvas"}).prop({width:300,height:300});
```

Then you can reference using the DOM:

```
const canvas = document.getElementById("canvas");
const canvas = $("#canvas");
```

Or you can reference using JQuery:

```
const canvas = document.getElementById("canvas");
const canvas = $("#canvas");
```

Once you have a canvas object, you obtain a 2D graphics context and can start drawing:

```
const ctx     = canvas.getContext("2d");
```

Practically, all the Canvas API consists of is methods and properties called from the graphics context. Before drawing, you set properties such as font, fill color, and stroke color:

```
ctx.fillStyle = "red";
ctx.strokeStyle = "rgba(255,127,0,0.7)";
ctx.lineWidth = 10;
```

And then *fill* or *stroke* rectangles and arbitrary paths containing lines and curves. These commands will draw a red 50 x 50 pixel square with a 10 pixel wide yellow semi-transparent border at position 50,50:

```
ctx.fillRect(50,50,50,50);
ctx.strokeRect(50,50,50,50);
```

You can draw other shapes, texts, and images on the same canvas. The context properties will not change unless they are redefined.

You can also draw using path commands. You need to start the path with `ctx.beginPath()`, and call a sequence of commands that moves to points and draws lines and curves, and when you are done you can close the path (if it's a closed path) and call `fill()` and/or `stroke()` to draw it using the current styles.

The following code draws some shapes, paths, shadows, gradients, and text:

```
ctx.strokeStyle = "blue";
ctx.lineWidth = 2;
ctx.shadowBlur = 10;
ctx.shadowColor = "green";
ctx.shadowOffsetX = ctx.shadowOffsetY = 5;
ctx.setLineDash([5,2,1,2]);
ctx.beginPath();
ctx.moveTo(150,200);
ctx.lineTo(150,150);
ctx.lineTo(100,150);
ctx.bezierCurveTo(100,200,150,250,200,250);
ctx.lineTo(200,200);
ctx.closePath();
ctx.stroke();
const text = "Canvas";
ctx.font = "24px monospace";
const textWidth = ctx.measureText(text).width;
const gradient = ctx.createLinearGradient(200,100,200 + textWidth,100);
gradient.addColorStop(0,"magenta");
gradient.addColorStop(1, "yellow");
ctx.fillStyle = gradient;
ctx.shadowColor = "transparent";
ctx.fillText("Canvas", 200, 100);
ctx.setLineDash([0]);
ctx.strokeStyle = "gray";
ctx.beginPath();
ctx.moveTo(50,200);
ctx.lineTo(50,250);
ctx.lineTo(100,250);
ctx.arcTo(100,200,50,200,50);
ctx.stroke();
ctx.beginPath();
ctx.arc(275,150,50,1.57,3.14,false);
ctx.lineTo(275,150);
ctx.fill();
ctx.globalAlpha = 0.75;
ctx.beginPath();
ctx.arc(175,75,40,0,6.28,false);
ctx.clip();
const image = new Image(100,100);
image.onload = function() {
    ctx.drawImage(this, 125, 25, this.width, this.height);
}
image.src = "pluto.jpg";
```

The following diagram shows the result. You can try and run the full code, which is available in `Examples/example-8-canvas.html`:

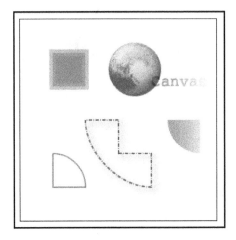

Some shapes drawn in an HTML Canvas context. Code: *Examples/example-8-canvas.html*

Some essential Canvas commands are listed in the following table. All commands are methods of the current Canvas context:

| Method or property | Description |
|---|---|
| `fillStyle` | Sets the color to be used in the `fill()` commands. |
| `strokeStyle` | Sets the color to be used in the `stroke()` commands. |
| `lineWidth` | Sets the line width to be used in the `stroke()` commands. |
| `lineCap` | Sets the style of the line caps, for example `butt` (default), `round`, or `square`. |
| `lineJoin` | Sets the style of the line joins, for example 'round', 'bevel', or 'miter' (default). |
| `font` | Sets the font to be used in the `strokeText()` or `fillText()` commands. |
| `globalAlpha` | Sets the global opacity (0 = transparent, 1 = opaque) for the context. |

| | |
|---|---|
| `shadowBlur, shadowColor, shadowOffsetX, shadowOffsetY` | Sets shadow properties. The default color is transparent black. The default numeric values are zero. |
| `fillRect(x,y,w,h)` | Fills a rectangle. |
| `strokeRect(x,y,w,h)` | Draws a border around a rectangle. |
| `setLineDash(dasharray)` | Receives an array for the dash, alternating lines and spaces. |
| `fillText(text,x,y);` | Fills text at the x and y positions (y is the baseline). |
| `strokeText(text, x, y);` | Draws a border around text at the x and y positions. |
| `createLinearGradient(x0, y0, x1, y1)` | Creates a linear gradient perpendicular to the line. Radial gradients and patterns are also supported. |
| `drawImage(image, x, y, w, h)` | Draws an image. |
| `beginPath()` | Starts a path. |
| `moveTo(x, y)` | Moves the cursor to a position in the path. |
| `lineTo(x, y)` | Moves the cursor to a position in the path, drawing a line along the way. |
| `bezierCurveTo(c1x, c1y, c2x, c2y, x, y), quadraticCurveTo(cx, cy, x, y)` | Draws curves with one (*quadratic*) or two (*Bezier*) control points in a path. |
| `arc(x, y, r, sa, ea)` | Draws an arc by specifying the center, radius, start, and end angles in a path. |
| `arcTo(sx, sy, r, ex, ey)` | Draws an arc by specifying the coordinates of the starting point, the radius, and the coordinates of the end point. |
| `rect(x, y, w, h)` | Draws a rectangle in a path with the coordinates of the top-left corner, width, and height. |
| `clip()` | Creates a clipping region with the shapes drawn by the path that will affect objects that are drawn afterwards. |
| `fill()` | Fills a path with the current color. |
| `stroke()` | Strokes the path with the current color. |

Selected HTML Canvas commands

---

[ 41 ]

# Data formats

Data used in visualizations is usually distributed in a standard format that can be shared. Even when the data is served from a database, the data is usually delivered in some standard format. Popular proprietary formats, such as Excel spreadsheets, are common, but most statistical data is stored or delivered in CSV, XML, or JSON formats.

# CSV

CSV stands for comma-separated values. It's a very popular data format for public data. A CSV file is a text file that emulates a table. It usually contains one header row with the names of the columns, and one or more data rows containing value fields. Rows are separated by line breaks, and the comma-separated fields in each row form columns. It maps perfectly to an HTML table. This is a simple CSV file containing the population and land area of seven continents (Data/sample.csv):

```
continent,population,areakm2
"North America",579024000,24490000
"Asia",4436224000,43820000
"Europe",738849000,10180000
"Africa",1216130000,30370000
"South America",422535000,17840000
"Oceania",39901000,9008500
"Antarctica",1106,13720000
```

There are no types in CVS. Quotes are used to contain text that might contain the delimiter. They are not necessary if the fields don't contain a comma.

CSV is also used to refer to similar files that don't use a comma as a delimiter. These files are more accurately called **delimiter-separated value** (**DSV**) files. The most common delimiters are tabs (TSV), vertical bars (|), and semicolons.

CSVs may become corrupt and unreadable, but it's text and you can fix it. Missing or unescaped commas are the most common problems.

# XML

**eXtensible Markup Language** (**XML**) is a very popular data format. Ajax responses from Web services are usually returned as text or XML. It has standard native support in JavaScript via the DOM APIs and doesn't require additional parsing. Although it is still common to find data in XML format, CSV and JSON alternatives, if available, are usually smaller and easier to work with.

This is an example of an XML file with the same data as the CSV file shown earlier (`Data/sample.xml`):

```
<continents>
    <continent>
        <name>North America</name>
        <population>579024000</population>
        <area unit="km">24490000</area>
    </continent>
    <continent>
        <name>Asia</name>
        <population>4436224000</population>
        <area unit="km">43820000</area>
    </continent>
...
    <continent>
        <name>Antarctica</name>
        <population>1106</population>
        <area>13720000</area>
    </continent>
</continents>
```

XML files can be validated if an XML Schema is available. You can extract data from a well-formed XML file with DOM or with XPath (which is easier). There are many tools in all languages to manipulate XML. XML is also very easy to generate. Its main disadvantage is verbosity and size.

# JSON

JSON stands for JavaScript Object Notation. It looks a lot like a JavaScript object, but it has stricter formation rules. It's probably the easiest format to work with. It's compact and easy to parse, and it's gradually replacing XML as a preferred data format in Web services.

The following data file containing continent data is shown in JSON format
(Data/sample.json):

```
[
    {
        "continent": "North America",
        "population": 579024000,
        "areakm2": 24490000
    }, {
        "continent": "Asia",
        "population": 4436224000,
        "areakm2": 43820000
    }, {
        "continent": "Europe",
        "population": 738849000,
        "areakm2": 10180000
    }, {
        "continent": "Africa",
        "population": 1216130000,
        "areakm2": 30370000
    }, {
        "continent": "South America",
        "population": 422535000,
        "areakm2": 17840000
    }, {
        "continent": "Oceania",
        "population": 39901000,
        "areakm2": 9008500
    }, {
        "continent": "Antarctica",
        "population": 1106,
        "areakm2": 13720000
    }
]
```

JSON is the preferred format for data manipulation in JavaScript. There are many online
tools you can use to transform CSV and XML files into JSON.

# Loading and parsing external data files

Unless you have a very small or static dataset, it will usually not be embedded in your web
page. You will probably use an asynchronous request to load it from a separate file after
your HTML page is already loaded and then parse it. This section covers topics related to
loading and parsing external files.

# Using a Web server

Most of the examples in this book consist of a single file (not considering the external libraries loaded using the `<script>` tags), and you can run them by simply opening them in a browser. You don't even need a Web server. Just click on the file and view it in your browser. But this won't work in examples that load external files via Ajax. For those files, you do need a Web server.

If you are using an HTML editor, such as PHPStorm or Brackets, it automatically starts a Web server for you and serves the page to your default browser. If you have Python installed in your system (it is native in macOS and Linux, and you can install it in Windows), you can run a simple server from the directory where your files are installed. The syntax depends on which Python version you have installed. You can check by opening a console and typing:

```
python -v
```

Now move to the directory where your HTML files are stored and run one of the following commands. If you have Python 3.x , run:

```
python3 -m http.server
```

If your version is 2.x, run:

```
python -m SimpleHTTPServer
```

Now you can open your files using `http://localhost:8080/your-file-name.html`.

# Loading files using standard JavaScript

The standard way to load data into a Web page is using asynchronous JavaScript and XML, or Ajax. It uses the standard built-in `XMLHttpRequest` object, supported by all modern browsers.

To load a file using `XMLHttpRequest`, you need to create the `XMLHttpRequest` object, choose an HTTP method, use the object to open an HTTP connection to the file's URL, and send the request. You must also create a callback function that listens to the object's `'readystatechange'` event and test the object's `readystate` property.

When this property contains `XMLHttpRequest.DONE`, the request is done and you can extract the data. But it's not finished yet! If the request finished successfully (the object *status* property equals 200), you need to extract the data from the object. In a CSV file, the data will be in the `responseText` property (it's in a different place if it's XML). Only then can you finally parse its contents and create your data array. This is shown in the following code (`Examples/example-9-ajax.html`):

```
const httpRequest = new XMLHttpRequest();
httpRequest.open('GET', 'Data/sample.csv');
httpRequest.send();
    httpRequest.onreadystatechange = function(){
        if (httpRequest.readyState === XMLHttpRequest.DONE) {
            if (httpRequest.status === 200) {
                const text = httpRequest.responseText;
                parse(text);
            }
        }
    }
function parse(text) {
    // parse the CSV text and transform it into a JavaScript object
}
```

# Loading files using JQuery

You never have to use standard JavaScript to load files, but it's good to know how it works. It's much, much simpler to load files using the *JQuery* library (`Examples/example-10-ajax-jquery.html`):

```
$.ajax({
    url: 'Data/sample.csv',
    success: function(text){
        parse(text)
    }
});
```

You can also load and parse JSON files in a single step using *JQuery*:

```
$.getJSON('/Data/sample.json', function(object) {
    // use the JavaScript object
}
```

# Loading files using the standard Fetch API

In all modern browsers, you can also load external files using the Fetch API. It's the new JavaScript standard for loading files asynchronously, and we will be using it in all examples that load external files in this book, but it may not work in some older browsers. In that case, you should revert to standard JavaScript or JQuery.

The `fetch()` command is a reactive method based on JavaScript promises. A basic fetch request is shown as follows (`Examples/example-12-fetch.html`):

```
fetch('Data/sample.csv')
  .then(response => response.text())
  .then(function(text) {
      parse(text);
  });
```

You can also parse JSON files using `fetch()`:

```
fetch('Data/sample.json')
  .then(response => response.json())
  .then(function(object) {
      // use the JavaScript object
  });
```

# Parsing JSON

Although JSON is based on JavaScript, a JSON file is not a JavaScript object. It's a string. To convert it into an object and access its properties with the dot operator, you can use `JSON.parse()`:

```
const obj = JSON.parse(jsonString);
```

Sometimes you need to convert a JavaScript object back into JSON format. You might also do this for debugging. You can do this with `JSON.stringify()`:

```
const jsonString = JSON.stringify(obj);
```

If you parsed the example JSON file at the beginning of this section, the JavaScript object will actually be an array of objects, and you can list its contents (in the JavaScript console) using the following code (`Examples/example-14.html`):

```
obj.forEach(function(item) {
    console.log(item.continent, +item.population, +item.areakm2);
  });
```

# Parsing CSV

There is no native CSV parser in JavaScript, but if you have a very small and simple CSV file, you can parse it using JavaScript string manipulation tools or regular expressions, splitting by newlines (\n) to select each row, and then splitting by the delimiter to select each data cell within each row.

Larger data files are more complex, since the preceding code depends on a specific format and does not deal with commas inside quoted strings, missing data, and so on. In this case, you should use a CSV parser. Most examples in this book use the PapaParse CSV parser (papaparse.com) by Matt Holt, which is open source and free. The following code shows how to convert CSV into a JavaScript object using PapaParse:

```
const csvData = Papa.parse(csvText, {header: true}).data;
```

If you parsed the example CSV file at the beginning of this section, you will receive an array of objects, and you can list the contents (in the JavaScript console) using the following code (Examples/example-15.html):

```
csvData.forEach(function(item) {
    console.log(item.continent, +item.population, +item.areakm2);
});
```

The + before the last two properties converts them into numbers. If you don't do that they will be loaded as strings, even though they are numbers.

# Loading multiple files

Sometimes you need files from different sources that need to be loaded and then manipulated within a page. You load these using Promise.all(), as shown next. The code in the promise will only be executed when all the files are loaded (Examples/example-16.html):

```
const files = ['/path/to/file.json', '/path/to/file.csv'];
var promises = files.map(file => fetch(file).then(resp => resp.text()));
Promise.all(promises).then(results => {
    const jsonData = JSON.parse(results[0]);
    const csvData = Papa.parse(results[1], {header: true}).data;
    // use the two data objects
});
```

# Displaying a map

Without any charting library, using just standard JavaScript, you can load a JSON file and draw a world map using Canvas. The data is a special JSON format that stores geographical shapes: GeoJSON. Its general structure is as follows:

```
{"type":"FeatureCollection",
  "features":[
     {"type":"Feature",id:"AFG","properties":{"name":"Afghanistan"},
"geometry":{"type":"Polygon","coordinates":[[[61.210817,35.650072],...]]
     },{"type":"Feature", "id":"AGO", "properties":{"name":"Angola"},
"geometry":{"type":"MultiPolygon","coordinates":[[[[16.326528,-5.87747,...]
]
     },
     // many other lines
   ]
 }
```

Using JavaScript, you can load this file, parse it, and access each longitude and latitude pair. Then you can scale the values so that they fit into the coordinate system of your Canvas, and draw each shape using Canvas path commands. This is done in the following code (Examples/example-17.html):

```
<canvas id="map" width="1000" height="500"></canvas>
<script>
    var canvas = document.getElementById("map");
    var ctx = canvas.getContext("2d");

    // Map ocean background
    ctx.fillStyle = 'white';
    ctx.fillRect(0, 0, canvas.width, canvas.height);

    // countries border and background
    ctx.lineWidth = .25;
    ctx.strokeStyle = 'white';
    ctx.fillStyle = 'rgb(50,100,150)';

    // load and draw map
    fetch('Data/world.geojson')
    .then(response => response.text())
    .then((jsonData) => {
        let object = JSON.parse(jsonData);
        drawMap(object.features);
    });
    function scaleX(coord) {
        return canvas.width * (180 + coord) / 360;
    }
```

```
        function scaleY(coord) {
            return canvas.height * (90 - coord) / 180;
        }
    function drawPolygon(coords) {
        ctx.beginPath();
        for(let i = 0; i < coords.length; i++ ) {
            let latitude = coords[i][1];
            let longitude = coords[i][0];
            if(i == 0) {
                ctx.moveTo(scaleX(longitude), scaleY(latitude));
            } else {
                ctx.lineTo(scaleX(longitude), scaleY(latitude));
            }
        }
        ctx.stroke();
        ctx.fill();
    }
    function drawMap(data) {
        data.forEach(obj => {
            if(obj.geometry.type == 'MultiPolygon') {
                obj.geometry.coordinates.forEach(poly =>
drawPolygon(poly[0]));
            } else if(obj.geometry.type == 'Polygon') {
                obj.geometry.coordinates.forEach(poly =>
drawPolygon(poly));
            }
        });
    }
</script>
```

The result is shown as follows:

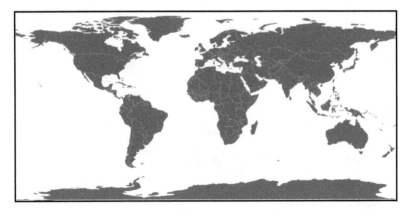

A world map created using GeoJSON, JavaScript, and Canvas code

# Extracting and transforming data

If you are lucky enough to find your data in CSV, XML, or JSON, you can load it and start using it right away. But what if your data is only available as HTML tables, or worse, as a PDF file? In these cases, you need to extract your data and transform it into a usable format.

If it's a very simple HTML table, sometimes you can select it and copy and paste it into a spreadsheet and preserve the rows and columns. Then you can export it as a CSV. Sometimes you will need to do extra work, perhaps removing garbage characters, styles, and unnecessary columns. This is risky, since you may also lose data or introduce errors during the process.

# Online tools

You can also use online tools that try to convert HTML tables into XML, CSV, and JSON. Let's try an example. The NASA JPL site has a Web page containing data about the moon and the planets in our solar system (nssdc.gsfc.nasa.gov/planetary/factsheet). To use that data, you will need to have it in a standard format such as JSON, CSV, or XML, but it's only available as an HTML table, shown as follows:

**Planetary Fact Sheet - Metric**

| | MERCURY | VENUS | EARTH | MOON | MARS | JUPITER | SATURN | URANUS | NEPTUNE | PLUTO |
|---|---|---|---|---|---|---|---|---|---|---|
| Mass ($10^{24}$kg) | 0.330 | 4.87 | 5.97 | 0.073 | 0.642 | 1898 | 568 | 86.8 | 102 | 0.0146 |
| Diameter (km) | 4879 | 12,104 | 12,756 | 3475 | 6792 | 142,984 | 120,536 | 51,118 | 49,528 | 2370 |
| Density (kg/m$^3$) | 5427 | 5243 | 5514 | 3340 | 3933 | 1326 | 687 | 1271 | 1638 | 2095 |
| Gravity (m/s$^2$) | 3.7 | 8.9 | 9.8 | 1.6 | 3.7 | 23.1 | 9.0 | 8.7 | 11.0 | 0.7 |
| Escape Velocity (km/s) | 4.3 | 10.4 | 11.2 | 2.4 | 5.0 | 59.5 | 35.5 | 21.3 | 23.5 | 1.3 |
| Rotation Period (hours) | 1407.6 | -5832.5 | 23.9 | 655.7 | 24.6 | 9.9 | 10.7 | -17.2 | 16.1 | -153.3 |
| Length of Day (hours) | 4222.6 | 2802.0 | 24.0 | 708.7 | 24.7 | 9.9 | 10.7 | 17.2 | 16.1 | 153.3 |
| Distance from Sun ($10^6$ km) | 57.9 | 108.2 | 149.6 | 0.384* | 227.9 | 778.6 | 1433.5 | 2872.5 | 4495.1 | 5906.4 |
| Perihelion ($10^6$ km) | 46.0 | 107.5 | 147.1 | 0.363* | 206.6 | 740.5 | 1352.6 | 2741.3 | 4444.5 | 4436.8 |
| Aphelion ($10^6$ km) | 69.8 | 108.9 | 152.1 | 0.406* | 249.2 | 816.6 | 1514.5 | 3003.6 | 4545.7 | 7375.9 |
| Orbital Period (days) | 88.0 | 224.7 | 365.2 | 27.3 | 687.0 | 4331 | 10,747 | 30,589 | 59,800 | 90,560 |
| Orbital Velocity (km/s) | 47.4 | 35.0 | 29.8 | 1.0 | 24.1 | 13.1 | 9.7 | 6.8 | 5.4 | 4.7 |
| Orbital Inclination (degrees) | 7.0 | 3.4 | 0.0 | 5.1 | 1.9 | 1.3 | 2.5 | 0.8 | 1.8 | 17.2 |

An HTML table containing data that can be used in a chart

Let's first try an online conversion service. Searching for HTML-to-CSV conversion, I found an online conversion service at at `www.convertcsv.com` with several CSV conversion tools. Open the **HTML Table to CSV** link and either paste the source code in the input box, or provide its URL. There are some options you can configure, such as choosing the delimiter. Click on the **Convert HTML to CSV** button, and the following text will appear in the output box:

```
,MERCURY,VENUS,EARTH,MOON,MARS,JUPITER,SATURN,URANUS,NEPTUNE,PLUTO
Mass (1024kg),0.330,4.87,5.97,0.073,0.642,1898,568,86.8,102,0.0146
Diameter
(km),4879,"12,104","12,756",3475,6792,"142,984","120,536",...,2370
Density (kg/m3),5427,5243,5514,3340,3933,1326,687,1271,1638,2095
Gravity (m/s2),3.7,8.9,9.8,1.6,3.7,23.1,9.0,8.7,11.0,0.7
... several rows not shown ...
Number of Moons,0,0,1,0,2,79,62,27,14,5
Ring System?,No,No,No,No,No,Yes,Yes,Yes,Yes,No
Global Magnetic Field?,Yes,No,Yes,No,No,Yes,Yes,Yes,Yes,Unknown
,MERCURY,VENUS,EARTH,MOON,MARS,JUPITER,SATURN,URANUS,NEPTUNE,PLUTO
```

This is valid CSV, but some fields were interpreted as strings, not numbers (some diameters, for example). You might also wish to remove some unnecessary rows, such as the last one, or data you don't need. You can edit the file later and write a script to fix the numbers using regular expressions. Download the result and save it in a file, and then try loading the file using JavaScript.

Since this is a third-party online service, I can't guarantee it will still exist when you read this book, but you should find similar services that perform the same conversion. If not, you can always write an extraction script yourself. A good tool for that is *XPath*, supported by many extraction libraries and browsers, described in the next section.

# Extracting data with XPath

Since HTML is a structure document, you can use a computer program to navigate that structure and extract selected text nodes, attributes, and elements. Most Web extraction tools are based on XPath: an XML standard that can be used to navigate in a XML structure and select elements, attributes, and text nodes using path notation. Although HTML is not as strict as XML, it has similar structures that can be represented as XPath paths and is supported by many Web scraping tools.

For example, the first lines of the previous web page have the following structure:

```
<html>
  <head>
    <title>Planetary Fact Sheet</title>
  </head>
  <body bgcolor=FFFFFF>
    <p>
    <hr>
    <H1>Planetary Fact Sheet - Metric</H1>
    <hr>
    <p>
    <table> ...
```

It's not XML or XHTML, since attributes are not within quotes and tags don't close, but you can still use XPath to extract data from it. This path will give you the title:

```
/html/head/title/text()
```

Any one of these one will return the `bgcolor` attribute (its name and value) from the body tag:

```
/html/body/@bgcolor
/html/body/attribute::bgcolor
```

This one will return the contents of the `<H1>` header:

```
/html/head/h1/text()
```

This one is tricky. If this was XML, it would be `/html/head/p/hr/H1`, because all XML tags must close, but HTML parsers automatically close the `<p>` and `<hr>` tags because there can't be an `<h1>` header inside them. HTML is also case insensitive, so using `H1` or `h1` doesn't make any difference with these parsers. Still, this may still confuse some parsers. You can play it safe by using:

```
/html/head//H1/text()
```

The `//` or double slash means that between `<head>` and `<H1>` there can be any number of levels. This is compatible with the XML or HTML absolute path.

You can experiment with XPath using your browser's JavaScript console, writing XPath expressions inside `$x(expression)`. Let's try it out using the *Planetary Fact Sheet* page. Open the page in your browser and then open a console window, and type the following:

```
$x("//table")
```

This will select all the tables in the document. In this case, there is only one. You can also view the source code or inspect the page to discover the absolute path:

```
$x("/html/body/p/table")
```

Enter this command and the console will reveal the HTML fragment corresponding to your selection. Now let's select the row that contains diameters. It's the third row in the table. You can ignore the existing <thead> or <tbody> tags using the //. XPath counts child nodes starting with 1, not 0 as in JavaScript. The command returns a single <tr> element in an array. We can extract it using [0]:

```
$x("//table//tr[3]")[0]
```

This will select the following fragment:

```
<tr>
    <td align="left"><b><a href="planetfact_notes.html#diam">Diameter</a>
(km)</b></td>
    <td align="center" bgcolor="F5F5F5">4879</td>
    <td align="center" bgcolor="FFFFFF">12,104</td>
    <td align="center" bgcolor="F5F5F5">12,756</td>
    <td align="center" bgcolor="FFFFFF">3475</td>
    <td align="center" bgcolor="F5F5F5">6792</td>
    <td align="center" bgcolor="FFFFFF">142,984</td>
    <td align="center" bgcolor="F5F5F5">120,536</td>
    <td align="center" bgcolor="FFFFFF">51,118</td>
    <td align="center" bgcolor="F5F5F5">49,528</td>
    <td align="center" bgcolor="FFFFFF">2370</td>
</tr>
```

To select the diameter of the earth, you need to add one more path step:

```
$x("//table//tr[3]/td[4]")[0]
```

The result is as follows:

```
<td align="center" bgcolor="F5F5F5">12,756</td>
```

To extract the text, you need to include the text() function at the end of the XPath expression. You also need to extract the data from the $x() function result, using the data property:

```
const result = $x("/html/body/p/table/tbody/tr[3]/td[4]/text()")[0].data
```

This will return the result as a string. You can then use regular expressions to remove the comma and then convert the result to a number:

```
const value = +data.replace(/\,/g,'');
// removes commas and converts to number
```

You might want to automate that with a programming library if you need to extract lots of data, such as all the planetary diameters. The `$x()` command only works in the browser console, but many programming languages support XPath libraries and APIs. You can also use tools such as Scrapy (in Python) or testing tools such as Selenium (in several languages) that support XPath selectors for extracting data from HTML.

XPath is a very powerful data extraction language, and this was only a very brief introduction. But there are also alternatives, such as XQuery (another XML standard with a query syntax) and CSS selectors (used by *JQuery* and also supported by Scrapy and Selenium).

# Summary

This chapter provided a refresher on several fundamental technology concepts that will help you create visualizations with Chart.js. Even though Chart.js tries to hide all the underlying complexity from you, it is still a JavaScript library and basic knowledge of JavaScript, DOM, and CSS are important.

This chapter also described the main data formats used for statistical data: CSV, XML, and JSON. It also described how to load external files in these formats and how to parse them. Additionally, you learned some ways to obtain data not in these formats by extracting it from HTML pages.

In the next chapter, we will begin using Chart.js to create data visualizations.

# Chart.js - Quick Start 3

This chapter provides a quick start to creating web-based data visualizations with Chart.js. You will learn how to set up the library and configure a basic web page where you can include a chart. We will walk through a complete step-by-step example, describing how to create a bar chart and configure it with labels, tooltips, titles, interactions, colors, animations, and more. By using Chart.js to create a full-featured chart, you will have a better understanding of the main concepts when we explore the details later on.

In this chapter, you will learn about the following topics:

- How to install and set up Chart.js
- How to create a simple bar chart
- How to configure axes, colors, and tooltips
- How to add animation and respond to simple events
- How to create a horizontal and a stacked bar chart

# Introduction to Chart.js

Chart.js is an open source community-maintained JavaScript data visualization library based on HTML5 Canvas. At the time of writing, it is available as version 2.7.3, and comes with eight customizable chart types. It's very easy to create a chart using Chart.js. It can be as simple as loading the JavaScript library into your page, choosing a chart type, and providing it with an array of data.

All charts are configured with a default look and feel, as well as basic interactive features. You can focus on the data and quickly create a simple responsive and interactive chart that fits nicely in your page. You don't have to worry about configuring padding or margins, fitting labels in axes, adding tooltips, or controlling transitions. But if you need to change something, there are many configuration options available.

# Installation and setup

To set up a web page for Chart.js, you just need to load the library. If you already have a website set up, you can download Chart.js from www.chartjs.org, store it where you can load it from a web page, and import it using the <script> tag, as follows:

```
<script src="../js/Chart.min.js"></script>
```

You can also use npm or bower to install Chart.js if you have a modular development environment, as shown in the following code. Chart.js integrates well with ES6 modules, *Angular*, *React*, and *Vue* applications:

```
npm install chart.js --save
bower install chart.js --save
```

The simplest way to get started is to link to a library file provided by a **Content Delivery Network (CDN)**. You can obtain a list at cdnjs.com/libraries/Chart.js, choose the version and CDN provider of your choice, and copy one of the links. Unless you want to inspect the code, use the minified link (that ends in min.js). It's best not to use the bundle version, since it includes some extra non-Chart.js libraries (a better practice is to include third-party libraries separately when needed).

Using any text or code editor, copy the link to the `src` attribute of a `script` tag placed somewhere in the `<head>` of your HTML file, as follows:

```
<script
src="https://cdnjs.cloudflare.com/ajax/libs/Chart.js/2.7.2/Chart.min.js">
</script>
```

If you have a development environment, such as Visual Studio Code, PHPStorm, or Brackets, you may wish to set up a template file that includes the Chart.js CDN script tag for new pages.

Another way to explore Chart.js and follow the examples in this book, is to use an online code editor, such as *CodePen* or *JSFiddle*. It's also a great way to share your charts and code.

Using JSFiddle (`https://jsfiddle.net/`), you just need to add the Chart.js CDN to the **Resources** tab, as shown in the following screenshot, and then you can use the tabs to write the HTML, CSS, and JavaScript code for your charts:

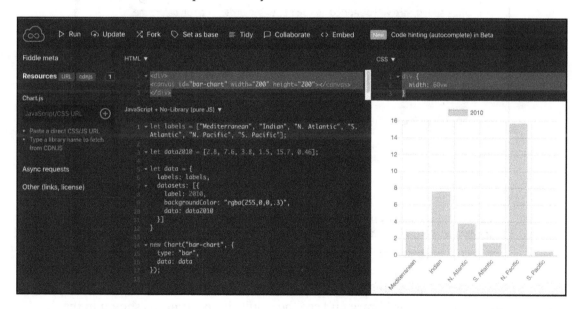

Using *JSFiddle* (*jsfiddle.net*) as an online code editor

To configure Chart.js in *CodePen* (`https://codepen.io/`), click the **Settings** menu and then the **JavaScript** tab. Search for Chart.js, and click the first option to add the CDN to your environment, as demonstrated in the following screenshot:

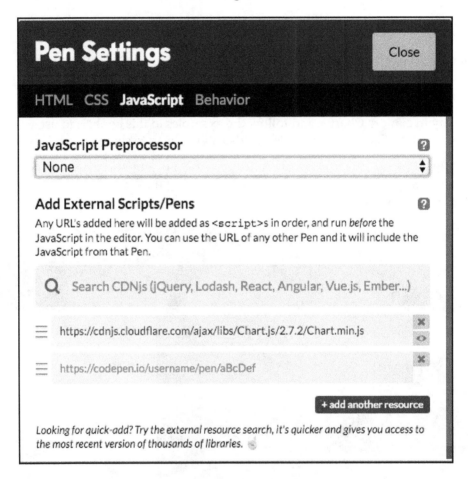

Adding Chart.js support to *CodePen* (*codepen.io*)

You can now use the Chart.js library and see the results in real time, as shown in the following screenshot:

Using CodePen (codepen.io) as an online code editor

# Creating a simple bar chart

Now that you have a working environment set up, let's get started and create a simple bar chart. You can type in the code as we go along, but you can also download the full working examples from the GitHub repository for this chapter. Each screenshot and code listing in this book contains a reference to the file used to produce it.

# Setting up the graphics context

Charts are displayed inside the graphics context provided by an HTML Canvas object. There are many ways to create one; the simplest way is to use plain HTML. Place a `<canvas>` element somewhere inside `<body>`. It should have an ID attribute, as follows:

```
<canvas id="my-bar-chart" width="200" height="200"></canvas>
```

Chart.js graphics are responsive by default. The chart will fit in the available space: the `height` and `width` attributes won't affect the actual size of the chart (unless you change the defaults).

You can obtain a JavaScript handle to the `canvas` object using DOM (or JQuery) in any script block or file loaded by your HTML file, as shown in the following code snippet (the script block will be ignored in most JavaScript listings in this book):

```
<script>
    const canvas = document.getElementById("my-bar-chart");
</script>
```

You can also dynamically create a `<canvas>` object using **Document Object Model (DOM)**, or JQuery. In this case, an `ID` attribute is not strictly necessary, since the variable itself can be used as a handle, but it's good practice to define one, as follows:

```
canvas canvas = document.createElement("canvas");
canvas.setAttribute("id","my-bar-chart");
document.body.appendChild(canvas);
```

A chart is created using the `Chart()` constructor. It receives two arguments: the graphics *context* of the canvas where the chart will be displayed, and an *object* containing the chart data, as demonstrated in the following code:

```
const chartObj = {...}; // the chart data is here
const context = canvas.getContext("2d");
new Chart(context, chartObj); // this will display the chart in the canvas
```

If your `canvas` object has declared an `ID` attribute, you don't need a `context` object. You can simply use the `ID` attribute as the first argument, as follows:

```
new Chart("my-bar-chart", chartObj);
```

The object that contains the chart data requires at least two properties: `type`, which selects one of the eight different kinds of Chart.js charts; and `data`, which references an object containing the datasets and properties of the data to be displayed, as follows:

```
const chartObj = {type: "bar", data: dataObj};
```

Normally, the chart object is configured inside the constructor, as follows:

```
new Chart("my-bar-chart", {type: "bar", data: dataObj});
```

This is the basic setup for any chart created with Chart.js. It won't show any chart yet, because we didn't provide any data, but if your library loaded correctly, you should see an empty axis. The code is in the `Templates/BasicTemplate.html` file.

If nothing shows up in your screen, there may be a syntax error in your code. Check your browser's JavaScript console. It's always a good idea to keep it open when you are working with JavaScript, so that errors can be detected and fixed quickly.

# Creating a bar chart

A bar chart displays a list of categories associated with values represented by the length of the bars. To create a simple bar chart, we need a list of *categories*, as well as list of *values*.

Let's create a simple chart to display the volume of water in each ocean. We will need an array of categories, as follows:

```
const labels = ["Arctic", "North Atlantic", "South Atlantic",
                "Indian", "North Pacific", "South Pacific",
                "Southern"];
```

In addition, we will also need a corresponding array of values, as follows:

```
const volumes = [18750,146000,160000,264000,341000,329000,71800]; // 10^3
km3
```

The `data` object should contain a `labels` property, which will refer to the `categories` array, and a `datasets` property, which contains an array with at least one `dataset` object. Each `dataset` object has a `label` property, and a `data` property, which will receive the data for our chart (the `volumes` array), as follows:

```
const dataObj = {
    labels: labels,
    datasets: [
        {
            label: "Volume",
            data: volumes
        }
    ]
}
```

Charts already come preconfigured with scales, axes, default colors, fonts, animation, and tooltips. Include the `dataObj` object from the preceding code as the `data` property of the chart object (`chartObj`), and you will have an interactive and responsive bar chart similar to the one shown as follows:

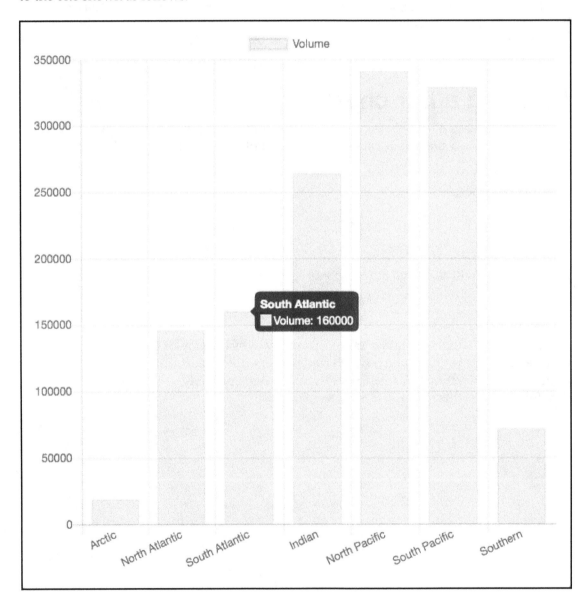

A simple bar chart (code: *Pages/BarChart1.html*)

Try resizing the window and see how the labels and scales adapt to the new display. Move your mouse over the bars and see how the tooltips display the chart's information. Click on the dataset label and toggle its visibility. In the following sections, we will configure some of its appearance and behavior.

The full listing is shown as follows:

```
<!DOCTYPE html>
<html lang="en">
<head>
<script
src="https://cdnjs.cloudflare.com/ajax/libs/Chart.js/2.7.2/Chart.min.js">
</script>
</head>
<body>
<canvas id="ocean-volume-bar-chart" width="400" height="400"></canvas>
<script>
  const labels = ["Arctic", "North Atlantic", "South Atlantic",
                  "Indian", "North Pacific", "South Pacific", "Southern"];
  const volumes = [18750,146000,160000,264000,341000,329000,71800];

  const dataObj = {
      labels: labels,
      datasets: [
          {
              label: "Volume",
              data: volumes
          }
      ]
  }
  new Chart("ocean-volume-bar-chart", {type: "bar", data: dataObj});
 </script>
</body>
</html>
```

Try typing in the preceding code in your development environment, or download it from Pages/BarChart1.html.

# Configuring colors, fonts, and responsiveness

Charts created with Chart.js are born responsive and fit nicely into your screen, but they are also born gray. In this section, you will discover how to change some style properties.

## Dataset configuration for bar charts

Besides the `data` and `label` properties, each dataset object can contain a number of optional configuration properties. Most of them are used to configure fill and border colors and widths. They are briefly described in the following table:

| Property | Value | Description |
|---|---|---|
| data | Number[] | An array of numbers containing the data to display (this is mandatory) |
| label | String | A label for the dataset |
| backgroundColor | String or String[] | The fill color of the bar |
| borderColor | String or String[] | The color of the border |
| borderWidth | Number or Number[] | The width of the border |
| hoverBackgroundColor | String or String[] | The fill when the mouse is over the bar |
| hoverBorderColor | String or String[] | The border color when the mouse is over the bar |
| hoverBorderWidth | Number or Number[] | The border width when the mouse is over the bar |
| borderSkipped | bottom, left, top, right | Selects which edge of the bar with no border (the default is bottom for bar, and left for horizontalBar ) |
| yAxisID and xAxisID | An Axis ID (see Chapter 5, *Scales and Grid Configuration*) | Used in axis configuration |

Dataset properties for bar charts

You can change the gray colored bars by adding color properties in each `dataset` object, or by configuring global defaults that affect all charts. The `backgroundColor` property receives a string containing a color specified in a legal CSS format. For example, if you want to have solid red bars, you can use the following formats:

- `red`
- `rgb(255,0,0)`
- `rgba(100%,0,0,1)`
- `#ff0000, #f00`
- `hsl(0,100%,50%)`
- `hsla(0,100%,50%,1)`

The `borderColor` property controls the color of the label icon. It also configures the color of the bars if the `borderWidth` is specified with a value greater than zero, as follows:

```
const dataObj = {
    labels: labels,
    datasets: [
        {
            label: "Volume",
            data: volumes,
            borderWidth: 2,
            backgroundColor: "hsla(20,100%,80%,0.8)",
            borderColor: "hsla(0,100%,50%,1)"
        }
    ]
}
new Chart("ocean-volume-bar-chart", {type: "bar", data: dataObj});
```

The preceding code should produce the result shown as follows. The full code is available at `Pages/BarChart2.html`:

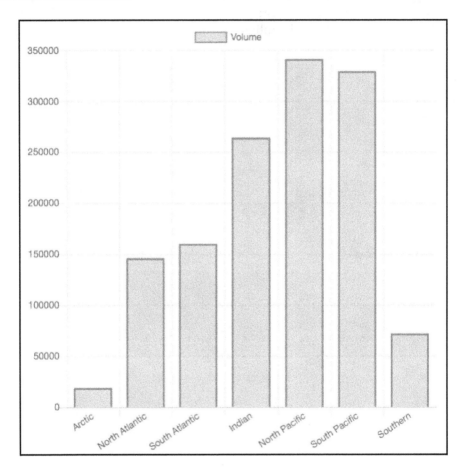

Applying color attributes to a bar chart (code: *Pages/BarChart2.html*)

# Options configuration

Defaults are configured per chart with an options configuration object included in the `chart` object (the second parameter of the constructor), as demonstrated in the following block of code:

```
new Chart("ocean-volume-bar-chart",
    {
        type: "bar",
```

```
        data: dataObj,
        options: {} // configure options here
    });
```

There are many defaults that you can change. You might, for example, wish to have more control over the size of your chart, which resizes automatically. That happens because charts are responsive by default. You can turn responsiveness off by overriding the responsive property, which has a default true value, as follows:

```
options: {
    responsive: false
}
```

Now, your chart no longer resizes automatically. However, what if you do want to undertake resizing, but don't care about the aspect ratio? Then, you can override the maintainAspectRatio property, as follows:

```
options: {
    maintainAspectRatio: false
}
```

You might want this if your canvas object is located inside a parent <div> container, which controls its size and is configured with CSS. In the following code (Pages/BarChart4.html), the canvas will occupy 80% of the size of its parent container, as follows:

```
<style>
    #canvas-container {
        position: relative;
        height: 80%;
        width: 80%;
    }
</style>
<div id="canvas-container">
  <canvas id="ocean-volume-bar-chart" width="200" height="200"></canvas>
</div>
```

If you try to resize the chart, it will, by default, maintain its aspect ratio (and no longer fit in the page), unless the `maintainAspectRatio` property is set to `false`, as follows:

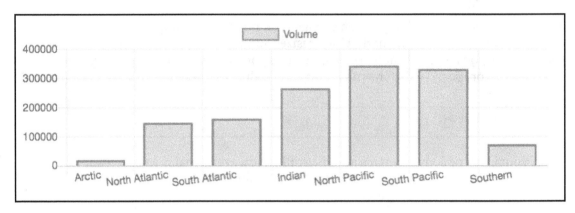

Configuring the aspect ratio of a chart to make it fit in a canvas (code: *Pages/BarChart4.html*)

# Text and fonts

Text can be included in many different objects. Each data object can have a list of categories, each dataset can have a legend, the chart can have a title, and tooltips can have titles and other information. Some text is visible or invisible by default. You can configure the visibility, font families, font sizes, and colors of any text inside a chart.

Fonts can be applied globally (for all charts) using default configurations. Using the `options` configuration object, they can be applied locally to titles and legends, which are also configured as objects.

In our chart, we have a single dataset, which makes the legend superfluous. You can hide it by changing the `legend.display` property to `false`, as follows:

```
options: { // configure options here
    ...
    legend: {
        display: false
    }
}
```

We can also give the chart a title and configure its font size, color, and family, as follows:

```
options: { // configure options here
    maintainAspectRatio: false,
    legend: {
```

```
        display: false
    },
    title: {
        display: true,
        text: ['Volume of the oceans','in thousands of cubic km'],
        fontFamily: "TrebuchetMS",
        fontSize: 24,
        fontColor: 'rgb(0,120,0)',
    }
}
```

It's not enough to simply add the title to the `text` property. Since the `display` property is `false` by default, you must explicitly define it to be `true` for the title to be displayed. With these changes, your chart should look similar to the following:

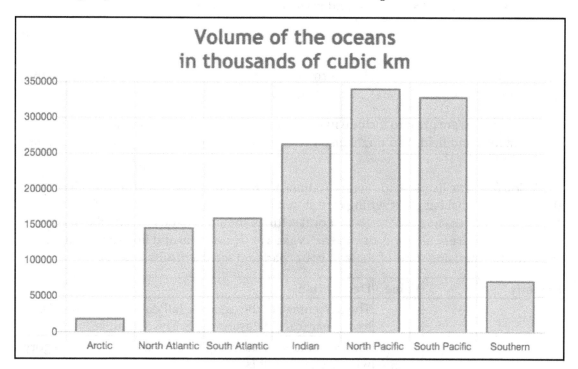

Adding a title and defining font properties (code: *Pages/BarChart5.html*)

You can configure the style of all of the text in the chart, including individual tooltip titles and bodies, scales, and major and minor ticks, as we will see in the following chapters.

# Global defaults

Local configuration options override global default configurations, which can be configured using the `Chart.defaults.global` object. You can configure properties, such as fonts, colors, axes, gridlines, ticks, animations, tooltips, and element properties, either globally (for all charts), or locally (for a specific chart).

To specify a global font family, you can use the following code:

```
Chart.defaults.global.defaultFontFamily = "Helvetica Neue";
```

This will affect all of the text in the chart. You can also define defaults for specific text elements by changing the properties, such as `Chart.defaults.global.legend`, `Chart.defaults.global.title`, and many more, as follows:

```
Chart.defaults.global.legend.fontSize = 10; // all legend text will be size
10
```

The default color used in charts is `rgba(0,0,0,0.1)` `(lightgray)`. You can change this using `Chart.defaults.global.defaultColor`.

Global properties are great to include in a separate `.js` file, so that your charts have a consistent look and field. You might also prefer to use them even when you have a single chart.

The following table lists specific configurations for bar charts that can be applied locally or globally. The global bar chart settings are stored in `Chart.defaults.bar` and `Charts.defaults.horizontalBar`. Local settings should be stored inside the `options` object under `scales.xAxes[]` or `scales.yAxes[]`, for vertical and horizontal bar charts, respectively. Try using some of these in your chart and see the results you get:

| Property | Value | Description |
|---|---|---|
| barPercentage | | The percentage of the category (all datasets) width taken by the bar (each dataset) width. The default is 0.9. |
| categoryPercentage | Number | The percentage of the sample width taken by the category width. The default is 0.8. |
| barThickness | | This manually sets the bar width (ignores categoryPercentage and barPercentage). |
| maxBarThickness | | This limits the bar thickness to this number. |

Option configuration properties for charts

# Transitions, interactions, and tooltips

All charts are also born with basic transitions, animations, and interactive tooltips. For a simple chart, you might not need to change anything; but in case you want more control, you can configure these behaviors with local and global properties.

## Transition duration

You can create charts that change the way they look on user interaction. They will automatically transition to the new values gracefully and smoothly. Transition animations are configured with default ease algorithms and durations, but you can change them by editing the properties of the `Chart.defaults.global.animation` object, or override any defaults locally by using the `options.animation` object.

For example, in the following chart code, all transitions last five seconds (`Pages/BarChart6.html`):

```
new Chart("ocean-volume-bar-chart", {
    type: "bar",
    data: {...},
    options: {
        ...
        animation: {
            duration: 5000
        }
    }
});
```

## Updating charts

You can use JavaScript functions and libraries to change your data dynamically, but the changes will not be reflected immediately in your chart. After changing data, you have to call `update()` in order to redraw it. For this, you will need a variable reference to the `chart` object, as follows:

```
const ch = new Chart("ocean-volume-bar-chart", {...});
```

The following example toggles the data in the chart, replacing the values in the dataset with a different array, and changing labels, titles, and colors. The `toggle()` function is registered as a click event listener on the canvas. Whenever you click anywhere in the canvas it will run, change the values of several properties, and call `update()`,which forces the chart to transition to the new data and appearance, as follows:

```
const labels = ["Arctic", "North Atlantic", "South Atlantic", "Indian",
                "North Pacific", "South Pacific", "Southern"];

const area   = [15558,41900,40270,70560,84000,84750,21960];   // km2 *
10^3
const volume = [18750,146000,160000,264000,341000,329000,71800];
//km3 * 10^3
const canvas = document.getElementById("ocean-volume-bar-chart");
const ctx = canvas.getContext("2d");
const ch = new Chart(ctx, {
    type: "bar",
    data: {
        labels: labels,
        datasets: [
            {
                label: "Volume",
                data: volume,
                borderWidth: 2,
                backgroundColor: "hsla(20,100%,80%,0.8)",
                borderColor: "hsla(0,100%,50%,1)"
            }
        ]
    },
    options: {
        maintainAspectRatio: false,
        title: {
            display: true,
            text: ['Volume of the oceans','in thousands of cubic km'],
            fontFamily: "TrebuchetMS",
            fontSize: 24
        },
        legend: {
            display: false
        }
    }
});

canvas.addEventListener("click", toggle);

function toggle(event) {
    if(ch.data.datasets[0].label == "Volume") {
```

```
        ch.data.datasets[0].data = area;
        ch.data.datasets[0].label = "Area";
        ch.data.datasets[0].borderColor = "hsla(120,100%,50%,1)";
        ch.data.datasets[0].backgroundColor = "hsla(140,100%,80%,0.8)";
        ch.options.title.text = ['Surface area of the oceans',
                                'in thousands of square km'];
    } else {
        ch.data.datasets[0].data = volume;
        ch.data.datasets[0].label = "Volume";
        ch.data.datasets[0].backgroundColor = "hsla(20,100%,80%,0.8)";
        ch.data.datasets[0].borderColor = "hsla(0,100%,50%,1)";
        ch.options.title.text = ['Volume of the oceans',
                                'in thousands of cubic km'];
    }
    ch.update();
}
```

The following screenshot shows the same chart before and after being clicked. The full code
is available at `Pages/BarChart7.html`:

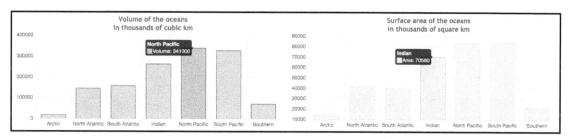

Screenshots of same chart after and before a click. Code: *Pages/BarChart7.html*

# Tooltips

The animation duration does not affect tooltips, which have their own configuration.
Besides animation, you can configure colors, fonts, spacing, shape, and behaviors in
tooltips. You can also declare callback functions that change the appearance and content at
every interaction. If you need to add more information to a tooltip, Chart.js allows you to
create sophisticated HTML tooltips containing images and text.

For example, the following configuration creates black tooltips that contain default title colors. The tooltip configuration options contain callbacks that set text colors that match the colors of the bars, as follows:

```
options: {
    ...
    title: {...},
    legend: {...},
    animation: {...},
    tooltips: {
        backgroundColor: 'rgba(200,200,255,.9)',
        titleFontColor: 'black',
        caretSize: 5,
        callbacks: {
            labelColor: function(tooltipItem, chart) {
                return {
                    borderColor: 'black',
                    backgroundColor:
                    chart.data.datasets[0].backgroundColor
                }
            },
            labelTextColor:function(tooltipItem, chart){
                return chart.data.datasets[0].borderColor;
            }
        }
    }
}
```

You can run the preceding code in the `Pages/BarChart8.html` file.

# Working with larger and multiple datasets

From what we have seen so far, you should already be able to create a simple bar chart. In this section, we will explore some configuration options related to large datasets, which you will probably load as an external file, and multiple datasets, which can be plotted on the same chart.

# Loading data

Many times, your data will be available online and you may want to load it dynamically. It's also a good idea to keep your data and code in separate files. If you have data in a CSV file, you can load it into your JavaScript code and use it to generate the chart.

JavaScript loads data asynchronously using Ajax. You can use standard Ajax, JQuery, or the ES6 fetch function, which functions like a JavaScript promise. After you load the CSV file, you need to parse it. If you only need one set of category labels and values, you can handle it without a parser.

In this example, we will use a CSV file that contains the amount of plastic waste disposed of in the oceans by the 20 greatest pollutants. You can find the following code in the GitHub repository for this chapter in `Data/waste.csv`:

```
Country,Tonnes
China,8819717
Indonesia,3216856
Philippines,1883659
...
United States,275424
```

The following code loads and parses the file, splitting the data into rows, and then splitting each row by a comma to assemble a `labels` array and a `values` array (we could also have used a CSV parser). This process transforms the data into arrays in a format that can be used by Chart.js, as follows:

```javascript
fetch('../Data/waste.csv')
  .then(response => response.text())
  .then((data) => {
    const labels = [],
          values = [];
    const rows = data.split("\n");

    rows.forEach(r => {
        const item = r.split(",");
        labels.push(item[0]);
        values.push(+item[1]);
    });

    labels.shift(); // remove the header
    values.shift(); // remove the header

    console.log(labels); // print to check if the arrays
    console.log(values); // were generated correctly

    draw(labels, values);

});
```

The `draw()` function contains the code to set up a canvas, and create and display the bar chart, as follows:

```
function draw(labels, values) {
    const canvas = document.getElementById("bar-chart");
    const ctx = canvas.getContext("2d");

    new Chart(ctx, {
        type: "bar",
        data: {
            labels: labels, // the labels
            datasets: [
                {
                    label: "Tonnes of plastic",
                    data: values, // the data values
                    borderWidth: 2,
                    backgroundColor: "hsla(20,100%,80%,0.8)",
                    borderColor: "hsla(0,100%,50%,1)"
                }
            ]
        },
        options: {
            maintainAspectRatio: false,
            title: {
                display: true,
                text: 'Tonnes of plastic waste',
                fontSize: 16
            },
            legend: {
                display: false
            }
        }
    });
}
```

You can view the full code in `Pages/BarChart9.html`. The result is shown as follows:

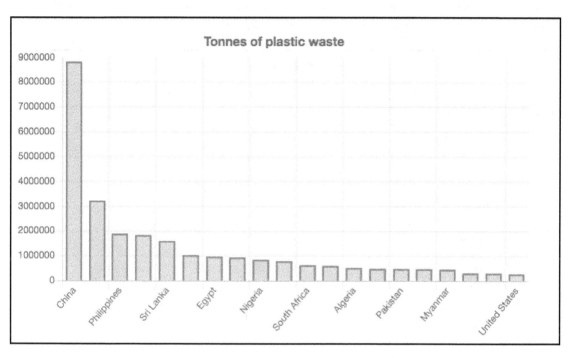

A bar chart created with data loaded from an external file (code: *Pages/BarChart9.html*)

# Horizontal bar chart

When you have a lot of data to display and compare, it might fit better in a horizontal bar chart. You can easily convert a vertical bar chart into a horizontal one by changing the `type` to `horizontalBar`, as follows:

```
new Chart(ctx, {
    type: "horizontalBar",
    data: {...}
}
```

The preceding chart seems better as a horizontal chart, since the category labels don't have to be turned sideways. You can see the full code in `Pages/BarChart10.html`. The following screenshot shows what the chart looks like now:

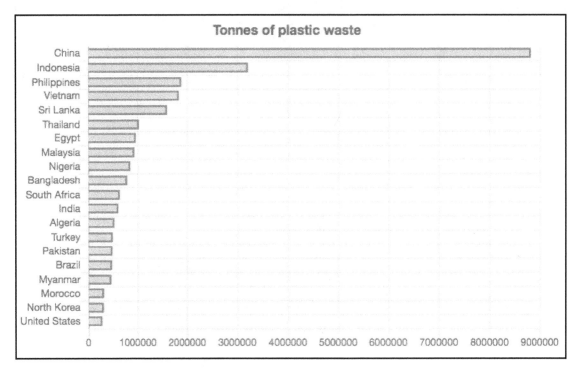

A horizontal bar chart (code: *Pages/BarChart10.html*)

# Adding extra datasets

You can add more datasets to a bar chart, and configure it with a new legend label, colors, and data arrays. In the following example, we will load a larger `.csv` file, which contains the data for plastic waste disposal in 2010, and a forecast for 2025. It has one extra column, as follows:

```
Country,2010,2025
China,8819717,17814777
Indonesia,3216856,7415202
Philippines,1883659,5088394
...
United States,275424,336819
```

This time, the code will generate two `data` arrays and a single `labels` array. The data and labels that belong to the same category have the same index, as follows:

```
fetch('../Data/waste2.csv')
  .then(response => response.text())
  .then((data) => {
    const labels = [],
          values2010 = [],
          values2025 = [];

    const rows = data.split("\n");

    rows.forEach(r => {
        const item = r.split(",");
        labels.push(item[0]);
        values2010.push(+item[1]/1000000); // divide by 1 million to make
        values2025.push(+item[2]/1000000); // the chart easier to read
    });

    labels.shift();
    values2010.shift();
    values2025.shift();

    draw(labels, [values2010, values2025]);

});
```

The new values will be included in a second dataset, in the `datasets` array, as follows.

```
function draw(labels, values) {
    const canvas = document.getElementById("bar-chart");
    const ctx = canvas.getContext("2d");

    new Chart(ctx, {
        type: "horizontalBar",
        data: {
            labels: labels,
            datasets: [
                {
                    label: "2010",
                    data: values[0],
                    backgroundColor: "hsla(20,100%,50%,0.7)",
                },{
                    label: "2025",
                    data: values[1],
                    backgroundColor: "hsla(260,100%,50%,0.7)",
                }
            ]
```

```
        },
        options: {
            maintainAspectRatio: false,
            title: {
                display: true,
                text: 'Millions of tonnes of plastic waste',
                fontSize: 16
            }
        }
    });
}
```

The full code is in `Pages/BarChart12.html`. With two datasets, there are two bars for each category. There is also one legend item for each dataset. The result is shown in the following screenshot:

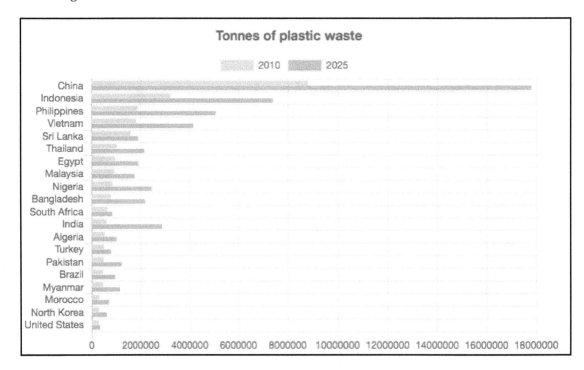

A bar chart with two datasets (code: *Pages/BarChart12.html*)

With two or more datasets, you may want to configure the width of the bars using the configuration option properties, `barPercentage` and `categoryPercentage`. The former controls the width of the individual bars for each category, and the latter determines the space taken by all of the bars in one category. These properties should be defined in `options.scales.xAxes[]` if you are using a bar chart, and `options.scales.yAxes[]` if it is a `horizontalBar` (see `Pages/BarChart12.html`), as follows:

```
options: {
    maintainAspectRatio: false,
    title: {
        display: true,
        text: 'Tonnes of plastic waste',
        fontSize: 16
    },
    scales: {
        yAxes: [{
            barPercentage: .3,
            categoryPercentage: .5
        }]
    }
}
```

# Stacking bars

Bars are usually placed side-by-side for comparison. However, if the values are part of a whole, you can stack bars in different datasets to emphasize this relationship. We can stack the volumes of the world's oceans, since their sum reveals the total volume of ocean water in the world. The following data object places the volume of each ocean in a separate dataset, as follows:

```
const dataObj = {
    labels: ["Volume"], // there is only one category
    datasets: [
        {
            label: "Arctic", data: [18750],
            backgroundColor: "hsla(0,100%,50%,0.5)"
        }, {
            label: "North Atlantic", data: [146000],
            backgroundColor: "hsla(60,100%,50%,0.5)"
        }, {
            label: "South Atlantic", data: [160000],
            backgroundColor: "hsla(120,100%,50%,0.5)"
        }, {
            label: "Indian", data: [264000],
```

```
                    backgroundColor: "hsla(180,100%,50%,0.5)"
            },{
                    label: "North Pacific", data: [341000],
                    backgroundColor: "hsla(240,100%,50%,0.5)"
            },{
                    label: "South Pacific", data: [329000],
                    backgroundColor: "hsla(300,100%,50%,0.5)"
            },{
                    label: "Southern", data: [71800],
                    backgroundColor: "hsla(340,100%,50%,0.5)"
            },
        ]
    };
```

To transform a bar chart into a stacked chart, you have to configure the settings for the $x$ and $y$ axes, enabling the stacked property as follows:

```
const optionsObj = {
    maintainAspectRatio: false,
    title: {
        display: true,
        text: 'Volume of oceans (km3)',
        fontSize: 16
    },
    legend: {
        position: 'right'
    },
    scales: {
        xAxes: [{
            stacked: true
        }],
        yAxes: [{
            stacked: true
        }]
    }
}
new Chart("ocean-volume-bar-chart",
        {type: "bar", data: dataObj, options: optionsObj});
```

The expected result is shown in the following screenshot. The full code is in `Pages/BarChart13.html`:

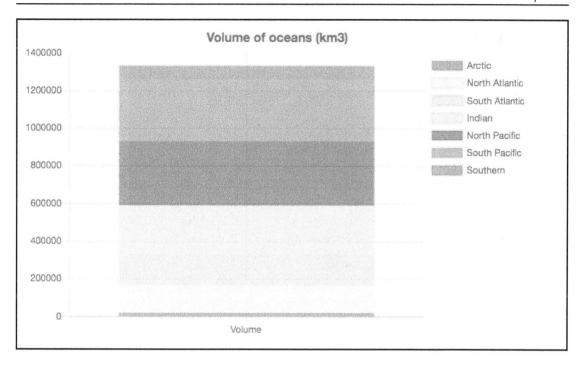

A stacked bar chart can be used to display data as parts of a whole (code: *Pages/BarChart13.html*)

# Summary

In this chapter, we learned how to install Chart.js in a web application and how to quickly create a simple interactive and responsive bar chart, which can be included in a web page. We also learned how to configure the default look and feel of a chart, by changing basic properties, such as colors, fonts, responsiveness, animation duration, and tooltips. With this knowledge, you can already start using Chart.js to display simple data visualizations in your web pages.

This chapter also explored some real-world issues, such as loading external files, and how to deal with larger datasets, by filtering data and configuring the chart in order to display the information more efficiently.

In the following chapters, we will explore Chart.js in greater detail, create all eight different types of charts, learn how to configure several other properties, and deal with more complex datasets.

# References

**Books and websites:**

- Chart.js official documentation and samples: `https://www.chartjs.org/docs/latest/`

**Data sources:**

- Volumes of the World's Oceans (based on ETOPO1): `Chapter03/Pages/BarChart1.html` and others. `https://www.ngdc.noaa.gov/mgg/global/etopo1_ocean_volumes.html`
- Plastic waste: `Chapter03/Data/waste.csv`. Jambeck et al. *Plastic waste inputs from land into the ocean*. Science magazine. 13 February 2015

# 4
# Creating Charts

This chapter covers several charts that can be created with Chart.js to efficiently communicate quantitative information and relationships. The choice of a chart depends on the type of data, how each set of values is related to one another, and what kind of relationships you want to show. In the previous chapter, we learned how to efficiently display data in bar charts and compare quantitative information related to different categories. In this chapter, you will create line and radar charts to compare sequences of one-dimensional data, pie and doughnut charts to compare proportions, scatterplots and bubble charts to represent two or more dimensions, and polar area charts to display quantitative data in a radial grid.

In this chapter, you will learn about the following topics:

- Line and area charts
- Radar and polar area charts
- Pie and doughnut charts
- Scatterplots and bubble charts

## Line and area charts

Line charts are used to display a correlation between two sets of data, where one of the sets should contain categorical or ordered data (ascending or descending). The most common application of a line chart is the time series, where the ordered set consists of instants of time. If arbitrary categories are used, it should be possible to establish some kind of connected sequence with them (for example, an ordered sequence of steps).

Line charts display estimates. The points that correlate the datasets are connected with straight or curved lines that represent estimated values. Line charts can be used to predict intermediate values and reveal trends.

# Creating a simple line chart

Just like the bar chart, you need to load the Chart.js JavaScript library, place a `<canvas>` object somewhere in the `<body>` of your page, and create a new chart referring to the ID of the canvas, and an object with the chart data. The `chart` object should specify `line` as the chart type. The following code is the minimum you need to create a line chart with the global defaults provided by Chart.js:

```
<html>
<head>
    <script src=".../Chart.min.js"></script>
</head>
<body>

<canvas id="my-line-chart" width="400" height="200"></canvas>

<script>
    const values =
        [1.17,1.35,1.3,1.09,0.93,0.76,0.83,0.98,0.87,0.89,0.93,0.81];
    const labels =
["Jan","Feb","Mar","Apr","May","Jun","Jul","Aug","Sep","Oct","Nov","Dec"];

    const dataObj = {
        labels: labels,
        datasets: [{ data: values }]
    }
    const chartObj = {
        type: "line",
        data: dataObj
    };
    new Chart("my-line-chart", chartObj);
</script>
</body></html>
```

This data contains average global temperatures for 2016, obtained from NASA. The result is shown as follows. As you can see, the default line chart has a gray line and a gray fill. You can change these defaults using the *options* or *dataset* configurations. The full code is in `LineArea/line-1.html`:

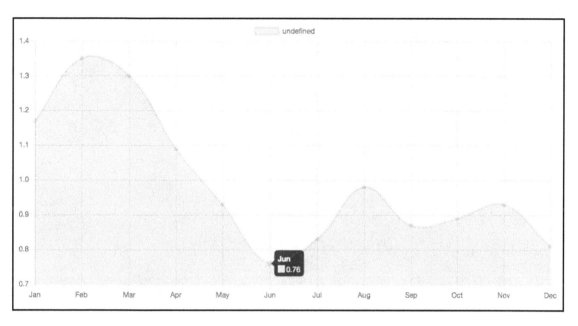

Simple line chart with default Chart.js properties showing average global temperatures in 2016 (code: *LineArea/line-1.html*)

# Dataset configuration

Dataset-specific options can be applied to control attributes, such as color and width of each line. Adding a `borderColor` attribute to the dataset will set the color of the line (and legend box), as follows:

```
let dataObj = {
    labels: labels,
    datasets: [{
        data: values,
        borderColor: 'hsla(300,100%,50%,1)'
        backgroundColor: 'transparent';
    }]
}
```

The following chart shows the effect of setting `borderColor` and `backgroundColor` for a dataset. This configuration only affects one dataset. You can also configure properties that affect all datasets. In this example, the legend was also removed using the options configuration (explained in a separate section). You can see the full code in `LineArea/line-2.html`, as shown in the following screenshot:

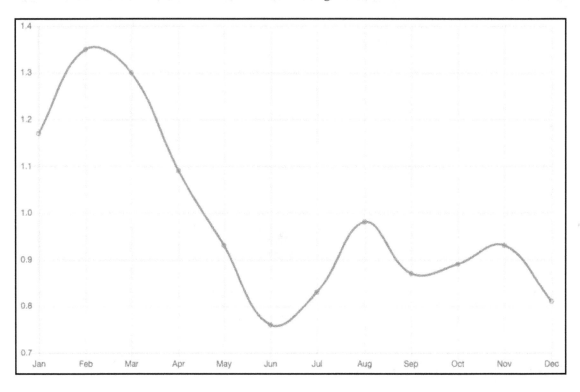

Simple line chart with average global temperatures measured in 2016 (code: *LineArea/line-2.html*)

The following listed dataset properties can be declared for each object of the `datasets` array. Many are also shared by other charts that display numerical data, such as radar, scatter, and bubble charts:

| Property | Value | Description |
| --- | --- | --- |
| data | Number[] | An array of numbers containing the data to display (mandatory). |
| label | String | A label for the dataset (appears in legend and tooltips). |

| | | |
|---|---|---|
| `backgroundColor` | A CSS color property value string | The fill color under (or above) the line. Position depends on the `fill` property. |
| `borderColor` | A CSS color property value string | The color of the line. |
| `borderWidth` | `Number` | The width of the line in pixels. |
| `borderDash` | `Number[]` | The canvas `setLineDash` method. An array describing the width of alternated line and space. For example, `[5, 10]` will create a dashed line with 5 pixel dashes and 10 pixel spaces. |
| `borderDashOffset` | `Number` | The canvas `lineDashOffset` property. An offset for line dashes. If zero (default), a `[10,10]` dash will start with a 10 pixel line. If 10, it will start with the 10 pixel space. If 5, it will start with a 5 pixel line, followed by a 10 pixel space, 10 pixel line, and so on. |
| `borderJoinStyle` | `'bevel'`, `'round'`, or `'miter'` (default) | The canvas `lineJoin` property. |
| `borderCapStyle` | `'butt'` (default), `'round'`, or `'square'` | The canvas `lineCap` property. |
| `pointBackgroundColor` | `Color` or `Color[]` | The background color of the point. |
| `pointBorderColor` | `Color` or `Color[]` | The border color of the point. |
| `pointBorderWidth` | `Number` or `Number[]` | The border width of the point. |
| `pointRadius` | `String` or `String[]` | The radius of the point. |
| `pointStyle` | `circle` (default), `cross`, `line`, `crossRot`, `dash`, `rectRounded`, `rectRot`, `star`, or `triangle` | The style of the point. A string or a DOM reference to an `Image` object. |
| `pointHoverBackgroundColor` | `Color` or `Color[]` | The background color of the point when the mouse hovers over it. |

| pointHoverBorderColor | Color or Color[] | The border color of the point when the mouse hovers over it. |
|---|---|---|
| pointHoverBorderWidth | Number or Number[] | The width of the point when the mouse hovers over it. |
| pointHoverRadius | Number or Number[] | The radius of the point when the mouse hovers over it. |
| pointHitRadius | Number or Number[] | The invisible radius of the point that reacts to the mouse hover (to show a tooltip). |
| cubicInterpolationMode | 'default' or 'monotone' | The default algorithm employs a cubic weighted interpolation. It doesn't guarantee monotonicity (so, if values increase or decrease, the default algorithm may deviate from this behavior). |
| lineTension | Number | The cubic bezier line tension (this applies only to default interpolation mode). If zero, the chart will draw straight lines. |
| fill | false, start, end, origin, or dataset index (relative or absolute) | This property describes how the space between lines is filled. false turns the feature off. start fills the space above or before the line, end fills the opposite space, origin fills to the origin of the chart, and index values fill the space between two datasets. A number represents the absolute index of a dataset. A string containing a signed number (for example: +2) represents a relative dataset (for example: the preceding two datasets). |
| spanGaps | 'bottom', 'left', 'top', or 'right' | If false, a null value or *NaN* (not zero) will cause a break in the line. The default is false. |
| showLine | Boolean | If false, the line for this dataset is not shown (only points will be displayed). |

| | | |
|---|---|---|
| steppedLine | true = 'before', false (default), or 'after' | Draws line as a sequence of steps. If true or before, the initial point is used. If after, the final value is used. The default is false, which disables this algorithm. |
| yAxisID and xAxisID | An axis ID (see Chapter 7, *Advanced Chart.js*) | This is used in axis configuration. |

Dataset properties for line charts

Data points represent the actual data in a dataset, and serve as an anchor for tooltips. There are several different data point styles that can be selected with the pointStyle property. These are shown as follows:

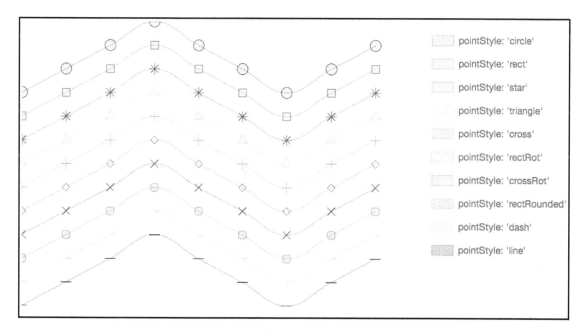

Point styles available for line charts (code: *LineArea/line-3-pointStyle.html*)

Data points can also configure radius, background color, border color, and tooltip behaviors. In a line chart, only the points represent actual values. The lines are just estimates. Depending on the kind of data you are displaying or the amount of points you have to display, it may not make sense to show them. You might also want to render them differently.

There are several options to control the algorithm that draws the lines. The `lineTension` property is a number (usually between 0 and 0.5) that configures the cubic Bezier interpolation of each line, drawing smooth curves between each point. If you set it to zero, the chart will draw straight lines, as demonstrated in the following diagram:

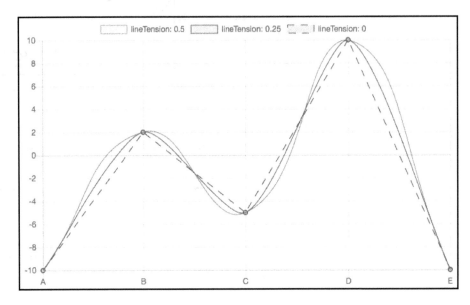

Comparing different values for the lineTension property (code: *LineArea/line-4-tension.html*)

If you are plotting discrete values, you may prefer to draw the lines as *steps*. You can place the step on a line based on the first or the second point of the line segment by choosing between the `before` or `after` strategies for the `steppedLine` property. The effects are shown as follows:

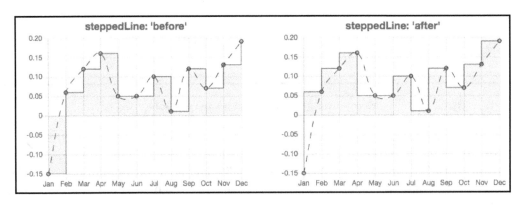

The effect of using different strategies for the steppedLine property (code: LineArea/line-5-stepped.html)

# Options configuration for line charts

The same general options we used for bar charts can be used to configure line charts, but there are some chart specific options, too. All charts come preconfigured with defaults, which can be overridden using local or global properties. One of the ways to remove the shading for all charts that use lines (instead of setting transparency per dataset) is to declare the fill global property for line elements as false, as follows:

```
Chart.defaults.global.elements.line.fill = false;
```

However, you can configure options per-chart setting properties in the options configuration object. We improved the way our first line chart was rendered, removing the legend, which is not necessary as there is only one dataset (see `LineArea/line-2.html`), as follows:

```
let chartObj = {
    type: "line",
    data: dataObj,
    options:{
        legend: {
            display: false
        }
    }
};
new Chart("my-line-chart", chartObj);
```

Data points can be completely hidden by setting `pointRadius` to zero in each dataset. However, you can also configure them for all datasets and charts globally by setting the values of the properties in `Chart.defaults.global.elements.point.radius`. This hides all points from all charts that use points, as follows:

```
Chart.defaults.global.elements.point.radius = 0;
```

If you have a very large number of points, you may not want to draw the lines. To hide the line of a specific dataset, you can set its `showLine` property to `false`, but you can also configure line drawing for all lines with the options properties listed as follows.

They can be set locally for the current chart or globally for all charts:

| Property | Value | Description |
|---|---|---|
| showLines | true or false | If this property is `false`, the lines between the points are not drawn. The default for line charts is `true`. The default for scatter charts is `false` . |
| spanGaps | true or false | A *null* value or *NaN* (not zero) causes a break in the line if this property is `false`. The default is `false`. |

Configuration properties for line charts

Global options for line elements are configured using the `Chart.defaults.line` object. To hide all lines as default, use the following code:

```
Chart.defaults.line.showLines = false;
```

Locally, they are defined directly inside the `options` object. You can override the default in a chart with the following code:

```
options: { showLines: true }
```

# Line charts with more than one dataset

Each dataset is displayed in a line chart by a separate line. The following example adds a new set of values to our chart, that is, the average monthly temperatures measured in 1880. We can now plot both datasets in the same grid and compare them with the average temperatures in 2016, as follows:

```
// NASA/GISS Temperature anomalies from 1880 to 2016
let values2016 =
   [1.17,1.35,1.3,1.09,0.93,0.76,0.83,0.98,0.87,0.89,0.93,0.81];
let values1880 =
   [-0.3,-0.21,-0.18,-0.27,-0.14,-0.29,-0.24,-0.08,-0.17,-0.16,-0.19,
   -0.22];
Chart.defaults.global.elements.line.fill = false;

let labels =
   ["Jan","Feb","Mar","Apr","May","Jun","Jul","Aug","Sep","Oct","Nov",
   "Dec"];

let dataObj = {
    labels: labels,
    datasets: [{
        label: '2016',
```

```
        data: values2016,
        borderColor: 'hsla(300,100%,50%,1)',
        borderDash: [5, 5],
    },{
        label: '1880',
        data: values1880,
        borderColor: 'hsla(200,100%,50%,1)'
    }]
  }
// the rest of the code is identical
```

The result of the preceding code is shown in the following chart. The full code is in
LineArea/line-6-datasets.html. The chart reveals that the average temperature
anomalies in 2016 are approximately 1° C higher than the measurements in 1880:

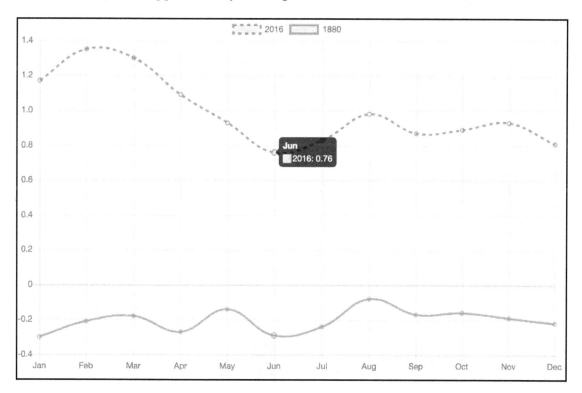

Line chart with two datasets (code: *LineArea/line-6-datasets.html*)

The `fill` property can be used with a Boolean value to turn on/off shading for all lines, but it can also be used as a `dataset` property to configure a shading strategy for individual datasets. In this case, it receives a string identifying an axis line: `'start'`, `'end'`, or `'origin'`, which will shade the chart between the line and an axis line (smallest, largest, or zero axis, respectively). It can also shade between lines, specifying a relative number as a string: `'-1'` will shade between the current dataset and the previous one, `'+2'`, will shade from the current dataset to the dataset that is two positions higher in the `dataset` array. You can also refer to an absolute index of the `dataset` array. The following chart compares the effects of some of these fill strategies:

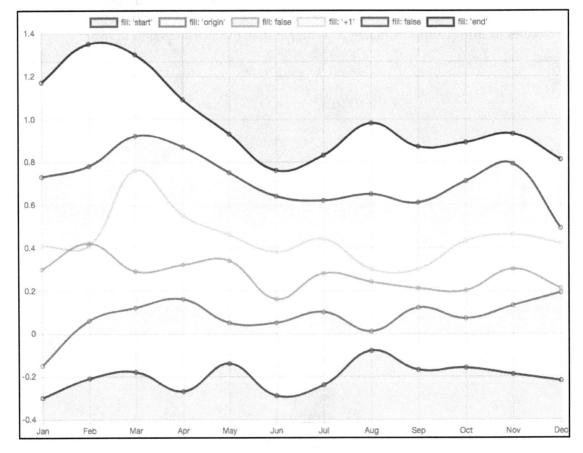

Fill strategies for line charts (code: *LineArea/line-7-fill.html*)

# Loading data from external files

Line charts are great for revealing trends and relationships in large amounts of data. Public data is widely available in standard formats, such as CSV and JSON, but usually needs to be downscaled, parsed, and converted to a data format expected by Chart.js before using. In this section, we will extract data from a public data file and turn it into a trend-revealing visualization.

For all examples that use external files, you need to open your files using a web server. Double-clicking on the HTML file and opening it in your browser won't work. If you are not running your files with a web server, see the section *Loading data files*, in `Chapter 2`, *Technology Fundamentals*, on how to configure a web server for testing.

The temperature data in the previous example was extracted from a JSON file obtained from the NASA **Goddard Institute for Space Studies** (**GISS**) website (`data.giss.nasa.gov/gistemp`), which includes monthly measurements for each year between 1880 and 2016. It would be very interesting to plot the numbers for all months in a single chart. We can do by this loading the file and using JavaScript to extract the data we want.

The following is a fragment of the JSON file from the GISS site. It's also available from the GitHub repository for this chapter in `Data/monthly_json.json`:

```
[
    {"Date": "2016-12-27", "Mean": 0.7895,  "Source": "GCAG"},
    {"Date": "2016-12-27", "Mean": 0.81, "Source": "GISTEMP"},
    {"Date": "2016-11-27", "Mean": 0.7504,  "Source": "GCAG"},
    {"Date": "2016-11-27", "Mean": 0.93, "Source": "GISTEMP"},
    {"Date": "2016-10-27", "Mean": 0.7292,  "Source": "GCAG"},
    {"Date": "2016-10-27", "Mean": 0.89, "Source": "GISTEMP"},
    /* ... many, many more lines ... */
    {"Date": "1880-02-27", "Mean": -0.1229,  "Source": "GCAG"},
    {"Date": "1880-02-27", "Mean": -0.21, "Source": "GISTEMP"},
    {"Date": "1880-01-27", "Mean": 0.0009,  "Source": "GCAG"},
    {"Date": "1880-01-27", "Mean": -0.3,  "Source": "GISTEMP"}
]
```

Files should be loaded asynchronously. You can use any Ajax library for this (for example, JQuery) or use standard ES2015 features, supported by all modern browsers. In this book, we will use the standard JavaScript `fetch()` command (in the GitHub repository, there are also JQuery alternatives for most examples).

The `fetch()` command is reactive. It will wait until the whole file is loaded into memory before moving to the first `then()` step, which processes the response and extracts the JSON string (using the `text()` method). The second `then()` step only starts after all of the contents are placed in a string, made available for parsing in the final step, as follows:

```
fetch('monthly_json.json')
    .then(response => response.text())
    .then((json) => {
        const dataMap = new Map();
        ...
    });
```

Before using a JSON file (which is a string), we need to parse it so that it will become a JavaScript object, from which we can read individual fields using the dot operator. This can be done with the standard JavaScript command, `JSON.parse()`, as follows:

```
const obj = JSON.parse(json);
```

If you are using JQuery or some other library instead of `fetch()`, you might prefer to use a function that loads and parses JSON. In this case, you should not run the preceding command.

The data contains two measurements, labeled `GCAC` and `GISTEMP`. We only need one of them, so we will filter only the objects that have `GISTEMP` as `Source`. We will also reverse the array so that the earlier measurements appear first in the chart. We can do all of this in one line, as follows:

```
const obj = JSON.parse(json).reverse()
                    .filter(field => field.Source == 'GISTEMP');
console.log(obj);
```

The last line will print the following code in your browser's JavaScript console:

```
Array(1644)
 [0 ... 99]
0:{Date: "1880-01-27", Mean: -0.3, Source: "GISTEMP"}
1:{Date: "1880-02-27", Mean: -0.21, Source: "GISTEMP"}
2:{Date: "1880-03-27", Mean: -0.18, Source: "GISTEMP"}
3:{Date: "1880-04-27", Mean: -0.27, Source: "GISTEMP"}
 ...
```

Now, it's easy to select the data we need to build a dataset for each year. The best way to do that is to create a `Map` storing each value and month, and use the year as a retrieval key. Split the date components to extract the year and month, and then store these values and the temperature anomaly in a new object (with properties: `year`, `month`, and `value`) for each `Map` entry.

These steps are performed in the following code:

```
const dataMap = new Map();
obj.forEach(d => {
    const year = d.Date.split("-")[0], month = d.Date.split("-")[1];
    if(dataMap.get(year)) {
        dataMap.get(year).push({year: year, month: month, value: d.Mean});
    } else {
        dataMap.set(year, [{year: year, month: month, value: d.Mean}]);
    }
});
console.log(dataMap); // check the structure of the generated map!
draw(dataMap);
```

The resulting map will contain one key for each year in the dataset. The value of each entry will be an array of 12 objects, one for each month. Use your browser's JavaScript console to inspect the generated map.

The `draw()` function will convert `dataMap` into a format that Chart.js can use. For each entry it will create a `dataset` object and add it to the `datasets` array. Each `dataset` object contains a `data` property with an array of data values (one per month), and dataset configuration properties, such as line color and label. The map's key (year) is the label, and the colors are generated in a gradient sequence using the year to change the hue, as follows:

```
function draw(dataMap) {
    const datasets = [];
    dataMap.forEach((entry, key) => {
        const dataset = {
            label: key, // the year
            data: entry.map(n => n.value),
            // array w temperature for each month
            borderColor:     'hsla('+(key*2)+',50%,50%,0.9)',
            //gradient
            backgroundColor: 'hsla('+(key*2)+',50%,50%,0.9)',
            borderWidth: 1,
            pointRadius: 0 // hide the data points
        };
        datasets.push(dataset);
    });
    ...
```

Now we can assemble the data object and instantiate the line chart, as follows:

```
const months = ["Jan","Feb", ...,"Oct","Nov","Dec"];
Chart.defaults.global.elements.line.fill = false;
const chartObj = {
    type: "line",
```

```
        data: {
            labels: months,
            datasets: datasets
        }
    };
    new Chart("my-line-chart", chartObj);
}
```

The final result is shown as follows. The full code is available in `LineArea/line-8-load-fetch.html` (fetch version), and `LineArea/line-8-load-jquery.html` (JQuery Version):

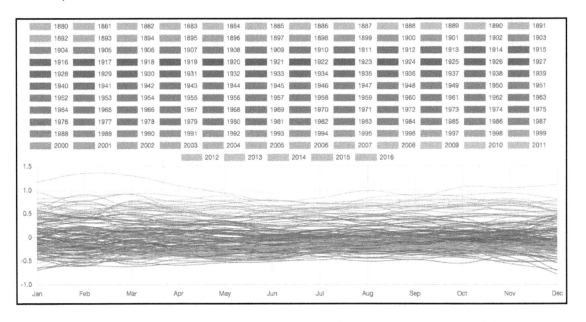

Line chart using external data showing temperature variation from 1880 to 2016 (data: NASA/GISS; and code: *LineArea/line-8-load-fetch.html* for fetch version, or *LineArea/line-8-load-jquery.html* for JQuery version)

It looks nice, but there is too much information. We could filter out some results, but we can also just reduce the amount of labels. The `options.legend.labels.filter` property supports a `callback` function that we can use to filter out selected labels. In the following code, it will only display labels that are 20 years apart:

```
const chartObj = {
    type: "line",
    data: {
        labels: labels,
        datasets: datasets
    }
```

```
options:{
    legend: {
        labels: {
            filter: function(item, chart) {
                return new Number(item.text) % 20 == 0;
            }
        }
    }
};
```

The result is shown as follows and the full code is in `LineArea/line-10-filter.html`.
Now only a few legends are shown, and the colors differ enough to relate them to different
parts of the chart. Although there is still a lot of information in the chart, the colors are
sufficient to reveal a trend toward increasing temperatures:

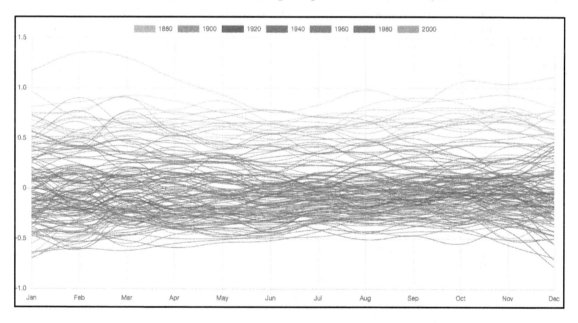

Line chart using external data after filtering out excess labels (code: *LineArea/line-10-filter.html*)

# Stacked area charts

A line chart could be used to show how much CO2 that each country releases in the atmosphere each year. It would reveal if a country's emissions were increasing, stable, or decreasing, but such a line chart would not be very useful to show the *total* amount of CO2 released in the air, and how each country contributes to this total. You can display this kind of information using a stacked area chart.

There is no special `area` type chart in Chart.js. Instead, you can create a simple overlapping area chart configuring the fill properties for each dataset in a line chart. To create a stacked area chart, you will need to set the stacked property to `true` in the *x* and y-axes.

Let's try an example. We will use a JSON file containing data about carbon emissions (in kilotonnes) from selected countries from 1960 to 2014. It's based on a CSV file containing data for all countries, which is available for download from the World Bank public database. I created a JSON Version of this file containing only the six greatest polluters, adding up all of the other countries in a single entry. This is the file we will use (`Data/world_bank_co2_kt.json`), as follows:

```
{ "labels":[1960,1961,...,2013,2014],
  "entries":[
     {"country":"Others",
      "data":[983835.74025,1015886.52639,
       ...,10073290.7688,10300830.9827]},
     {"country":"Russian Federation",
      "data":[0,0,... ,1778561.006,1705345.684]},
     {"country":"India",
      "data":[120581.961,130402.187,... ,2034752.294,2238377.137]},
     {"country":"Japan",
      "data":[232781.16,283118.069,... ,1246515.976,1214048.358]},
     {"country":"China",
      "data":[780726.302,552066.85,... ,10258007.128,10291926.878]},
     {"country":"European Union",
      "data":[2359594.88616257,2445945.66448806,...
       ,3421472.348,3241844.353]},
     {"country":"United States",
      "data":[2890696.1,2880505.507,2987207.873,...
       ,5159160.972,5254279.285]}
  ]}
```

As in the previous example, we need to load the file and parse the JSON string, as follows:

```
fetch('world_bank_co2_kt.json')
        .then(response => response.text())
        .then((json) => {
    draw(JSON.parse(json));
  });
```

The next step is to set up an array of `labels` and `datasets` from the data. The JSON file already contains an array with the years, so all you have to do is copy it directly into the chart's data object `labels` property. The `datasets` array is assembled iterating through each entry in the data file's entries array to extract the label of the dataset (from the `country` property) and the data array (from the `data` property). We will use the array's index to generate different colors, as follows:

```
function draw(datasetsObj) {
    const datasets = [];
    datasetsObj.entries.forEach((entry, index) => {
        const color = 'hsla('+(index+5)*50+',75%,75%,1)';
        const dataset = {
            label: entry.country,
            data: entry.data,
            borderColor: color,
            backgroundColor: color,
            borderWidth: 3,
            fill: 'start', // fills the space below each line
            pointRadius: 0
        };
        datasets.push(dataset);
    });

    const dataObj = {
        labels: datasetsObj.labels, // copied from the JSON data
        datasets: datasets
    }

    new Chart("my-area-chart", {type: "line", data: dataObj });
```

The result of this code is shown as follows. The full code is in `LineArea/line-11-area.html`. The step between 1990 and 1992 is caused by a lack of data in previous years, mostly from Warsaw Pact countries and the Soviet Union:

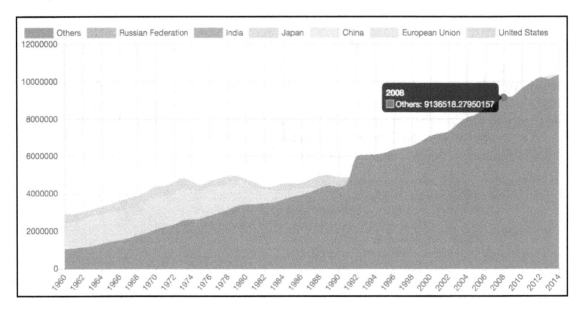

An area chart with overlapped (not stacked) datasets (code: *LineArea/line-11-area.html*)

The `Chart` is probably not what you would expect. It's not stacking the data. The other dataset is overlapping all of the other datasets.

Datasets could be stacked in two ways: on the $x$ axis, or on the $y$ axis, so you have to tell Chart.js how you want to do it. In this example, it doesn't make sense to add up the years, but it does to add up carbon emissions, so we have to stack the $y$ axis. This is done by setting the `scales.yAxes[0].stacked` property to `true`, in the options configuration object, as follows:

```
const chartObj = {
    type: "line",
    data: dataObj,
    options:{
        scales: {
            yAxes: [{
                stacked: true
            }]
        },
            legend: {
            labels: {
```

```
            boxWidth: 20,
        }
      }
    }
};
```

In the preceding options configuration, we have also reduced the size of the legend boxes to half (the `boxWidth` property). You can see the final result as follows. The full code is in `LineArea/line-12-area-stacked.html`:

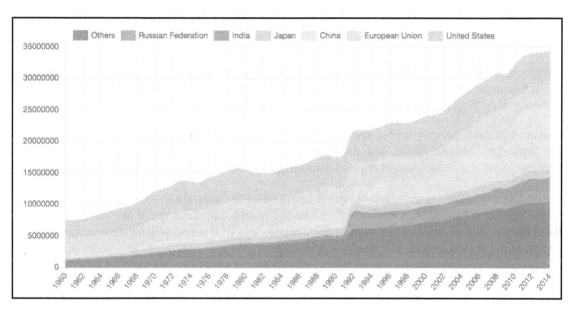

A stacked area chart showing total and per-country CO2 emissions (code: *LineArea/line-12-area-stacked.html*)

Now the chart reveals that the step from 1990 to 1992 is mostly due to Russia, for which the World Bank didn't have any carbon emission data before 1990, when it was the Soviet Union.

# Radar charts

Radar charts are line charts plotted on a radial axis. They can be used with one or more datasets that contain at least three values each. There is only one axis, which starts from the center. Each line begins and ends at the same point and, for that reason, radar charts are usually used to display values that are either cyclic in nature (such as hours, months, schedules, or repeating events), a sequential list of categories which end at the same place where it begins (such as round-trip), or categories that have no specific order. A radar chart can be used to compare different datasets by revealing strong and weak points, or showing outliers and commonality in data. It usually works best with a small number of datasets (that is, no more than three or four).

Radar charts are usually a poor choice for large datasets. In these cases, it's usually better to use a Cartesian line chart or a bar chart. Radial distances are also harder to perceive, although this limitation can be minimized with the grid.

The configurable properties for radar charts are the same as line charts. You can even reuse the same datasets and labels. The data property of each dataset must contain an array of numbers and the `chart` object should be configured with `type='radar'`.

In the following example, a radar chart is being used to compare three different travel schedules for a 30-day trip. Each dataset lists the number of days spent in each city. Using this chart, a tourist can quickly visualize how the days of the trip will be distributed, per city, making it easier to choose the best schedule:

```
let dataObj = {
    labels: ["Lisbon", "Paris", "Berlin", "Moscow", "Rome",
    "Barcelona"],
    datasets: [
        {
            label: "Trip schedule #1",
            data: [5,5,5,5,5,5],
            borderColor: 'red',
            backgroundColor: 'hsla(0,75%,75%,.25)'
        },{
            label: "Trip schedule #2",
            data: [7,3,3,3,7,7],
            borderColor: 'blue',
            backgroundColor: 'hsla(240,75%,75%,.25)'
        },{
            label: "Trip schedule #3",
            data: [4,7,7,7,3,2],
            borderColor: 'yellow',
            backgroundColor: 'hsla(60,75%,75%,.25)'
        }
```

```
        ]
    }

const chartObj = {
    type: "radar",
    data: dataObj,
    options: {
        scale: {
            ticks: {
                beginAtZero: true,
                stepSize: 1 // show one gridline per day
            }
        }
    }
};
new Chart("my-radar-chart", chartObj);
```

Instead of a `scales` property containing *x* axes and *y* axes, a radar chart has a single `scale` property. The grid structure is configured within the `ticks` property (more about scales at the end of this chapter).

The result is shown as follows. You can see the full code in `Radar/radar-1.html`:

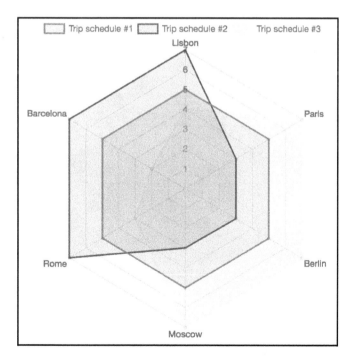

Radar chart comparing three different trip schedules for a 30-day trip (code: *Radar/radar-1.html*)

Radar charts are great for cyclic data, such as the months in a year. Let's try to transform the Cartesian line chart we created in the previous section into a radar chart with the same data. Most of the code is the same. You only need to change the chart type, but some minor changes in the configuration will make it look better.

The following code shows a slightly modified draw() function that uses the same NASA/GISS monthly temperature data, but draws the lines in a radar chart:

```
const months = ["Jan", "Feb", "Mar", ... , "Sep", "Oct", "Nov",
"Dec"];

function draw(datasetMap) {
    const datasets = [];

    datasetMap.forEach((entry, key) => {
        const dataset = {
            label: key,
            data: entry.map(n => n.value),
            borderColor:     'hsla('+(key*2)+',50%,50%,.9)',
            backgroundColor: 'hsla('+(key*2)+',50%,50%,0.1)',
            borderWidth: 1,
            pointRadius: 0, // don't show the data points
            lineTension: .4 // do draw lines as curves (not default in
                                radar)
        };
        datasets.push(dataset);
    });

    const dataObj = {
        labels: months,
        datasets: datasets
    }

    const chartObj = {
        type: "radar",
        data: dataObj,
        options: {
            animation: {
                duration: 0
            },
            scale: {
                ticks: {
                    max: 1.5
                }
            },
            legend: {
                labels: {
```

```
                boxWidth: 20,
                filter: function(item, chart) {
                    return new Number(item.text) % 20 == 0
                                 || item.text % 2016 == 0;
                }
            }
        }
    }
};

new Chart("my-radar-chart", chartObj);
}
```

The default line tension is 0 for radar charts, which draws straight lines. Since the values are averages, we selected a value between 0 and 0.5 for the `lineTension` property to make the chart draw curved lines.

The full code is available in `Radar/radar-3.html`. The result is shown as follows:

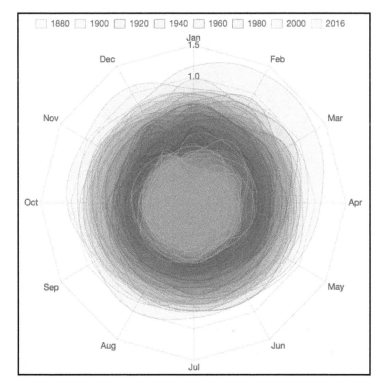

A radar chart showing the increase in global temperatures from 1880 to 2016 (code: *Radar/radar-3.html*)

The variation in color is sufficient to reveal that temperatures are increasing year after year. However, if you wish for more precision, you can try filtering out some `datasets` and display only the data for every two decades, as follows:

```
datasets: datasets.filter(d => d.label % 20 == 0 || d.label % 2016 == 0)
```

The result, showing only eight years is demonstrated as follows. The full code is in `Radar/radar-4.html`:

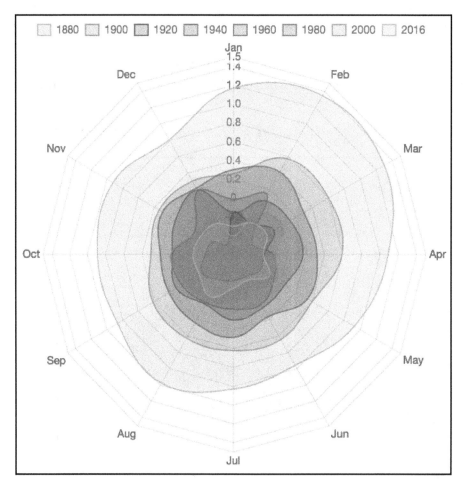

A radar chart showing the increase in global temperatures every 20 years from 1880 to 2016 (code: *Radar/radar-4.html*)

# Pie and doughnut charts

Pie and doughnut charts are used to display numerical proportion between data as parts of a whole. Each data value is represented as a slice, which represents a proportional quantity. These charts are very popular but are also widely criticized. Since we don't perceive angles very well, it's much harder to compare data displayed in a pie chart, than in a bar or line chart. Using pie charts to compare only very small sets of data can avoid or reduce these problems.

A pie chart is usually used to display a single dataset. The `type` property of the chart object should be `pie`. Doughnut charts are equivalent to pie charts, but they are created with `type: doughnut`. You can also transform any pie chart into a doughnut by simply changing the dataset property `cutoutPercentage` to `50` (or some other value different than zero).

# Creating a simple pie chart

Let's create a simple pie chart to compare CO2 emissions among the world's greatest polluters for a single year. You can use the same data we used for the area chart, but you will need to choose one of the datasets, place the country names in a `labels` array, the data for one year in the `data` array, and generate colors for each slice. All this can be done in JavaScript (see `Pie/pie-2-fetch.html`), but for the sake of simplicity and to focus on the construction of a simple pie chart, we will include the data directly in the HTML file, as shown in the following code block:

```
const dataset = [1.21, 1.71, 2.24, 3.24, 5.25, 10.29, 10.3]; // 2014 data
const labels = ["Japan", "Russian Federation", "India", "European Union",
                "United States", "China", "Others"];
const colors = [];

dataset.forEach((entry, index) => { // generate some colors
    colors.push('hsla('+((index+5)*50)+',75%,75%,1)');
});
```

The `datasets` array contains a single dataset, as follows:

```
const dataObj = {
    labels: labels,
    datasets: [{
        data: dataset,
        backgroundColor: colors,
        borderWidth: 3
    }]
}
```

The chart type should be `pie`, as follows:

```
const chartObj = {
    type: "pie",
    data: dataObj,
    options:{
        title: {
            text: "CO2 emissions (billions of tonnes)",
            display: true,
            fontSize: 24
        },
        legend: {
            labels: {
                boxWidth: 20,
            },
            position: 'right'
        }

    }
};
new Chart("my-pie-chart", chartObj);
```

The results are shown as follows. You can also see the full code in `Pie/pie-1.html`. Note that slices don't have any labels. You can only see the value of each slice if you hover the mouse over it. It will be shown in a tooltip:

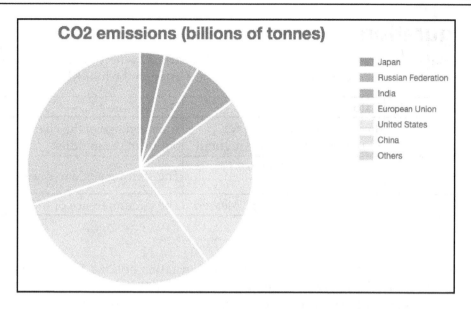

A simple pie chart showing CO2 emissions by the greatest polluters in billions of tonnes (code: *Pie/pie-1.html*)

# Dataset properties for pie charts

Besides `data` and `labels` properties, several other properties (listed as follows) can be used in each dataset object to configure the colors and style of each slice. All properties receive an array of attributes, and each attribute is applied to the corresponding slice:

| Property | Value | Description |
|---|---|---|
| backgroundColor | Array of CSS color strings | The fill color of the slice |
| borderColor | Array of CSS color strings | The border color of the slice |
| borderWidth | Array of numbers | The border width of the slice |
| hoverBackgroundColor | Array of CSS color strings | The fill color of the slice when the mouse hovers over it |
| hoverBorderColor | Array of CSS color strings | The border color of the slice when the mouse hovers over it |
| hoverBorderWidth | Array of numbers | The border width of the slice when the mouse hovers over it |

Dataset options for pie and doughnut charts

# Configuration options

Common configuration options are inherited for pie charts, but there are also some options that are specific to pie and doughnut charts. These are listed in the following table:

| Property | Value | Description |
|---|---|---|
| cutoutPercentage | Number. Defaults: 0 for 'pie', and '50' for doughnut | A percentage of the chart that is cut out from the middle |
| rotation | Number. Default: *-0.5 \* Math.PI* | The starting angle to draw the arcs |
| circumference | Number. Default: *2 \* Math.PI* | The circumference of the pie |

Configuration options for pie and doughnut charts

These options are merged (and override) global configuration options. Default options for each type of chart can also be set through the Chart.defaults.doughnut and Chart.defaults.pie objects, which support the same properties listed earlier.

# How to show values in the slices

Currently, there is no native Chart.js way to show values or percentages in a pie chart without tooltips. But you can achieve this using a plugin or extension. In the following example, we will use a very simple library called Chart.Piecelabel.js. You can download it from github.com/emn178/Chart.PieceLabel.js and include it your page using a script tag:

```
<script src="../JavaScript/Chart.PieceLabel.js"></script>
```

That's it! Now you can add the `pieceLabel` property to the `options` object, and configure labels for the slices. You can display absolute values or percentages, place the labels inside, at the border or outside the slices, draw the text on the arc and configure several font attributes. The following is a selection of these properties (you can check the library's documentation for more properties):

| Property | Value | Description |
|---|---|---|
| render | 'percentage' (default) or 'value' | Displays the percentage or the value of the slice. |
| precision | Number | The precision (number of digits after the decimal point) for percentages (does not work with other values). |
| fontSize, fontColor, fontSize, and fontFamily | CSS property value strings | Changes font attributes for the label. |
| textShadow | true or false | Applies a shadow to the label (the shadow attributes, such as offset and color, can also be configured with additional properties). |
| position | 'default', 'border' or 'outside' | Places the label in the different positions. |
| arc | true or false | Draws the text aligned with the arc. Works better when the position is 'outside'. |

Some configuration options for the *Chart.PieceLabel.js* plugin

To include labels in the pie chart you created in the previous example, add the following property to the `options` object of your chart (see `Pie/pie-3-plugin.html`):

```
options:{
    pieceLabel: {
        fontColor: '#000',
        render: 'value',
        textShadow: true,
        position: 'border'
    },
    ...
```

Run the script and you have labels containing the value represented by each slice, as shown in the following chart:

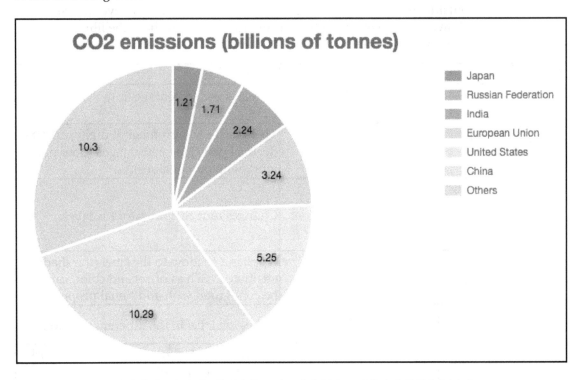

A simple pie chart using the Chart.PieceLabel.js extension to display labels on each slice (code: *Pie/pie-3-plugin.html*)

If you want even more customization, you can try other plugins such as ChartJS-Datalabels and ChartJS-Outlabels, which support sophisticated label placement options. These two plugins will be explored in Chapter 6, *Configuring Styles and Interactivity*.

# Preparing data for pie and doughnut charts

Pie charts can't be used with any type of data. They should only be used to display part-whole relationships and contain not much more than half a dozen data values. The following screenshot shows what happens when you create a pie or doughnut chart with too much data. In this example, we loaded a doughnut chart containing the populations of almost 200 countries. It may be art, but not really a useful visualization:

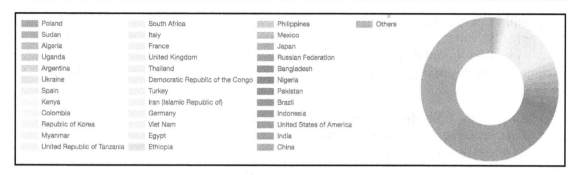

Abusing a pie chart (code: Pie/pie-4-evilpie.html; see also *Pie/pie-6-evilpie.html*)

Even if you reduce this dataset to less than 20 values, it would still not be efficiently displayed in a pie chart. There aren't enough colors, and it would be difficult to place labels inside or beside so many slices, not considering the fact that angles are much harder to compare. In such cases, you should switch to a bar chart, which can be used to efficiently compare 20 values or even more.

The following screenshot shows a bar chart created with the same data, filtered to show the 35 most populous countries:

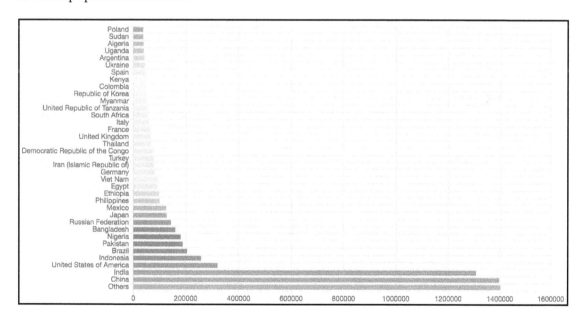

A bar chart is a better choice than a pie chart to compare large datasets (code: Pie/pie-5-evilpie-as-bar.html; see also *Pie/pie-7-evilpie-as-bar.html*)

If you still want to use a pie chart, you need to reduce the data sample, but it's not enough to simply filter out data (for example, by including only the most populous countries). Since a pie chart should display part-whole relationships, but you also need to add the excluded items (for example, add up the populations of the smaller countries, as in the CO2 emissions example).

This is done in the following example: it loads and parses a CSV data file, sorts the data by population, creates an array of objects with the largest countries, and finally, adds up all of the other populations into a new others entry.

To parse the CSV, we are using the popular `PapaParse` library (`github.com/mholt/PapaParse`). You can include it in your page using the following code:

```
<script
src="https://cdnjs.cloudflare.com/ajax/libs/PapaParse/4.6.0/papaparse.min.j
s">
</script>
```

`PapaParse` reads CSV and transforms the data into a JavaScript array, where each row is an object with the column headers as keys. To obtain the data from any CSV file where the first row contains the headers (which is the most common case), use the following code:

```
const data = Papa.parse(csv, {header: true}).data;
```

Now, for each array item, you can access the values using `item.header` or `item['header']`.

The following code loads the CSV, parses it, and calls a function to reduce the data. The reduced data is then passed to the `drawData()` function that will use Chart.js to draw the pie, as follows:

```
const numberOfEntries = 6; // change this to include more countries

fetch('../Data/WPP2017_UN.csv')
    .then(response => response.text())
    .then((csv) => {
        const data = Papa.parse(csv, {header: true}).data;
        const reduced = reduceData(data);
        drawData(reduced);
});
```

The `reduceData()` function filters the countries with the largest population (that is, by sorting by population, and then slicing the array), and adds the populations of the remaining countries to create the `others` entry, as follows:

```
function reduceData(array) {
    array.sort((a, b) =>  a["2015"] - b["2015"]);

    const topEntries =
        array.slice(array.length - numberOfEntries,array.length)
            .map(d => ({country: d["Country or region"], data:
            +d["2015"]}));

    let others = array.slice(0, array.length - numberOfEntries);
    const sumOthers = others.map(d => +d["2015"]).reduce((a,b)  => a+b, 0);
    others = {country: "Others", data: sumOthers};
    topEntries.push(others);
    return topEntries;
}
```

The `drawData()` function prepares the data so that it can be used by Chart.js, and uses the result to populate the chart's labels, `datasets[0].data` and `datasets[0].backgroundColor`, as follows:

```
function drawData(data) {
    const dataset = [], labels = [], colors = [];
    let count = 0;
    data.forEach(d => {
        dataset.push(Math.round(d.data/1000));
        labels.push(d.country);
        colors.push('hsla('+(count++ *
        300/numberOfEntries)+',100%,70%,.9)');
    });

    const dataObj = {
        labels: labels,
        datasets: [
            {
                data: dataset,
                backgroundColor: colors,
                borderWidth: 5,
                hoverBackgroundColor: 'black',
                hoverBorderColor: 'white'
            }
        ]
    }

    const chartObj = {
```

```
        type: "doughnut",
        data: dataObj,
        options: {
            title: {
                display: true,
                position: 'left',
                fontSize: 24,
                text: "World population (millions)"
            },
            legend: {
                position: 'right'
            },
            pieceLabel: {
                fontColor: '#000',
                render: 'value',
                textShadow: true,
                position: 'border'
            }
        }
    };
    new Chart("my-pie-chart", chartObj);
}
```

You can see the full code in `Pie/pie-8-filter.html`. The final result, showing six countries compared to all of the others, is shown as follows:

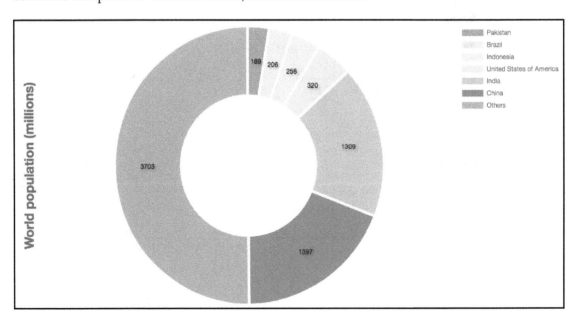

A doughnut chart comparing the most populous countries with the rest of the world (code: *Pie/pie-8-filter.html*)

# Changing the circumference

Pie and doughnut charts don't have to be complete circles. You can set the value of the circumference property (in radians) and use less than 360 degrees (2 * *Math.PI* radians). Using Math.PI as the circumference, you get a half-pie or half-doughnut chart. These charts are good to compare two or three values and may fit better in reduced spaces.

We modified the previous chart in the following example. It compares the 2017 populations of China and India with the rest of the world using a half-doughnut. The following fragment contains the relevant code. You can see the full code in Pie/pie-9-halfpie.html:

```
const numberOfEntries = 2;
// ...
const chartObj = {
    type: "doughnut",
    data: dataObj,
    options: {
        circumference: Math.PI, // creates the half-pie
        rotation: Math.PI / 2,  // rotates the half-pie 180 degrees
        title: {...},
        legend: {...},
        pieceLabel: {...}
    }
};
new Chart("my-pie-chart", chartObj);
```

The resulting chart is shown as follows. The `rotation` property doesn't contain the amount of rotation, but a position (that is, the starting angle from where the arcs are drawn), and the default rotation position is -*Math.PI/2*, so the value of *Math.PI/2* actually rotates it 180 degrees, not 90 degrees, as it might seem (for that, use Math.PI to move it to a perpendicular position):

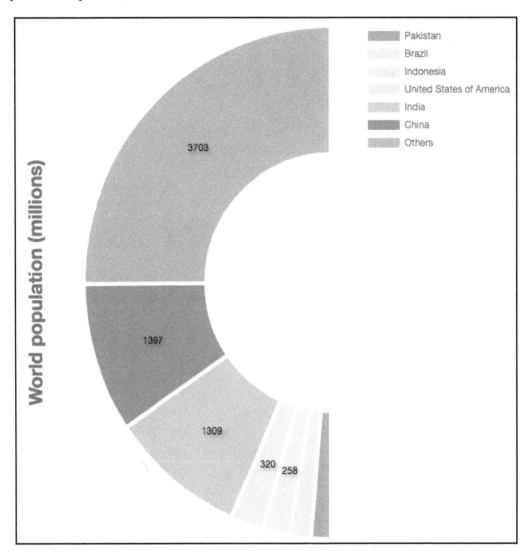

Changing the circumference and rotation properties of a doughnut chart (code: *Pie/pie-9-halfpie.html*)

# Pie and doughnut charts with multiple datasets

Normally, you only display a single dataset with a pie chart, but multiple datasets are supported. They are displayed as concentric circles. Labeling the data in this case is mandatory, since it's impossible to visually compare the sizes of the slices.

The following example uses two datasets containing country population estimates from 1980 and 2015 to create a doughnut chart with the 1980 values in the inner circle, and the 2015 values in the outer circle. The relevant code fragments are shown as follows. You can see the full code in `Pie/pie-10-multiset.html`:

```
const dataset2015 = [189,206,258,320,1309,1397,3703],
      dataset1980 = [78,121,147,230,697,994,2191];

const labels = ["Pakistan", "Brazil", "Indonesia", "United States of
                America", "India", "China", "Others"];

const colors2015 = [], colors1980 = [];

let count = 0;
labels.forEach(d => {
    count++;
    colors2015.push('hsla('+(count * 300 / labels.length)+', 100%,
    50%, .9)');
    colors1980.push('hsla('+(count * 300 / labels.length)+', 100%,
    75%, .9)');
});

const dataObj = {
    labels: labels,
    datasets: [
        { data: dataset2015, backgroundColor: colors2015 },
        { data: dataset1980, backgroundColor: colors1980 }
    ]
}
const canvas = document.getElementById("my-pie-chart");
const ctx = canvas.getContext("2d");

const chartObj = {
    type: "doughnut",
    data: dataObj,
    options: {
        animation: { // to draw on canvas use this callback
            onComplete: function() {
                ctx.fillText("Population in 1980",
                            canvas.width/2 - 140,canvas.height/2);
                ctx.fillText("Population in 2015",
```

```
                                          canvas.width/2 + 70,canvas.height - 10);
                }
            } // ...
        }
    };

    const chart = new Chart("my-pie-chart", chartObj);
    chart.update();
```

The label in the center of the doughnuts was created by drawing directly on the canvas. If you need to do that, you must use a callback. The `onComplete` callback (configured under `options.animation`) is called when the chart has finished drawing. If you don't use a callback, Chart.js may erase whatever you draw. This behavior will be detailed in `Chapter 6`, *Configuring Styles and Interactivity*.

The result is shown as follows:

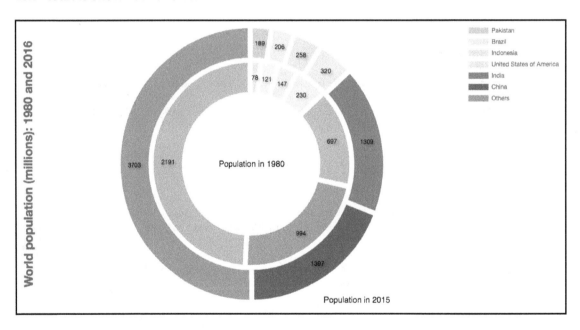

A doughnut chart with two datasets (code: Pie/pie-10-multiset.html)

These charts may be visually attractive, but they can introduce some serious perception errors. The outer arcs are perceived to be much larger than they actually are. It's an optical illusion. A population growth in the preceding chart won't be noticed unless the difference is significant. You can visualize this problem if you invert the order of the datasets, placing the 1980 values on the outer circle. This is shown in the following chart, where it seems that some populations grew in proportion to the whole, when all of them actually decreased. This chart is lying to us:

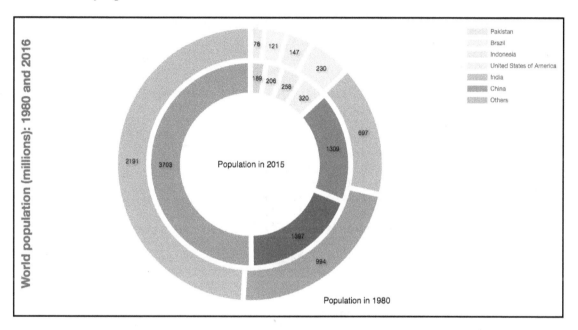

Multiple datasets cannot be compared in pie and doughnut charts: the smaller values seem to be larger (code: Pie/pie-11-evilmultiset.html)

# Polar area charts

Polar area charts are like bar charts rendered on a radial axis. A bar chart is usually a better option if you need precision, but you might choose a polar area chart for its visual effects.

To create a polar area chart, you set up the data the same way you would for a bar chart, then change the type to `polarArea`. As in the radar chart, there is only one `scale` property and axis to configure.

In the following example, we use a polar area chart to compare the volumes of the world's oceans. It is based on the bar chart with the same data we created in Chapter 3, *Chart.js – Quick Start*.

```
const labels = ["Arctic", "Southern", "North Atlantic", "South
              Atlantic", "Indian", "South Pacific", "North Pacific"];
const volume = [18750, 71800,146000,160000,264000,329000,341000];
// km3*10^3

Chart.defaults.global.elements.rectangle.borderWidth = 1;

const chartObj = {
    labels: labels,
    datasets: [
        {
            label: "Volume",
            data: volume,
            borderWidth: 2,
            backgroundColor: [
                'hsla(260,100%,75%,.7',
                'hsla(245,100%,75%,.7',
                'hsla(230,100%,75%,.7',
                'hsla(210,100%,75%,.7',
                'hsla(195,100%,75%,.7',
                'hsla(180,100%,75%,.7',
                'hsla(165,100%,75%,.7']
        }
    ]
}
new Chart("my-polar-area-chart", {
    type: "polarArea",
    data: chartObj,
    options: {
        title: {
            display: true,
            position: 'left',
            fontSize: 24,
            text: "Volume of water (in 1000 cubic km)"
        },
        legend: {
            position: 'right'
        }
    }
});
```

You can see the full code in PolarArea/polar-area-1.html. The result is shown as follows:

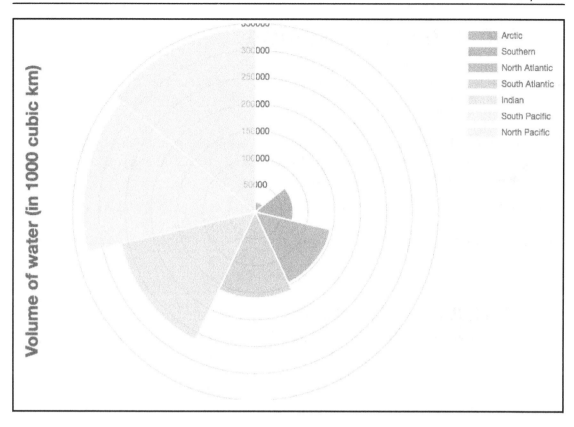

A polar area chart comparing the volume of water in each ocean (code: *PolarArea/polar-area-1.html*)

Polar area charts share the same dataset properties as pie and doughnut charts, which consist mostly of properties to set the border widths, border colors, and fill colors of the slices.

There is one configuration option specific to polar area charts, listed as follows:

| Property | Value | Description |
|---|---|---|
| startAngle | Number | The angle to start drawing the arcs |

Configuration options for polar area charts

You can draw polar area charts containing multiple datasets, but they will be overlapped. The current version of Chart.js (2.7.2) does not support stacking or other ways of showing multiple datasets in these charts. You can also see `PolarArea/polar-area-2.html` and `polar-area-3.html` for other ways to configure polar area charts.

# Scatter and bubble charts

Scatter charts or scatterplots are very popular in data science and statistics. They can be used to explore various kinds of correlations between variables, revealing trends, clusters, linear, and non-linear relationships. It's an essential tool in problem solving procedures and decision-making.

Scatter charts display the correlation between two variables by plotting their points in a system of Cartesian coordinates. Additional variables can be displayed by using different shapes and/or colors for the points.

A bubble chart is a scatter chart that uses circles with different radii to display an additional variable. It's also common to overlap scatter charts with other charts, such as line and bar charts, as to emphasize patterns and compare raw data with estimates, such as trendlines (best-fit).

# Creating a scatter chart

The `type` property should be `scatter`. Scatter charts support the same properties as line charts, but instead of an array of numbers, the data property should contain an array of point objects with the following structure:

```
{
    x: number,
    y: number
}
```

The following example creates a simple scatter chart with a single dataset. The data values consist of a sequence of numbers generated for the *x* property, and the sine function of each number for the *y* property:

```
const dataset = [];
  for(let i = 0; i <= 360; i+= 5) {
    const point = {
        x: i,
        y: Math.sin(i * Math.PI / 180)
    }
    dataset.push(point);
  }

const dataObj = {
    datasets: [
        {
            data: dataset,
```

```
                pointRadius: 2,
                backgroundColor: 'red'
            }
        ]
    }

    const chartObj = {
        type: "scatter",
        data: dataObj,
        options: {
            legend: {
                display: false
            },


        }
    };
    new Chart("my-scatter-chart", chartObj);
```

You can see the full code in `ScatterBubble/scatter-1.html`. **The result is shown as follows:**

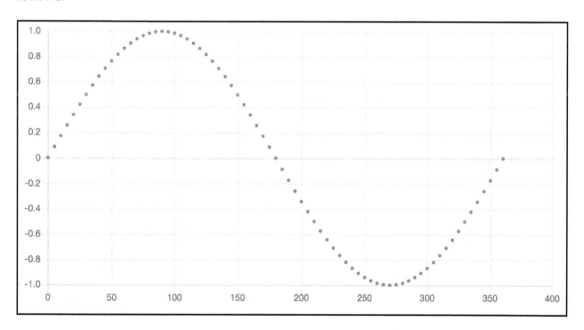

A simple scatter chart with x = n and y = sin(x) (code: *ScatterBubble/scatter-1.html*)

Multiple datasets can be displayed on the same chart. This following example generates two more mathematical functions and displays their graphs using the same scales:

```
const dataset1 = [], dataset2 = [], dataset3 = [];
  for(let i = 0; i <= 360; i+= 5) {
      const n = i * Math.PI / 180;
      const point1 = { x: n - Math.PI, y: Math.sin(n) }
      const point2 = { x: n - Math.PI, y: Math.cos(n) }
      const point3 = { x: Math.cos(n) + Math.sin(n), y: Math.cos(n) -
      Math.sin(n) }
      dataset1.push(point1);
      dataset2.push(point2);
      dataset3.push(point3);
  }

  const dataObj = {
      datasets: [
          {   data: dataset1,
              pointRadius: 2,
              backgroundColor: 'red'
          },{
              data: dataset2,
              pointRadius: 2,
              backgroundColor: 'blue'
          },{
              data: dataset3,
              pointRadius: 2,
              backgroundColor: 'green'
          }
      ]
  }

  const chartObj = {
      type: "scatter",
      data: dataObj,
      options: {
          legend: { display: false },
          scales: {
              yAxes: [{
                  ticks: {min: -2, max: 2}
              }]
          }
      }
  };
  new Chart("my-scatter-chart", chartObj);
```

You can see the full code in `ScatterBubble/scatter-3.html`. The result is shown as follows:

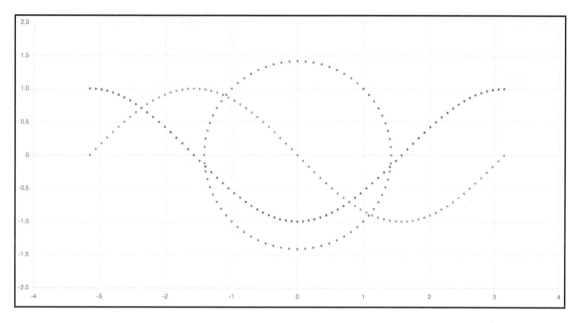

Scatterplot with multiple datasets (code: *ScatterBubble/scatter-3.html*)

# Revealing correlations with scatter charts

Scatter charts are great to show correlations between data. The following example will combine NASA/GISS global temperature data (`Data/monthly_json.json`) and CO2 emission data (`Data/co2_mm_mlo.csv`) measured in Mauna Loa, Hawaii, to discover if there is any correlation between the two. Since the Mauna Loa data is only available after 1959, we will only use the GISS data after that year.

Since we must load multiple files, we will use JavaScript promises. Each data source is parsed and the data is sent to the `combine()` function, which returns an array that can be used by Chart.js, as follows:

```
const canvas = document.getElementById("my-scatter-chart");
const files = ['../Data/monthly_json.json', '../Data/co2_mm_mlo.csv'];
var promises = files.map(file => fetch(file).then(resp => resp.text()));
Promise.all(promises).then(results => {
    const temperatures = JSON.parse(results[0]);
    const co2emissions = Papa.parse(results[1], {header: true}).data;
```

```
        const data = combine(temperatures, co2emissions);
        drawData(data);
});
```

The `combine()` function iterates through each object in the CO2 data, extracts the year and the month and uses it to obtain the corresponding mean temperature, then creates an object with the CO2 and temperature for each month/year. Each object is pushed into an array that is returned, as follows:

```
function combine(tempData, co2Data) {
    const entries = [];
    co2Data.filter(n => +n.year >= 1959).forEach(measure => {
        const year = measure.year, month = measure.month;
        let temperature = 0;
        tempData.filter(n => n.Source=='GISTEMP' && +n.Date.split("-")
        [0] >= 1959)
                .forEach(temp => {
                    if(+temp.Date.split("-")[0] == year
                        && +temp.Date.split("-")[1] == month) {
                            temperature = temp.Mean;
                    }
                });
        entries.push({ co2: measure.average, temp: temperature });
    });
    return entries;
}
```

The following `drawData()` function uses the array of objects that contains `co2` and `temp` properties to draw the scatter chart by copying these values into `{x, y}` objects:

```
function drawData(datasets) {
    const entries = [];
    datasets.forEach(entry => {
        const obj = { x: entry.co2, y: entry.temp };
        entries.push(obj);
    });
    const dataObj = {
        datasets: [
            {
                data: entries,
                pointRadius: 2,
                pointBackgroundColor: 'rgba(255,0,0,.5)'
            }
        ]
    }
    const chartObj = {
        type: "scatter",
        data: dataObj,
```

```
        options: { legend: { display: false } }
    };
    new Chart("my-scatter-chart", chartObj);
}
```

You can see the full code in `ScatterBubble/scatter-4.html`. The result is shown in the following chart and reveals a possible relationship between growing CO2 emissions and global temperatures. It also shows some data that we should have filtered out (if we had read the documentation that comes with the data), such as missing CO2 measurements, which appear as *-99.99*:

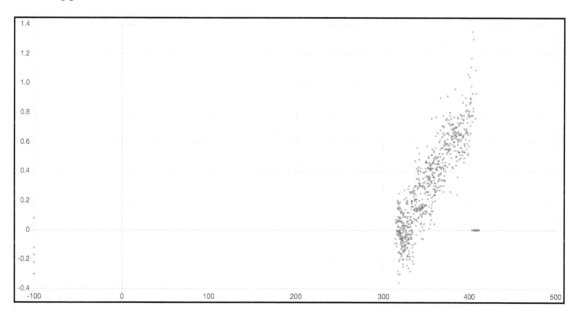

Comparing CO2 emissions (source: Mauna Loa) and global temperature (source: NASA; code: *ScatterBubble/scatter-4.html*)

We can filter out the bad measurements by adding an extra predicate to the `co2Data` filter, as follows:

```
co2Data.filter(n => +n.year >= 1959 && n.average > 0)
```

It's also a good idea to label the axes, so the viewer knows what kind of data is being compared. The following configuration adds axis titles and also a title for the chart. The full code is in `ScatterBubble/scatter-5.html`:

```
const chartObj = {
    type: "scatter",
    data: dataObj,
    options: {
```

```
            legend: { display: false},
            title: {
                display: true,
                text: 'CO2 emissions vs. Global temperatures',
                fontSize: 24
            },
            scales: {
                xAxes: [{
                    scaleLabel: {
                        labelString: 'CO2 emissions (ppm)',
                        display: true
                    }
                }],
                yAxes: [{
                    scaleLabel: {
                        labelString: 'Temperature anomaly (Celsius)',
                        display: true
                    }
                }],
            }
        }
    };
    new Chart("my-scatter-chart", chartObj);
```

The final chart is shown as follows:

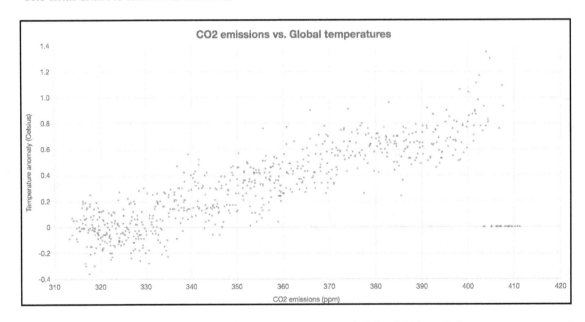

CO2 vs temperature scatter chart after filtering out wrong measurements (code: *ScatterBubble/scatter-5.html*)

# Scatter charts with large quantities of data

Scatter charts are great to reveal hidden patterns in large datasets. In the following example, we will use a huge file obtained from a public database (`geonames.org`) to plot a scatter chart showing the position of cities based on their latitude and longitude. The file contains a list of locations with populations above 15,000 (`Data/cities_15000.csv`). It contains over 100,000 entries (and because of this, it will take a few seconds to load). This is the general structure of the CSV file:

```
geonameid;asciiname;latitude;longitude;country_code;population;timezone1425
6;Azadshahr;34.79049;48.57011;IR;514102;Asia/Tehran
18918;Protaras;35.0125;34.05833;CY;20230;Asia/Nicosia
23814;Kahriz;34.3838;47.0553;IR;766706;Asia/Tehran
24851;Nurabad;34.0734;47.9725;IR;73528;Asia/Tehran
// + than 100 000 lines
```

To build the scatter chart, we need to process the file and convert latitudes and longitudes into the point data format. The axes also have to be configured to represent a cylindrical projection of the globe (limited by longitude: *-180* to *180* and latitude: *-90* to *90*). The following code configures the scales, loads the files, parses the data, builds the point object for each coordinate pair, and draws the chart:

```
fetch('../Data/cities15000.csv')
    .then(response => response.text())
    .then(csv => drawData(Papa.parse(csv, {header: true}).data));

function drawData(datasets) {
    const locations = [];
    datasets.forEach(city => {
        const obj = {
            x: city.longitude,
            y: city.latitude,
            name: city.asciiname
        }
        locations.push(obj);
    });

    const dataObj = {
        datasets: [
            {
                label: "Label",
                data: locations,
                pointRadius: .25,
                pointBackgroundColor: 'red'
            }
        ]
```

```
        }

    const chartObj = {
        type: "scatter",
        data: dataObj,
        options: {
            animation: { duration: 0 },
            title: { display: false },
            responsive: false,
            legend: { display: false },
            scales: {
                xAxes: [ { ticks: { min: -180, max: 180 } } ],
                yAxes: [ { ticks: { min: -90,  max: 90  } } ]
            },
            tooltips: {
                callbacks: {
                    title: (items,data) => locations[items[0].index].name
                }
            }
        }
    };

    new Chart("my-scatter-chart", chartObj);
}
```

You can see the full code in `ScatterBubble/scatter-6-world.html`. The result reveals a surprising hidden pattern (and correlation between land and humans). You can move the mouse over the points and it will reveal the name and coordinates of the location (this was configured using tooltip callbacks):

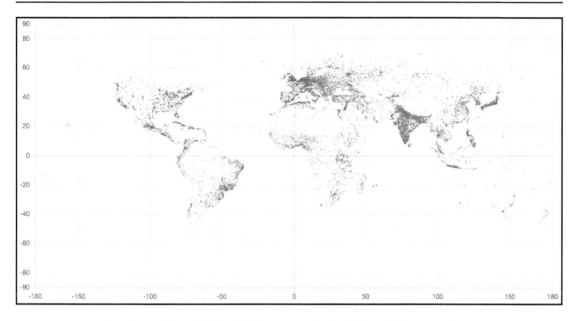

Scatter chart showing the position of over 100,000 human-populated locations (code: *ScatterBubble/scatter-6-world.html*)

# Bubble charts

Bubble charts are just like scatter charts, but they can display an extra variable in the diameter of the point (or shape). The `type` property should be `bubble`. Although they share the same dataset properties as scatter charts, most of them can receive callbacks in bubble charts, which allow a higher degree of interactivity. The data structure for bubble charts contains three properties, as follows:

```
{x: number, y: number, r: number}
```

The properties x and y are scaled automatically when the chart is scaled. The r property is the raw radius of the circle in pixels and is not scaled (but you can configure a callback if you need to scale it).

The following code (`ScatterBubble/bubble-1.html`) creates a simple bubble chart with a single dataset containing five entries. The color of each bubble is generated automatically according to the radius of the bubble using a callback:

```
const dataObj = {
    datasets: [
        {
            data: [{x:5, y:1, r:60},{x:3, y:1, r:30},{x:1, y:2, r:15},
```

```
                        {x:3, y:5, r:90},{x:2, y:4, r:20}],
            backgroundColor: function(context) {
                const point = context.dataset.data[context.dataIndex];
                return 'hsla('+(point.r * 4)+',100%,70%,.6)'
            }
        }
    ]
}

const chartObj = { type: "bubble", data: dataObj,
    options: {
        scales: {
            xAxes: [{ticks: {min: 0, max: 6}}],
            yAxes: [{ticks: {min: 0, max: 7}}]
        },
    }
};
new Chart("my-bubble-chart", chartObj);
```

The result is shown as follows. Note that if you resize the chart, the bubble sizes don't change:

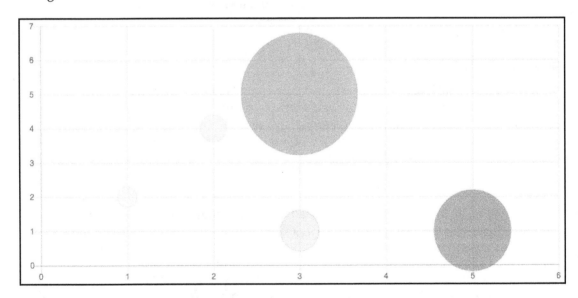

A simple bubble chart with one dataset (code: *ScatterBubble/bubble-1.html*)

Bubble charts are as not as informative as scatter charts when displaying large amounts of data, but they can still reveal interesting information. The following example converts the previously shown scatter chart into a bubble chart using the population of each location to generate the radius of the bubble.

Since bubbles may overlap, the dataset is sorted so that the smaller populations stay on top. The `scaleR()` function creates a simple scale to convert populations into circle radii, as follows:

```
fetch('../Data/cities15000.csv')
        .then(response => response.text())
        .then(csv => {
            const data = Papa.parse(csv, {header: true}).data;
            drawData(data.sort((a, b) =>  b.population - a.population));
        });

function scaleR(value) {
    const r = Math.floor(value / 100000);
    return r != 0 ? r/10 : .25;
}
```

The `drawData()` function creates a data point object for the bubble chart, with three properties x, y containing the longitudes and latitudes, and the scaled population converted into a radius, as follows:

```
function drawData(datasets) {
    const coordset = [];
    datasets.forEach(city => {
        const obj = {
            x: city.longitude,
            y: city.latitude,
            r: scaleR(city.population)
        };
        coordset.push(obj);
    });
```

The data object includes the data array as its data, and configures the `backgroundColor` property as a callback that returns different colors for the bubbles depending on the value of the radius, as follows:

```
const dataObj = {
    datasets: [
        {
            label: "Label",
            data: coordset,
            backgroundColor: function(context) {
                const value =
```

```
                        context.dataset.data[context.dataIndex].r;
                        if(value > 20) return 'hsla(0,100%,50%,.4)';
                        if(value > 10) return 'hsla(30,100%,50%,.5)';
                        if(value > 5) return 'hsla(60,100%,50%,.6)';
                        if(value > 1) return 'hsla(120,100%,50%,.7)';
                        else return 'hsla(0,0%,50%,1)';
                    }
                }
            ]
        }

    new Chart("my-bubble-chart", {type: 'bubble', data: dataObj, options:
    {...}});
    }
```

You can see the full code in `ScatterBubble/bubble-2.html`. The result is shown as follows:

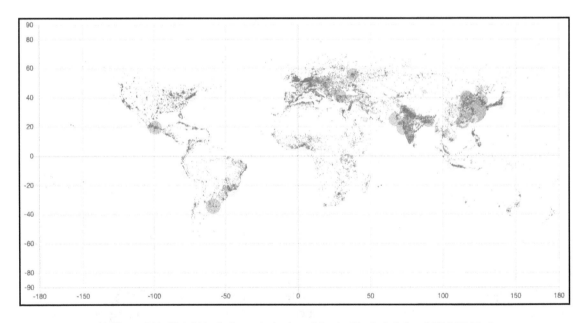

A bubble map of cities. The bubble's radius is proportional to the population of each location (code: *ScatterBubble/bubble-2.html*)

# Summary

In this chapter, we learned how to create all of the standard types of charts supported by Chart.js: bar, horizontal bar, line, area, pie, doughnut, polar area, radar, scatter, and bubble charts.

Different charts are more suited for certain types of datasets and purposes than others. We explored the same examples with different charts and saw how each type communicates different aspects of the data, revealing correlations, proportions, trends, and hidden patterns.

Each chart was introduced with a simple example, but we also created some real world visualizations using public CSV and JSON data, which needed to be downscaled, combined, filtered, and mapped to data formats expected by Chart.js.

We also experimented with several configuration properties, for graphical elements, datasets, and charts, allowing a high degree of customization. Many of these will be explored in greater detail in the next chapters.

# References

**Books and websites:**

- Chart.js official documentation and samples: `https://www.chartjs.org/docs/latest/`
- PieceLabel plugin (`Chart.PieceLabel.js`) `https://github.com/emn178/Chart.PieceLabel.js`

**Data sources:**

- Mauna Loa CO2 measurements: `Chapter04/Data/co2_mm_mlo.csv`. Dr. Pieter Tans, NOAA/ESRL (`www.esrl.noaa.gov/gmd/ccgg/trends/`) and Dr. Ralph Keeling, Scripps Institution of Oceanography (`scrippsco2.ucsd.edu/`).
- Ocean temperatures: `Chapter04/Data/monthly_json.json`. GISTEMP Team, *2019: GISS Surface Temperature Analysis (GISTEMP)*. NASA Goddard Institute for Space Studies. Dataset accessed 2019-02-01 at `https://data.giss.nasa.gov/gistemp/`. Hansen, J., R. Ruedy, M. Sato, and K. Lo, 2010: Global surface temperature change, Rev. Geophys., 48, RG4004, doi:10.1029/2010RG000345.

- Geographical database: `Chapter02/Data/cities1000.csv`. GeoNames geographical database: `www.geonames.org`.
- CO2 emissions per country in kilotons (1960-2014): `Chapter04/world_bank_co2_kt.json`. *World bank public data.* `https://data.worldbank.org`
- World population: `Chapter04/WPP2017_UN.csv`. *United Nations World Population Prospects 2017.* `https://www.un.org`

# Scales and Grid Configuration

5

In this chapter, you will learn how to configure the scales that control how your chart is displayed in a Cartesian or radial grid. Scales are used in all charts except pie and doughnut. Cartesian charts, such as line, bar, scatter, and bubble, use a pair of perpendicular axes, each one with a scale automatically calculated by Chart.js to position data points. Data in charts, such as polar area and radar, use a single scale, placing the data points at different positions that originate from the center. You can configure scales, altering the way the data points are presented, for example, by using a logarithmic scale instead of a default linear scale for numerical values. You may also choose a sequential time scale instead of a category scale. There are also many ways to configure styles and change the way axes, grid lines, ticks, and labels are shown in your chart.

In this chapter, we will cover the following topics:

- Configuring scales
- Cartesian axes, ticks, and grid lines
- Radial axes, ticks, and grid lines
- Advanced scales configuration

## Configuring scales

A *scale* is a transformation that enlarges or shrinks a data domain so that it fits a specific range. Chart.js scales data automatically, adjusting domain data values so they fit within the space reserved for the chart. A scale is represented by an *axis*, which is a directed line that represents the extent of the domain. The discrete values that are placed on an axis line are called `ticks`. A coordinate system with perpendicular or radial axes and discrete ticks forms a `grid`. Scales, axes, ticks, and grids exist in all charts, even if you don't see them. They control how the data points will be displayed in the chart.

Cartesian charts have two scales, each represented by perpendicular axes, *x* and *y*, and radial charts have one scale, represented by the radius and angle. Radial scales are always linear, but Cartesian scales can be linear, logarithmic, categorical, or temporal. Chart.js also allows you to create your own scales.

In most charts, the axes, grid lines, and tick labels are visible by default, but you may wish to remove unnecessary lines, lighten colors, dash lines, and hide unused legends to maximize the data-ink ratio of your chart. Font sizes and colors can be configured for all labels, and you can conditionally hide data using callbacks.

# Cartesian configuration options

Cartesian grids are used in scatter, bubble, bar, and line charts, and contain two sets of scales, one for each perpendicular axis. They are configured in an object assigned to the `options.scales` property:

```
options: {
    scales: {
        xAxes: [{...}, ..., {...}], // array of x-axis objects
        yAxes: [{...}, ..., {...}]  // array of y-axis objects
    }
}
```

You can have multiple axes of each type. They can be stacked, placed side by side, or positioned on opposite sides. Each axis may be linked to a specific dataset.

Polar area and radar charts use radial scales and configure a single `options.scale` property:

```
options: {
    scale: {
        {...} // axis object containing configuration for the radial axis
    }
}
```

All axis configuration objects in Cartesian charts and the `scale` property in radial charts contain a `display` property, which receives a Boolean value (`true` or `false`), making it visible or not. The following code fragments hide all axes, grids and labels from a Cartesian chart and a radial chart:

```
options: { // configuration for a Cartesian chart
    scales: { xAxes: [{display: false}], yAxes: [{display: false}] }
  }
options: { // configuration for a radial chart
    scale: { display: false }
  }
```

The result is shown here. You can use this effect to create sparklines (small minimalistic visualizations). See the full code in `Scales/scales-1-Cartesian-display.html` and `scales-2-radial-display.html`:

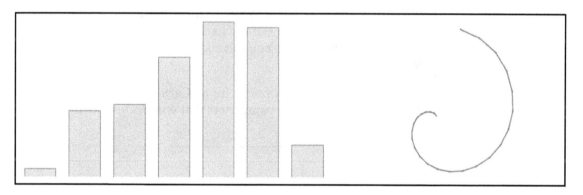

A Cartesian chart and a radial chart with hidden axes, gridlines, and tick labels.
Code: *Scales/scales-1-Cartesian-display.html* and *scales-2-radial-display.html*

Axes also support more than a dozen callback functions that can be used to configure labels, ticks, and other data displayed by each axis.

# Cartesian axes, ticks, and grid lines

There are five chart types that use Cartesian grids: bar, horizontalBar, line, scatter, and bubble. Every chart has two scales, one for each perpendicular axis. Each scale can be of four types:

- `type: 'linear'`: A numeric scale that can be used to compare values of the same order of magnitude.
- `type: 'logarithmic'`: A numeric scale to compare values that differ in order of magnitude.
- `type: 'category'`: A list of unordered categories.
- `type: 'time'`: An ordered list of instants. This scale requires the `moment.js` library.

In most charts, at least one of the scales is numeric (linear or logarithmic). In scatterplots and bubble charts, both scales are numeric. Time-series charts use a numeric scale and a time scale, but you can also use a category scale. You can also create correlation charts where both scales are categories.

The following table lists common configuration options for all Cartesian axes (the three last are objects, which contain specific configuration parameters that will be described in separate sections):

| Property | Value | Description |
|---|---|---|
| type | `'logarithmic'`, `'linear'` (default for both axes in scatter and bubble charts, and in the $y$ axis for line and bar charts), `'category'` (default in the $x$ axis for bar and line charts), `'time'` (requires the `moment.js` library) | Selects axis type. Note that some configuration properties are specific to certain types of axes, and others may not be supported. |
| position | top or bottom (default) for xAxes; left (default) or right for yAxes | The axis position. If there is more than one axis in the same position, it will be placed below or to the left of the existing axis. You can sort them using `weight`. See `Cartesian/Cartesian-1-position.html`. |
| weight | Number | Order axes when more than one axis is in the same position. Larger numbers are position the axes farther from the chart. See `Cartesian/Cartesian-2-weight.html`. |

| offset | true or false (default for all axes except type:'category' in bar charts) | If true, adds space to each side of the axis. |
|---|---|---|
| id | String | Labels an axis so it can be related to a dataset, when using multiple axes. |
| gridLines | Object | Configures grid lines. |
| scaleLabel | Object | Configures scale titles. |
| ticks | Object | Configures ticks. |

Configuration properties and objects for Cartesian scales

There are also 14 life cycle callback functions not listed here. These properties are always used inside objects of the `scales.xAxes` or `scales.yAxes` arrays. A typical configuration is shown as follows:

```
options: {
    scales: {
        xAxes: [{
            ticks: {...},
            scaleLabel: {...},
            gridLines: {...}
        }],
        yAxes: [{
            type: 'logarithmic',
            position: 'left',
            scaleLabel: {...},
        ]
    }
}
```

This multi-level nesting hierarchy may sometimes be confusing. A common error is to place a property in the wrong object; no error messages are shown but nothing happens. In this chapter, we will use *axis* to refer to any axis object inside xAxes or yAxes (such as `axis.ticks.minor`, `axis.scaleLabel`), or use its full path from the `scales` object (such as `scale.yAxes[0].ticks.minor`). The exception is when they are listed in tables, but in this case the parent object will be qualified.

# Numeric Cartesian scales

There are two types of numeric scales. In all charts that use numeric scales, `type:'linear'` is the default, but it's not always the best option. A linear chart is best to compare data points of the same magnitude, but when the samples contain some values that are hundreds of times larger than others, data correlations may be hard to find.

# Linear scales

A linear scale was used to for the following scatter chart, which plots the populations of several countries, comparing their population in 1980 (*y* axis) with their population in 2015 (*x* axis). The data is from the United Nations (see `Data/WPP2017_UNH.csv` in the GitHub repository for this chapter). The median line represents the points where the population is the same. Countries that appear in the shaded area above the middle line experienced a decrease in population:

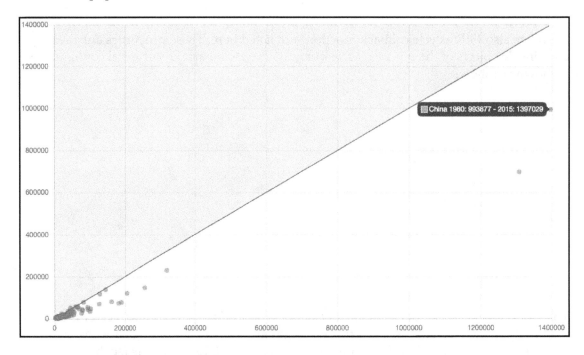

A chart showing population increase/decrease from 1980 to 2015. Due to the different order of magnitude between China, India, and the rest of the world, the linear scale is not the best choice

Code: *Numeric/numeric-1-linear.html*

The two dots on the right side of the chart are India and China. All the other countries are concentrated in the lower-left corner of the chart. This chart is very difficult to read because it mixes values of different orders of magnitude. Most countries have a small population (in the order of millions), and when compared to China and India (billions), they end up cluttered near the beginning of the scale. In these situations, we should use a logarithmic scale.

Tooltips reveal the name of each country represented in the chart. You can check the full code for this chart in `Numeric/numeric-1-linear.html`. It's a mixed chart, with datasets of different types (line and scatter). We will explore mixed charts in `Chapter 7`, *Advanced Chart.js*.

# Logarithmic scales

Declaring the *type* property of an axis object as logarithmic will render its data according to a logarithmic scale. Change one of the axes of the previous example to `type: 'logarithmic'` and the line will become a curve, as shown as follows. It seems that the distribution of data points has improved in this visualization. They are a bit closer and the chart reveals some data that was not visible before:

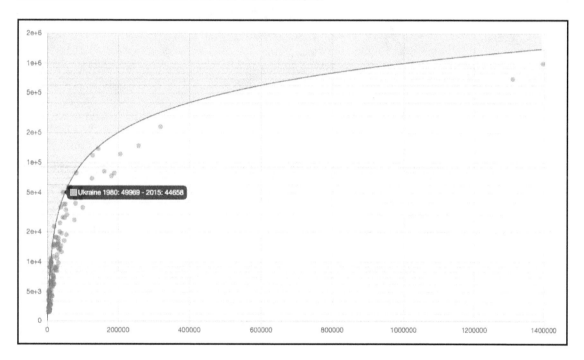

Making one of the scales logarithmic improves the scatter chart, revealing hidden data
Code: *Numeric/numeric-2-log.html*

We can improve it. Since both scales contain the same population data, we can declare the type of both axes as logarithmic, as shown as follows. Now the curve becomes a line again, the points are much closer and easier to compare, and even more hidden data is revealed:

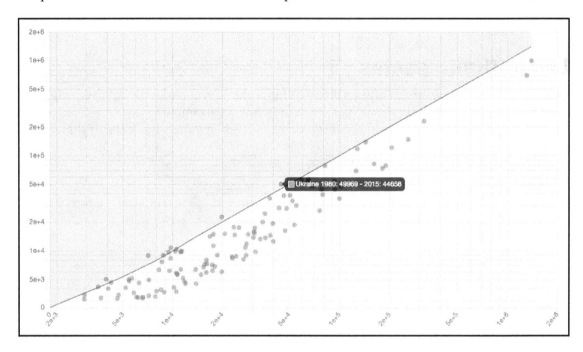

An even better scatterplot with two logarithmic axes
Code: *Numeric/numeric-3-log.html*

The full code for these last two examples is in `Numeric/numeric-2-log.html` and `numeric-3-log.html`.

# Configuring axis titles

You can add a label or title for each axis in any Cartesian chart using the `axis.scaleLabel` property (for example, `options.scales.xAxes[0].scaleLabel` configures the title for the first *x* axis). The following table lists the configurable properties of a `scaleLabel` object:

| Property | Value | Description |
|---|---|---|
| display | true or false (default) | Displays or hides the axis title |
| labelString | String (default is '') | The title for the axis |
| lineHeight | Number | Spacing above and below the text |
| fontColor, fontFamily, fontStyle | String | CSS font attributes |
| fontSize | Number | Font size in pixels |
| padding | Number | Spacing before and after the text |

Scale label (scale title) configuration for Cartesian scales. These properties are used in any axis.scaleLabel object.

The following code fragment adds titles for the *x* and *y* axes of a bar chart that we created in `Chapter 3`, *Chart.js – Quick Start*. Note that it's not enough to just add `axis.scaleLabel.labelString`, you also have to set `axis.scaleLabel.display: true`, since the titles are hidden by default:

```
scales: {
    xAxes: [{
        scaleLabel: {
            display: true,
            labelString: "Oceans",
            fontSize: 16
        }
    }],
    yAxes: [{
        scaleLabel: {
            display: true,
            labelString: "Volume in cubic km",
            fontSize: 16
        }
    }]
}
```

See the full code in `Cartesian/Cartesian-3-scaleLabel.html`. The result is shown as follows:

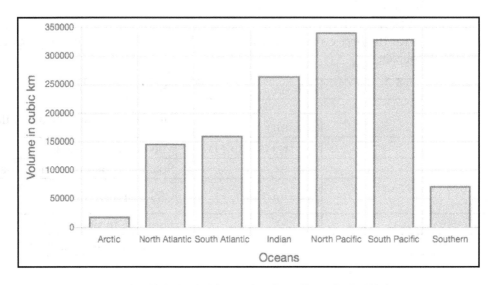

Axis titles added with the *scaleLabel* property. Code: *Cartesian/Cartesian-3-scaleLabel.html.*

# Configuring ticks

Ticks are discrete points placed along an axis. Their position determines how the data points will be plotted in relation to the axis. In numeric scales, the `axis.ticks` property configures numerical parameters such as the maximum and minimum values that an axis will display and the amount of ticks to show. In any Cartesian scale, it can be used apply styles to tick labels and configure padding and other positioning parameters. Tick markers are configured separately in the `axis.gridLines` property.

The following table lists tick properties that can be configured for any Cartesian scale:

| Property | Value | Description |
|---|---|---|
| `display` | `true` (default) or `false` | Shows or hides tick labels. |
| `fontSize` | Number | The font size in pixels. |
| `fontColor,`<br>`fontFamily,`<br>`fontStyle` | String | CSS font attributes. |

| reverse | true or false (default) | Reverses the order of tick labels. |
|---|---|---|
| callback | Function. Default: d=>d | The function receives the value of the tick. It can be used to hide ticks or change the values displayed. |
| labelOffset | Number. Default: 0 | Offsets the label from the center point of the tick. |
| mirror | true or false (default) | Flips labels around the axis to the inside of the chart. |
| padding | Number. Default: 10 | Space between tick label and the axis. |
| autoSkip | true (default) or false | If there is not enough space for horizontal labels, they are skipped. autoSkip:true always shows them. |
| maxRotation | Number. Default: 90 | Maximum rotation of label in the xAxis. |
| minRotation | Number. Default: 0 | Minimum rotation of label in the xAxis. |

Tick configuration for Cartesian scales. These properties are used in any *axis.ticks* object.

The following table lists additional tick properties supported by numeric scales (linear or logarithmic):

| Property | Value | Description |
|---|---|---|
| min | Number | The lower limit of the axis. |
| max | Number | The upper limit of the axis. |
| suggestedMin | Number | Will set this as the minimum, if the data's minimum is larger. |
| suggestedMax | Number | Will set this as the maximum, if the data's maximum is smaller. |
| beginAtZero | true (default) or false | Forces the axis to use zero as the lower limit. |
| stepSize | Number | Sets a minimum step size between ticks. Overrides precision. |
| maxTicksLimit | Number. Default is 11. | Explicitly sets a maximum number of ticks for the axis. |

Tick configuration for linear and logarithmic scales. These properties are used in any *axis.ticks* object of these scales

The following configuration was applied to one of the bar charts we created in `Chapter 3, Chart.js – Quick Start.` It uses the `axis.ticks.callback` property to add the word `ocean` as a suffix to the tick labels in the horizontal axis. The vertical axis was reversed, making the bars appear upside-down:

```
scales: {
    xAxes: [{
        ticks: {
            callback: d => d + ' ocean'
        }
    }],
    yAxes: [{
        ticks: {
            reverse: true,
        }
    }]
}
```

The result is shown here. See the full code in `Cartesian/Cartesian-4-ticks-style.html`:

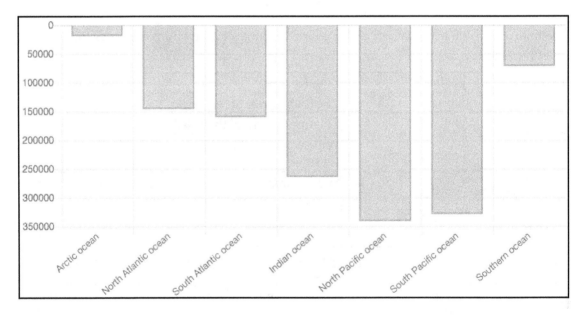

Tick configuration in Cartesian charts, reversing the vertical axis and adding text to labels in the horizontal axis with *axis.ticks.callback*.
Code: *Cartesian/Cartesian-4-ticks-style.html*

Chart.js automatically calculates the minimum range for each of the axes so that the data can be rendered in the most efficient way possible. But you can explicitly set minimum and maximum values using `axis.ticks.min` and `axis.ticks.max` properties. In this case, any parts of the chart that fall out of range will not be displayed. Alternatively, you can use `axis.ticks.suggestedMin` and `axis.ticks.suggestedMax`, which also limit the range, but only if no data values are left out. The following code applies these properties to a scatter chart, and adds more ticks (default maximum is `11`) by setting a smaller value for `axis.ticks.stepSize`:

```
scales: {
    xAxes: [{
        ticks: {
            padding: 10,
            stepSize: 20,
        }
    }],
    yAxes: [{
        ticks: {
            padding: 10,
            min: -0.6,
            suggestedMax: 0.6, // ignored, because data is larger

        }
    }]
}
```

The result of this configuration is shown as follows. The full code is in `Cartesian/Cartesian-5-ticks-minmax.html`:

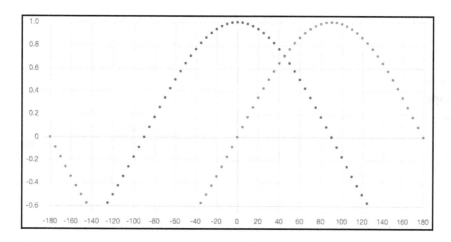

Tick configuration in numeric charts: step size and minimum value
Code: *Cartesian/Cartesian-5-ticks-minmax.html*

# Configuring grid lines

Cartesian grids support several properties that change their appearance on the screen. You can change colors, line widths, line styles, tick size, spacing for the grid lines, and different styles for the zero line. You can also show and hide grid lines, ticks, and borders, reducing the amount of unnecessary chart junk and making your chart more efficient.

These properties are configured in the `gridLines` object inside each object of the `xAxes` or `yAxes` arrays and are listed here:

| Property | Value | Description |
|----------|-------|-------------|
| display | true (default) or false | Shows or hides the grid lines for this axis. |
| color | A CSS color or array of colors; default is 'rgba(0,0,0,.1)' | The color of the grid lines. If an array is used, sets a color for each line. |
| lineWidth | Number; default is 1 | The width of the grid lines. |
| borderDash | Number[] | A dash array for the grid lines. |
| borderDashOffset | Number | The dash offset for the grid lines. |
| drawBorder | true (default) or false | Draws/hides the axis line. |
| drawOnChartArea | true (default) or false | Draws/hides grid lines inside the chart for the axis. |
| drawTicks | true (default) or false | Draws/hides the tick marks. |
| tickMarkLength | Number | The size of the tick mark. |
| zeroLineWidth | Number | The width of the zero line. |
| zeroLineColor | CSS color | The color of the zero line. |
| zeroLineBorderDash | Number[] | A dash array for the zero line. |
| zeroLineBorderDashOffset | Number | The dash offset for the zero line. |
| offsetGridLines | true or false | Moves the grid lines between labels (default in bar charts). |

Configuration of gridlines in Cartesian scales. These properties are used in any *axis.gridLines* object

Some grid-line configuration examples are shown here. This code applies different colors to the vertical grid lines and a dash array for the horizontal lines. The axis lines are hidden because `axis.gridLines.drawBorder` is `false`. A different width and color was applied to the zero lines on both axes:

```
scales: {
    xAxes: [{
        gridLines: {
            color: ['#fff','#d30','#b33',...,'#09b','#09e'],
            lineWidth: 2,
            zeroLineColor: 'black',
            zeroLineWidth: 5,
            drawBorder: false
        },
        ticks: {
            padding: 10,
            callback: function(d) {return d != 200 ? d : undefined;}
        }
    }],
    yAxes: [{
        gridLines: {
            zeroLineColor: 'black',
            zeroLineWidth: 5,
            lineWidth: 2,
            borderDash: [5, 5],
            drawBorder: false
        },
        ticks: { padding: 10 }
    }]
}
```

The result is shown in the following screenshot. The full code is in
`Cartesian/Cartesian-6-grid-styles.html`:

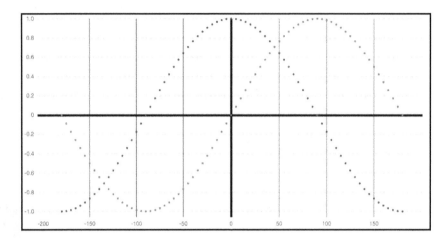

Vertical grid lines with different colors and horizontal lines with dash arrays. Both axis lines are hidden with *axis.gridLines drawBorder: false*
Code: Cartesian/Cartesian-6-grid-styles.html

Tick marks are lines that cross outside of the chart area. You can hide them with
`axis.gridLines.drawTicks:false` or make them longer or shorter with
`axis.gridLines.tickMarkLength`. You can hide `gridLines` inside the chart area with
`axis.gridLines.drawOnChartArea:false` and the axis line with
`axis.gridLines.drawBorder:false`. These properties were used to configure the
following chart (`Cartesian/Cartesian-7-grid-styles.html`):

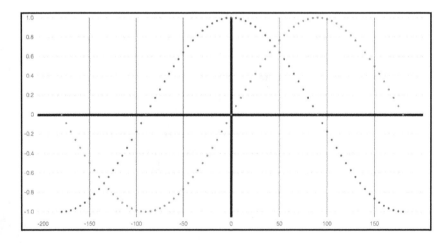

Vertical grid with an *axis.gridLines.tickMarkLength* of 15 pixels and *axis.gridLines drawOnChartArea: false*. Horizontal grid hides axis with *axis.gridLines drawBorder: false*
Code: *Cartesian/Cartesian-7-grid-styles.html*

This configuration hides `ticks` and `gridLines` to produce a minimalistic chart with a single centered *y* axis:

```
options: {
    scales: {
        xAxes: [{
                ticks: { display: false },
            gridLines: { display: false }
        }],
        yAxes: [{
                ticks: {
                mirror: true,
                padding: -(canvas.width/2)
            },
            gridLines: {
                drawBorder: false,
                drawOnChartArea: false,
                drawTicks: false,
                offsetGridLines: true
            }
        }]
    }
}
```

The result applied to a line chart is shown here. See the full code in `Cartesian/Cartesian-8-grid-minimal.html`:

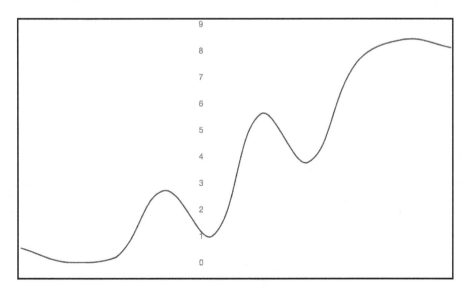

A chart with minimal grid markings Code: *Cartesian/Cartesian-8-grid-minimal.html*

# Category scales

Typical bar and line charts use a category scale for the $x$ axis, and a numeric scale for the $y$ axis. Multiple datasets reuse the same category data. In these charts, the values used for the category axis are obtained from the `labels` property of the data object. If a dataset has a `labels` property, its $x$ axis will automatically be defined as `type:category`.

# Configuring the axes

Category scales share the same axis configuration as numeric charts, but support some additional properties in the `axis` and `axis.ticks` objects. The `axis` object has one additional property that can be used to override the data object `labels` for an axis:

| Property | Value | Description |
|----------|-------|-------------|
| `labels` | Array of String | An array of labels to display. Overrides any other definition for labels, including data object properties: `labels`, `xLabels`, or `yLabels`. |

Additional axis configuration for category scales

The following code fragment shows category labels defined in three different properties. Since the single $x$ axis contains a `labels` property, it will override all previous definitions:

```
new Chart("my-chart",
    type: ...,
    data: {
        labels: ['One', 'Two', 'Three'], // used if others are not present
        xLabels: ['ONE', 'TWO', 'THREE'],   // overrides 'labels'
        datasets: [...]
    },
    options: {
        scales: {
            xAxes: [{
                type: 'category',
                labels: ['Label 1', 'Label 2', 'Label 3'] // overrides
                xLabels
            }]
        }
    }
});
```

You can create charts that have category scales for both *x* and *y* axes in Chart.js with the xLabels and yLabels properties in the data object. The first axis of each type will use them. The data and xLabels array have the same size. Each element in the xLabels array is related to a corresponding item from the data array, which contains values from the yLabels array. This creates a one-to-many relationship between the categories. There is a single *y* value shared by many *x* values.

In the following example, properties were set for all axes using Global.defaults.scale:

```
const yLabels = ["Water", "Land", "Air"]; // groups: multiple points
const xLabels = ["Ship", "Train", "Bike", "Cruiser",
                "Jet", "Bus", "Rocket", "Car"]; // items: single point
const data = ["Water", "Land", "Land", "Water", "Air", "Land", "Air",
             "Land"];

const dataObj = {
    xLabels: xLabels, // used by x-axis category scale
    yLabels: yLabels, // used by y-axis category scale
    datasets: [
        {
            data: data,
            pointRadius: 50, pointHoverRadius: 50,
            pointStyle: 'rectRot',
            showLine: false,
            backgroundColor: "hsla(20,100%,80%,0.8)",
            borderColor: "hsla(0,100%,50%,1)"
        }
    ]
}

Chart.defaults.scale.gridLines.drawBorder = false;
Chart.defaults.scale.gridLines.lineWidth = 10;
Chart.defaults.scale.gridLines.drawBorder = false;
Chart.defaults.scale.offset = true;
Chart.defaults.scale.ticks.padding = 20;

new Chart("correlation",
        {
            type: "line",
            data: dataObj,
            options: {
                legend: {display: false},
                scales: {
                    xAxes: [{type: 'category'}],
                    yAxes: [{type: 'category'}]
                },
                animation: {duration: 0},
```

```
                        tooltips: {displayColors: false}
            }
        });
```

The result is shown as follows. See the full code in `Category/category-1-one-to-many.html`:

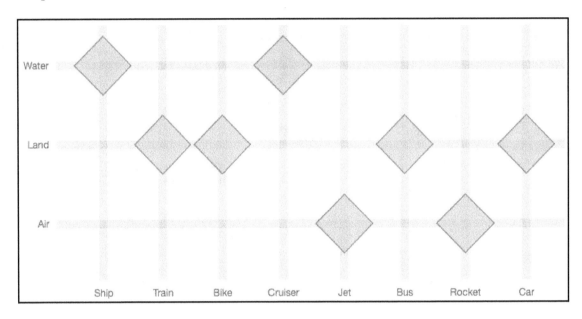

A correlation chart for one-to-many relationships created with two *type:'category'* axes.
Code: *Category/category-1-one-to-many.html*.

You can also create many-to-many categorical relationships, but it won't work with category scales. You have to set up a scatter chart with two numeric linear scales and then map the numbers back to categories using a callback. The following code shows how to do that:

```
const xLabels = ["Lake","River","Road","Railroad","Ocean","Air"];
  const yLabels = ["Car","Bus","Airplane","Sailboat","Cruiser","Train",
              "Bike"]
  const data = [
      {x: 1, y: 4}, {x: 1, y: 5}, {x: 2, y: 4}, {x: 3, y: 1}, {x: 3, y: 2},
      {x: 3, y: 7}, {x: 4, y: 6}, {x: 5, y: 5}, {x: 6, y: 3}
  ];

  const dataObj = {
      datasets: [
          {
              data: data,
```

```
                pointRadius: 20, pointHoverRadius: 20,
                pointStyle: 'rectRot',
                backgroundColor: "hsla(20,100%,80%,0.8)",
                borderColor: "hsla(0,100%,50%,1)"
            }
        ]
    }

Chart.defaults.scale.gridLines.drawBorder = false;
Chart.defaults.scale.gridLines.lineWidth = 2;
Chart.defaults.scale.gridLines.color = 'red';
Chart.defaults.scale.offset = true;
Chart.defaults.scale.ticks.padding = 10;
Chart.defaults.scale.ticks.min = 0;

new Chart("correlation",
        {
            type: "scatter",
            data: dataObj,
            options: {
                legend: {display: false},
                animation: { duration: 0 },
                scales: {
                    xAxes: [{
                        ticks: {
                            max: 7,
                            callback: function(value) {
                                return xLabels[value-1];
                            }
                        }
                    }],
                    yAxes: [{
                        ticks: {
                            max: 8,
                            callback: function(value) {
                                return yLabels[value-1];
                            }
                        }
                    }]
                }
            }
        });
```

The result is shown as follows. See the full code in `Category/category-2-many-to-many.html`:

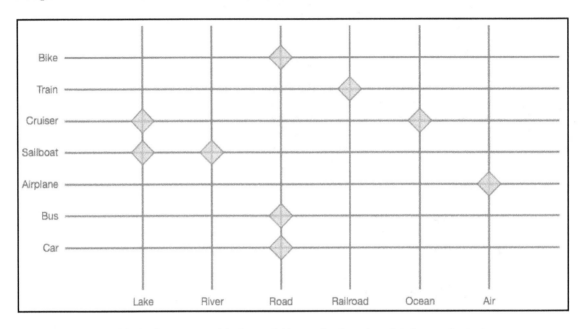

A correlation chart for many-to-many relationships created with two *type:'linear'* axes and numerical values mapped to categories
Code: *Category/category-2-many-to-many.html*

# Configuring ticks

Category scales extend the `axis.ticks` configuration for Cartesian charts with three additional properties, listed in the following table:

| Property | Value | Description |
|---|---|---|
| labels | String | The tick `labels` array. This overrides any previous declarations of this array. |
| min | String | A string in `axis.ticks.labels` that represents the lower limit for the categorical data. |
| max | String | A string in `axis.ticks.labels` that represents the upper limit for the categorical data. |

Additional tick configuration properties for category scales

The `axis.ticks.min` and `axis.ticks.max` properties depend on the order that the strings appear in the `axis.ticks.labels` array. If the order is reversed, the result could be an empty chart.

This is the bar chart we created in Chapter 3, *Chart.js – Quick Start*, with the category labels in reverse order and with five bars instead of seven. The missing bars were removed by the axis.ticks.min and axis.ticks.max properties for category scales, which accept strings:

```
scales: {
    xAxes: [{ // category axis
        display: true,
        ticks: {
            labels: labels.reverse(), // overrides labels array
            min: 'South Pacific',
            max: 'North Atlantic'
        }
    }]
}
```

The result is shown here. See the full code in `Category/category-3-minmax.html`:

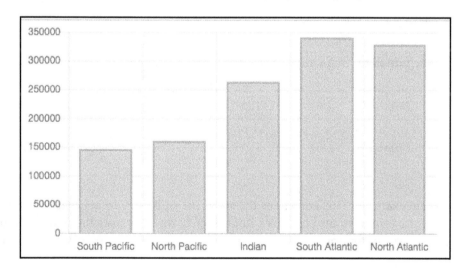

Using *axis.ticks.min* and *axis.ticks.max* to restrict the range of a category scale.
Code: *Category/category-3-minmax.html.*

# Configuring grid lines

Category scales share the same `axis.gridLines` configuration used by numeric scales.

# Time scales

You can use simple string categories to represent dates and temporal information, but by using an axis of the time type, you can parse, format, and generate temporal data. This allows greater flexibility and interactivity.

The time scale requires the moment.js library (momentjs.com). To use the time scale, you can either import the moment.js library or include the Chart.bundle.js library in your page. It's best to import moment.js since you might want to use other date and time functions. You can do that including by it in your page via CDN:

```
<script
src="https://cdnjs.cloudflare.com/ajax/libs/moment.js/2.24.0/moment.js">
</script>
```

The data is usually configured using the point structure, where the *x* property is a Date and the *y* property is some quantitative value. You can also use the t property instead of *x*. Many standard date formats are parsed automatically. These are some valid data points for time:

```
{x: new Date(), y: 1} // now
{t: '20190224', y: 2} // 2019-02-24
```

You can also include dates in a simple data object labels array:

```
new Chart("my-chart", {
    type: "bar",
    data: {
        labels: ['20190224', '20190227', '20190305'],
        datasets: [...],
    }
});
```

Here's a minimal example. This code uses the moment.js library to generate a list of dates using the moment.js library and creates a dataset of 10 dates. It uses the default values of all time-scale properties except axis.time.unit, which informs the unit that should be used:

```
const dataset = [];
let date = moment('20181120');
for(let i = 1; i <= 10; i+= 1) {
    dataset.push({t: date, y: Math.random() * 10});
    date = moment(date)
            .add( Math.floor(Math.random() * 10)+1, 'days').calendar();
}
const dataObj = {
```

```
            datasets: [{data: dataset, backgroundColor: 'hsla(290,100%,45%,.5)'}]
    }
    new Chart("my-chart", {
        type: "bar",
        data: dataObj,
        options: {
            legend: {display: false},
            scales: {
                xAxes: [{
                    type: 'time',
                    offset: true,
                    gridLines: { offsetGridLines: true },
                    time: {unit: 'day'}
                }]
            }
        }
    });
```

Offsets move bars and `gridLines` so that they stay within the chart. This is the default in bar charts with category scales, but not time scales. The result is shown here (`Time/time-1.html`). Note that the bars are not equally spaced, but the time intervals are. This is the default configuration, but you can change it, as we will see next:

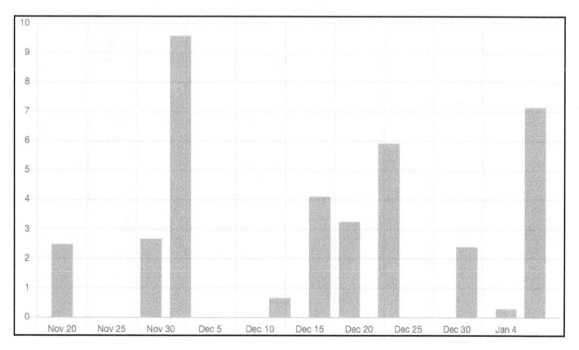

A bar chart using a time scale with default configuration. Code: *Time/time-1-html.*

# Configuring the time format

Properties that are specific for time scales are configured in the `axis.time` property. It receives an object. Some of these properties are listed as follows:

| Property | Value | Description |
|---|---|---|
| unit | millisecond, second, minute, hour, day, week, month, quarter, year | The unit of time to consider for the data. |
| stepSize | Number | The minimum step between values in the scale (this may group several values in a single tick). |
| displayFormats | Object, containing zero or more time units as String properties | This object is used to override the default string format used for each unit. See supported tokens below. |
| tooltipFormat | A string with a date format, such as MMMM, YYYY, or h:mm:ss | A format string to display data/time information in tooltips. See supported tokens below. |

Selected properties of the *axis.time* object

Time scales use `moment.js` formats, which are based on standard date/time formatting tokens. The default formats for each unit and the output they produce are listed as follows:

| Unit | Default format | Output example |
|---|---|---|
| Millisecond | h:mm:ss.SSS A | 2:07:36.976 PM |
| Second | h:mm:ss A | 2:07:36 PM |
| Minute | h:mm A | 2:07 PM |
| Hour | hA | 2 PM |
| Day | MMM D | Feb 24 |
| Week | ll | Feb 24 2019 |
| Month | MMM YYYY | Feb 2019 |
| Quarter | [Q]Q - YYYY | Q1 - 2019 |
| Year | YYYY | 2019 |

Default time unit formats used in time scales

If you wish to format date/time in a specific way, you can use the
`axis.time.displayFormats` property to override the default format for the time units
you are using:

```
time: {
    unit: 'month',
    displayFormats: {
        month: 'MMMM',    // will print January, February,... for month units
    }
}
```

You can combine the following tokens and create a string:

| Property | Tokens | Output |
|---|---|---|
| Day of month | D, Do, DD | 1 2 ... 31, 1st 2nd ... 31st, 01 02 ... 31 |
| Day of week | d, ddd, dddd | 0 1 ... 6, Sun Mon ... Sat, Sunday, Monday ... Saturday |
| Month | M, MM, MMM, MMMM | 1 2 ... 12, 01 02 ... 12, Jan Feb ... Dec, January February ... December |
| Quarter | Q, Qo | 1 2 3 4, 1st 2nd 3rd 4th |
| Year | YYYY, Y | 1970 1971 ... 2030, 1970 1971 ... 9999 |
| AM/PM | A, a | AM PM, am pm |
| AM/PM | A, a | AM PM, am pm |
| Hour | H, HH, h, hh | 0 1 ... 23, 00 01 ... 23, 1 2 ... 12, 01 02 ... 12 |
| Minute | m, mm | 0 1 ... 59, 00 01 ... 59 |
| Second | s, ss | 0 1 ... 59, 00 01 ... 59 |
| Millisecond | SSS | 000 001 ... 999 |
| Time zone | ZZ | -0700 -0600 ... +0700 |

Most common tokens for creating date-string formats

There are also other localized formats. See additional options in the documentation for
`moment.js` (momentjs.com/docs/#/displaying/format).

# Configuring the axes

Time scales support all properties for Cartesian scales and add two additional properties, listed in the following table. These properties are configured in each axis (for example, `scales.xAxes[0].bounds`):

| Property | Value | Description |
|---|---|---|
| bounds | data (default), ticks | Sets the scale boundary strategy. The default data will re-dimension the axes to fit the data. Using ticks, the chart will be truncated to fit the scales. |
| distribution | linear (default) or series | How the data is distributed on the axis. If series, the data values will be equally spaced. If linear, the instants will be equally spaced. |

Additional axis configuration properties for time scales

In the last example, the bars were unevenly positioned because the default distribution preserved the time instants. In this example, the bars will be evenly spaced, but the periods between them will not be uniform. The data is bounded by the ticks, instead of the data points, and the date format for the days displays the abbreviated month, day, and year:

```
xAxes: [{
    type: 'time',
    offset: true,
    gridLines: { offsetGridLines: true },
    distribution: 'series',
    bounds: 'ticks',
    time: {
        unit: 'day',
        displayFormats: {
            day: 'MMM D Y',
        }
    }
}]
```

The result is shown as follows. See the full code in `Time/time-2.html`:

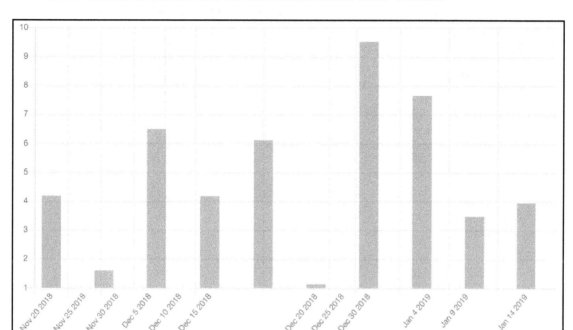

A bar chart with a time scale with equally-distributed bars, and tick bounds. Code: *Time/time-2.html*.

# Configuring ticks

Time scales extend the *axis.ticks* configuration for Cartesian charts with an additional property, listed here:

| Property | Value | Description |
|---|---|---|
| source | auto (default), data (default, if data in point format), labels (default, if data in array format) | Selects where to obtain the entries for the time scale. |

Additional tick configuration properties for time scales

The `axis.ticks.source` property allows you to select the source of the data for the time scale. If your dataset is a simple array and the dates are in the labels array, the default configuration will automatically get the dates from there. You can also set this property explicitly:

```
const dataset = [], labels = [];
let date = moment('20181120');
for(let i = 1; i <= 10; i+= 1) {
    labels.push(date);
    dataset.push(Math.random() * 10);
    date = moment(date)
            .add( Math.floor(Math.random() * 10)+1, 'days').calendar();
}

const dataObj = {
    labels: labels,
    datasets: [{
        data: dataset,
        backgroundColor: 'hsla(290,100%,45%,.5)'
    }]
}

new Chart("my-chart", { type: "bar", data: dataObj,
    options: {
        scales: {
            xAxes: [{
                // ... other configuration not shown
                ticks: { source: 'labels' }
            }]
        }
    }
});
```

The result is shown here. See the full code in `Time/time-3.html`:

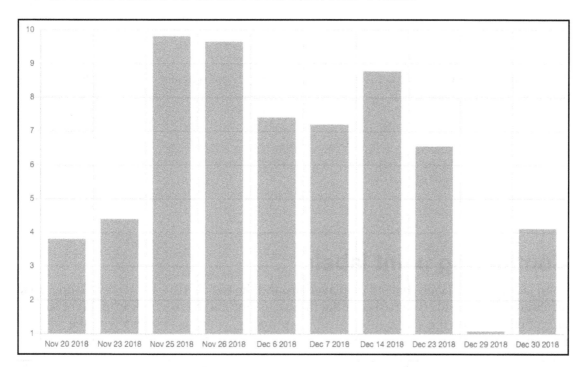

A bar chart with a time scale using the *labels* array as a source for the tick data. Code: *Time/time-3.html.*

# Configuring grid lines

Time scales share the same `axis.gridLines` configuration used by numeric scales.

# Radial scales

Two Chart.js chart types use radial scales: `radar` and `polarArea`. Radial charts that have a single scale are configured with the properties listed here. Some properties are similar to the properties used in Cartesian scales, but they have fewer configuration options:

| Property | Value | Description |
|---|---|---|
| pointLabels | Object | Configure point labels |
| ticks | Object | Configure chart ticks |

| angleLines | Object | Configures radial grid lines |
|---|---|---|
| gridLines | Object | Configure concentric grid lines |

Configuration objects for radial scales

These properties are used directly inside the `options.scale` object. For example:

```
options: {
    scale: {
        ticks: {...},
        angleLines: {...},
        gridLines: {...},
        pointLabels: {...}
    }
}
```

# Configuring point labels

Point labels are the labels that are displayed around the radial chart, at each angle line. Tick labels are placed inside the chart over the first angle line and have a backdrop. Point labels are configured with the `scale.pointLabels` property, which is an object with the following properties:

| Property | Value | Description |
|---|---|---|
| display | true (default in radar) or false (default in polar area) | Displays or hides the axis labels |
| callback | Function; default is d=>d | Returns the value label for each point |
| fontColor, fontFamily, fontStyle | Strings containing CSS font attributes | Font attributes |
| fontSize | Number | Font size in pixels |

Properties for point label configuration in radial axes

You can hide `pointLabels` using `display:false` in a radial chart (see the following diagram). If you are using a polar area chart, you can use `display:true` if you want to make them visible. See `Radial/radial-1-pointLabels-hide.html` and `radial-2-pointLabels-polar.html`.

The following code uses some other `pointLabel` properties to change the color of the labels in a radar chart and uses a callback to append text to each label:

```
scale: {
    pointLabels: { callback: (d) => 'Step ' + d, fontColor: 'red'}
}
```

See the full code in `Radial/radial-3-pointLabels-callback.html`. The result is shown as follows:

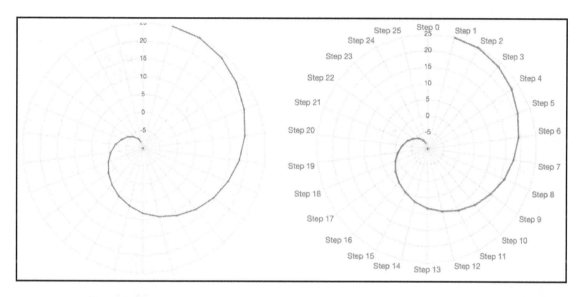

Radial scales point labels configuration. Left: Hiding labels with scale.pointLabels.display = *false*. Right: Changing color and appending text with a callback. Code: Radial/radial-1-pointLabels-hide.html and *radial-3-pointLabels-callback.html*.

# Configuring ticks

Ticks in radial axes are concentric circles (which can be rendered as circles or multi-sided regular polygons, with vertices at each angle line). Tick labels are placed on the circles with a backdrop behind them.

Ticks are configured in the `scale.ticks` object with the following properties:

| Property | Value | Description |
|---|---|---|
| display | true (default) or false | Shows or hides tick labels. |
| fontSize | Number | The font size in pixels. |
| fontColor, fontFamily, fontStyle | String | CSS font attributes. |
| reverse | true or false (default) | Reverses the order of tick labels. |
| callback | Function; default: d=>d | The function receives the value of the tick. It can be used to hide ticks or change the values displayed. |
| min | Number | The lower limit of the axis. |
| max | Number | The upper limit of the axis. |
| suggestedMin | Number | Will set this as the minimum, if the data's minimum is larger. |
| suggestedMax | Number | Will set this as the maximum, if the data's maximum is smaller. |
| beginAtZero | true (default) or false | Forces the axis to use zero as the lower limit. |
| stepSize | Number | Sets a minimum step size between ticks. |
| maxTicksLimit | Number; default is 11 | Explicitly sets a maximum number of ticks for the axis. |
| showLabelBackdrop | true or false; default is true | Draws a background behind tick labels over the grid lines. |
| backdropPaddingX backdropPaddingY | Number; default is 2 | Backdrop padding. |
| backdropColor | Color; default is rgba(255,255,255,.75) | Color of the label backdrops. |

Tick properties for radial scales

Tick properties are similar to those used in Cartesian linear charts. The following code shows some tick configurations applied to a radar chart:

```
scale: {
    ticks: {
        fontColor: 'blue',
        callback: (d) => d + ' m',
        reverse: true,
        min: 0,
    }
}
```

The result is shown here. See the full code in `Radial/radial-4-ticks.html`:

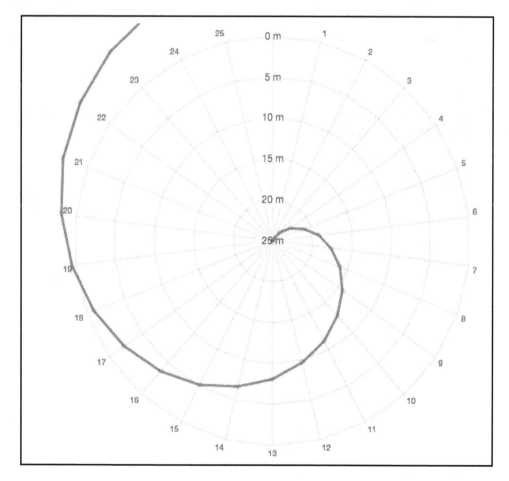

Radar chart with some tick configurations. *Code: Radial/radial-4-ticks.html.*

# Configuring grids and angle lines

The following properties are used to configure the radial lines (`scale.angleLines`) and concentric circles or polygons (`scale.gridLines`) of a radial grid. All properties listed are supported for both objects except circular, which is supported only by `scale.gridLines`:

| Property | Value | Description |
|---|---|---|
| display | true (default in radar) or false (default in polar area) | Shows or hides lines. |
| color | Color | Color of the lines. |
| circular | true (default in polar area) or false (default in radar) | In gridLines object only. If true, gridLines are circular. Otherwise, they are straight lines between points. |
| lineWidth | Number | The width of the lines. |

Configuration for grid and angle lines in radial grids

The following code configures several grid and angle line properties in a radial chart. It changes the grid lines to circular, and also changes the line width and colors:

```
scale: {
    gridLines: {
        circular: true,
        lineWidth: 2,
        color: 'hsla(240,100%,50%,.2)'
    },
    angleLines: {
        display: true,
        lineWidth: 2,
        color: 'hsla(120,100%,25%,.2)'
    }
}
```

The result applied to a radar chart is shown as follows. See the full code in `Radial/radial-5-grid-angle-lines.html`:

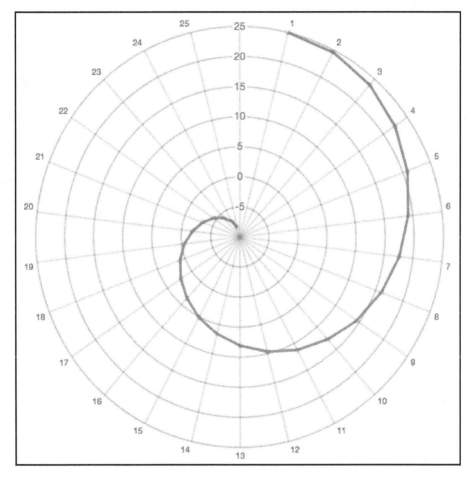

Radar chart with grid and angle lines configurations. *Code: Radial/radial-5-grid-angle-lines.html*

# Configuring advanced scales

This section contains a brief overview on some configurations that you will probably not use very often. For more details on these topics, refer to the official documentation.

# Multiple Cartesian axes

You only need two axes to plot data in a two-dimensional Cartesian grid, but you can add more if you need to. You may wish to repeat axis titles or tick labels on both sides of a chart for clarity. You may also wish to show two datasets with different scales (although this is usually a bad practice in data visualization).

If you have multiple axes, you can control their positions with the `axis.weight` and `axis.position` properties. Unless you connect an axis to a specific dataset using the `id` property, the first axis in the `yAxis` array will be used for all datasets. A dataset is linked to an axis using the `yAxisID` or `xAxisID` properties that reference the ID of an axis. See `Advanced/adv-1-position-evil.html` for an example.

The following code fragment configures three axes for a chart, and places them on different sides of the chart. It doesn't explicitly link any dataset, since they all use the same scales:

```
scales: {
    yAxes: [{
        id: 'y-axis-1',
        ticks: {min: -2,max: 2},
        scaleLabel: {display: true, labelString: "Left Axis"},
        position: 'left'
    },{
        id: 'y-axis-2',
        ticks: {min: -2, max: 2},
        scaleLabel: {display: true,labelString: "Right Axis"},
        gridLines: {display: false},
        position: 'right'
    }],
    xAxes: [{
        ticks: {min: -4, max: 4},
        scaleLabel: {display: true,labelString: "Top Axis"},
        position: 'top'
    }],
}
```

See the full code in `Cartesian/Cartesian-1-position.html`. The result is shown as follows:

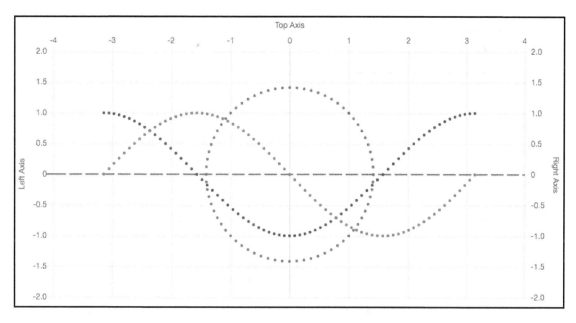

A chart with three axes, in different positions. Code: *Cartesian/Cartesian-1-position.html.*

You can also stack axes on the same side, as shown as follows. This is useful in categorical scales when you wish to add a context. In this example, an extra category scale was added for the oceans:

```
const labels = ["Arctic", "North Atlantic", "South Atlantic", "Indian",
                "North Pacific", "South Pacific", "Southern"];
 const labels2 = ["","Atlantic", "", "Pacific",""];
 // ...
 xAxes: [
     {
          weight: 10,
          labels: labels,
          ticks: {
               fontColor: 'black'
          }
     }, {
          weight: 20,
          labels: labels2,
          ticks: {
               fontColor: 'purple'
          },
```

```
            offset: true
        },
    ]
```

The result is shown as follows. See the full code in `Cartesian/Cartesian-2-weight.html`:

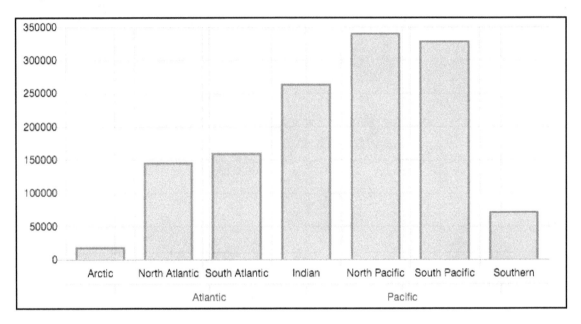

A chart with two category axes on the same side. Code: *Cartesian/Cartesian-2-weight.html.*

It might be a good idea to hide or configure the grid lines from the second category scale, so they won't leak into the chart area.

# Callbacks

If you need to filter or change individual tick labels, you can use life cycle callbacks. There are 14 of them and they are configured directly in each axis object. The following code a callback to filter ticks based on their value (increasing the step) and at a later stage, changes the value to be displayed (at this stage, the change no longer affects the chart):

```
yAxes: [
    {
        afterBuildTicks: function(axis) {
            log('afterBuildTicks')
            axis.ticks = axis.ticks.filter((d,i) => d % 100000 == 0);
```

```
        },
        afterTickToLabelConversion: function(axis) {
            log('afterTickToLabelConversion')
            axis.ticks.forEach((d,i) => axis.ticks[i] = +d/1000);
        }
    }
]
```

See the full code in `Advanced/adv-2-callbacks.html` and `adv-3-radial-callbacks.html`.

# The scale service

The scale service can be used to update scales during changes. You can use it to pass a partial configuration that will be merged with the current configuration. In the following code, it was used to set the minimum boundary for ticks in the linear scale, and append text to tick labels in the category scale:

```
Chart.scaleService.updateScaleDefaults('linear', {
    ticks: {
        min: -100000
    },
    afterTickToLabelConversion: function(axis) {
        axis.ticks.forEach((d,i) => axis.ticks[i] = +d/1000);
    }
});

Chart.scaleService.updateScaleDefaults('category', {
    afterTickToLabelConversion: function(axis) {
        axis.ticks.forEach((d,i) => axis.ticks[i] = d + " Ocean")
    }
});
```

See the full code in `Advanced/adv-4-scaleService.html`.

# Summary

In this chapter, you learned how to configure the different kinds of scales supported by Chart.js: the linear scale used in radial charts, such as radar and polar area, and the Cartesian scales used in scatter, bubble, line, and bar charts. You can configure scales in ways that change how data is presented, or style the grid lines and labels to add context to a chart.

We also compared different types of Cartesian charts, showing why sometimes it's better to use a logarithmic scale instead of a linear scale. We created category charts without any numeric scales and explored time scales.

In the next chapter, we will explore configuration in greater detail, efficiently using colors, fonts, and interactivity to control the appearance of charts using callbacks.

# References

**Books and websites:**

- Chart.js official documentation and samples: `https://www.chartjs.org/docs/latest/`Zoom plugin: `https://github.com/chartjs/chartjs-plugin-zoom`

# 6
# Configuring Styles and Interactivity

In this chapter, you will learn how to configure the look and feel of a chart so it will reflect a desired layout or style, follow good practices of chart design, and tune its interactive and responsive behavior. This includes configuring colors, gradients, patterns and fonts, setting margins, padding, borders, fills, backgrounds, line widths, dashes, positioning titles and legends, and configuring the behavior of transitions and animations. Some of these properties are easily configured using Chart.js configuration options, but others require plugins and extensions, which will also be introduced in this chapter.

In this chapter, you will learn the following:

- Default configuration
- Fonts
- Colors, gradients, patterns, and shadows
- Adding text elements and labels
- Interactions, data updates, and animation

## Default configuration

Every chart created in Chart.js comes previously configured with default properties. You can always override these properties in the `options` object when creating a new Chart instance, but you can also override them for all or for many of your charts, by setting the properties directly in the `Chart.defaults` object.

For example, the default line tension is 0.4 for any kind of chart. If you want all your charts to use only straight lines and have scales beginning at zero, you can make all pages load a `defaults.js` file that declares the following defaults:

```
Charts.defaults.global.elements.line.tension = 0;
Charts.defaults.scales.ticks.beginAtZero = true;
```

If you want to have only curved lines in the radar charts, you can override the property for all radar charts (but not any other kind of chart) using the following:

```
Charts.defaults.radar.elements.line.tension = 0.4;
```

Then, if you have a specific line chart where you would prefer to use curved lines, you can again override the property when you create the chart instance, using its `options` configuration object:

```
const chart = new Chart("my-chart", {      type: 'line', data: {...},
    options: {
      elements: {
        line: {
          tension: 0
          //overrides Charts.defaults.global.elements.line.tension
        }
      }
    }
});
```

Some options can even be configured for a specific dataset within a chart, which is the case with line tension. If you use `lineTension: 0.3` for a specific dataset in the `datasets` array, only the line corresponding to that dataset will exhibit the new tension:

```
datasets: [{
    data: [1,2,1],
    lineTension: 0.3
}]
```

The order is significant, and so is the hierarchy. Properties set in a more specific context will almost always override the values set in a more general context. And any global properties should be set *before* instantiating a chart. In the next sections, we will explore options that can be defined at different configuration levels, their object structure, and their default values.

# Global defaults

Properties in `Chart.defaults.global` contain configuration options for all types of charts, including graphical elements, titles and captions, layout properties, animation, tooltips, events, and plugins. But it doesn't include grids and scales, which are configured in the `Chart.defaults.scale` object. The options available in `Chart.defaults.global` are listed as follows. All these properties, except the default font and color settings, are also available as properties in the options configuration object of any chart instance:

| Object | Value | Description |
|--------|-------|-------------|
| defaultColor | CSS color | The default color for all chart elements. This property is overriden in several chart elements, so it's not really very useful. The default is `'rgba(0,0,0,0.1)'`. |
| defaultFontColor | CSS color (examples: `'lightblue'`, `'#9cf'`, `'#ff0000'`, `'rgb(100%,50%,25%)'`, `'hsl(60,100%,50%)'`, `'rgba(100%,50%,25%,0.6)'`, `'hsla(60,100%,50%,0.1)'`) | The default color for all text (unless overridden with a more specific font color property). The default is `'#666'`. |
| defaultFontFamily | CSS font-family name or list (example: `'Helvetica, "Helvetica Neue", sans-serif'`) | The default family for all text (unless overridden with a more specific font color property). The default is `'Helvetica Neue'`, `'Helvetica'`, `'Arial'`, sans-serif. |
| defaultFontSize | Font size in pixels | The default size in pixels for all text (unless overridden with a more specific font size property). The default is 12. |
| defaultFontStyle | CSS font-style (ex: `'bold'`, `'italic'`, `'normal'`) or any style available with the font that is being used (ex: `'condensed bold'`, `'light'`, and so on) | The default style for all text (unless overridden with a more specific font style property). The default is `'normal'`. |

| | | |
|---|---|---|
| `layout.padding` | The number or object with numerical properties for `top`, `left`, `right`, `bottom` | If the value is a number, the padding in pixels is applied to all sides of a chart. If it's an object, the individual values can be applied to different sides of the chart. |
| `maintainAspectRatio` | `true` or `false` | Maintains the aspect ratio of the canvas element. |
| `responsive` | `true` or `false` | Resizes the chart when the canvas is resized. The default is `true`. |
| `showLines` | `true` or `false` | If `true`, shows lines between point values. Default is `true`, but is overridden to `false` in scatter charts. |
| `title` | Object | See the *Legends and labels* section in this chapter. |
| `legend` | Object | See the *Legends and labels* section in this chapter. |
| `tooltips` | Object | See `Chapter 7`, *Advanced Chart.js*. |
| `hover` | Object | See `Chapter 7`, *Advanced Chart.js*. |
| `elements` | Object | See the *Chart elements* section in this chapter. |
| `events` | Object | See the *Animation* section in this chapter. |
| `plugins` | Object | See `Chapter 7`, *Advanced Chart.js*. |
| `animation` | Object | See the *Animation* section in this chapter. |

Configurable options in Charts.defaults.global that can be configured for all charts. Callbacks are not listed.

For example, the following configuration will turn off-line rendering between value points for any charts. Since this property is not overridden in line or radar charts, if you create a line chart, it won't have any lines. Only the points will be visible:

```
Chart.defaults.global.showLines = false;
```

This other configuration will turn off the legends for all charts (very useful for single-dataset charts):

```
Chart.defaults.global.legend.display = false;
```

# Scale defaults

Scales and grids can be globally configured in the `Charts.defaults.scale` object. The following table lists the top-level properties and some of the default properties of this object. Some of these defaults are overridden in specific charts. In these cases, changing them in this context may not have any effect:

| Object | Description | Default properties |
|--------|-------------|--------------------|
| display | Displays (`true`) or not (`false`) the scales for this chart. | The default is `true`. |
| offset | Adds extra space to left and right edges of the chart. | The default is `false` (overridden to `true` in bar charts). |
| gridLines | Default properties and callbacks for all scales (some are overridden in specific chart types). See `Chapter 5`, *Scales and Grid Configuration*. | `display = true`<br>`color = 'rgba(0,0,0,0.1)'`<br>`lineWidth = 1`<br>`drawTicks: true`<br>`drawOnChartArea = true`<br>`offsetGridLines = false` |
| scaleLabel | The default properties and callbacks for all scales (some are overridden in specific chart types). See `Chapter 5`, *Scales and Grid Configuration*, for details. | `display = false,`<br>`labelString = ''`<br>`lineHeight = 1.2`<br>`padding: {top: 4, bottom: 4}` |
| ticks | The default properties and callbacks for all scales (some are overriden in specific chart types). See `Chapter 5`, *Scales and Grid Configuration*, for details. | `display = true`<br>`beginAtZero = false`<br>`autoSkip = true`<br>`reverse = false` |

Options in Charts.defaults.scales that can be configured for scales of all charts.

For example, the following code will place the same labels on all axes in any charts that use Cartesian axes (`bar`, `horizontalBar`, `line`, `scatter`, `bubble`):

```
Chart.defaults.scale.scaleLabel.display = true;
Chart.defaults.scale.scaleLabel.labelString = 'default';
```

The `display` property is available in all scale components. With `display: false`, you can globally remove ticks, labels, gridlines, and other non-chart information from your default charts, overriding these properties in specific charts only when necessary. This is a good practice and will maximize the data-to-ink ratio of your charts.

The code fragments in this section are from `Config/defaults-1-global-config.html`, in the GitHub repository for this chapter.

# Graphical elements

**Graphical elements** are the primitives used to render visualizations of datasets in different types of charts. You can define defaults for them configuring the four objects in the `Chart.defaults.global.elements` context, listed as follows. Some of these properties are overridden in the defaults for certain charts, so changing them at this level may not cause any effect:

| Object | Description | Default properties |
|--------|-------------|--------------------|
| arc | The default properties for Canvas arcs, which are used in pie, doughnut, and polar area charts. | backgroundColor:"rgba(0,0,0,0.1)"<br>borderColor:"#fff"<br>borderWidth:2 |
| line | The default properties for Canvas lines, which are used in line and radar charts. See Chapter 2, *Technology Fundamentals*, for Canvas properties used in borderCapStyle and borderJoinStyle. See Chapter 4, *Creating Charts*, for fill strategies. | backgroundColor:"rgba(0,0,0,0.1)"<br>borderCapStyle:"butt"<br>//(see Chapter 2)<br>  borderColor:"rgba(0,0,0,0.1)"<br>  borderDash:[]<br>  borderDashOffset:0<br>  borderJoinStyle:"miter"<br>//(see Chapter 2)<br>  borderWidth:3<br>  capBezierPoints:true<br>  fill:true //(see Chapter 4)<br>  tension:0.4<br>  stepped: false |

| | | |
|---|---|---|
| Point | Value points are actually circles drawn with Canvas arcs. This object contains default properties for points in line, radar, scatter, or bubble charts. See Chapter 4, *Creating Charts,* for more point styles. | `backgroundColor:"rgba(0,0,0,0.1)"` `borderColor:"rgba(0,0,0,0.1)"` `borderWidth:1` `hitRadius:1` `hoverBorderWidth:1` `hoverRadius:4` `pointStyle:"circle"` `//(see Chapter 4)` `radius:3` |
| Rectangle | The default properties for Canvas rectangles used in bar and `horizontalBar` charts. One of the borders is not drawn (skipped). | `backgroundColor:"rgba(0,0,0,0.1)"` `borderColor:"rgba(0,0,0,0.1)"` `borderSkipped:"bottom" ("left"in` `horizontalBar)` `borderWidth:0` |

Options in Charts.defaults.global.elements that apply to elements in all charts

The following code will make all line and radar charts use red dashed 5-pixel lines as the default, unless they are overridden in their default configuration or `options` object. See `Config/defaults-2-global-elements.html`, as follows:

```
const line = Chart.defaults.global.elements.line;
line.borderDash = [5,5];
line.borderWidth = 5;
line.borderColor = 'red';
```

# Chart defaults

The `Chart.default` context contains an object for each chart type supported in Chart.js. The types are in the following table, which also lists some of the properties previously configured in each one. These properties may override the global defaults for chart styles and elements (`Chart.default.global`) and the default properties for scales (`Chart.default.scales`). You can define new defaults by changing these properties in the `Chart.default` context, or locally inside an options object:

| Object | Description | Default properties (selection) |
|---|---|---|
| bar | The default properties for bar charts | `hover.mode = 'label'` `scales.xAxes[0].type = 'category'` `scales.yAxes[0].type = 'linear'` |
| horizontalBar | The default properties for horizontal bar charts | `hover.mode = 'index'` `scales.xAxes[0].type = 'linear'` `scales.yAxes[0].type = 'category'` `elements.rectangle.borderSkipped = 'left'` |

| pie | The default properties and callbacks for pie charts | `circumference = 2 * Math.PI`<br>`cutoutPercentage = 0`<br>`hover.mode = 'single'` |
|---|---|---|
| doughnut | The default properties and callbacks for doughnut charts | `circumference = 2 * Math.PI`<br>`cutoutPercentage = 50`<br>`hover.mode = 'single'` |
| line | The default properties and callbacks for line charts | `hover.mode = 'label'`<br>`scales.xAxes[0] = {type: 'category', id: 'x-axis-0'}`<br>`scales.yAxes[0] = {type: 'linear', id: 'y-axis-0'}`<br>`showLines = true,`<br>`spanGaps = false` |
| radar | The default properties for radar charts | `elements.line.tension = 0`<br>`scale.type = 'radialLinear'` |
| polarArea | The default properties for polar area charts | `angleLines.display = false`<br>`gridLines.circular = true`<br>`pointLabels.display = false`<br>`ticks.beginAtZero = true`<br>`type = "radialLinear"`<br>`startAngle = Math.PI / 2` |
| scatter | The default properties for scatter charts | `hover.mode = 'single'`<br>`showLines = false`<br>`scales.xAxes[0] = {type: 'linear', id: 'x-axis-1'}`<br>`scales.yAxes[0] = {type: 'linear', id: 'y-axis-1'}` |
| bubble | The default properties for bubble charts | `hover.mode = 'single'`<br>`scales.xAxes[0] = {type: 'linear', id: 'x-axis-0'}`<br>`scales.yAxes[0] = {type: 'linear', id: 'y-axis-0'}` |

Default options in Charts.defaults for different types of charts

You can check the current values of your default properties by printing them to your JavaScript console and inspecting the object tree, with `console.log()`. The following code will print the context root:

```
console.log(Chart.defaults);
```

You can also inspect (and modify the properties of) the chart instance. In this case, you need to assign the new chart to a variable handle (see `Config/defaults-1-global-config.html`):

```
const chart = new Chart(...);
console.log("Chart Data, chart.config.data);
console.log("Chart Options, chart.options);
```

# Fonts

Chart.js uses Canvas to select and display local and installed fonts. The font configuration involves setting up to four font properties: family, size, style, and color. A `fontFamily` is a string containing a list of font-family names, a `fontStyle` contains a string with the name of a style supported by the corresponding font-family, a `fontColor` is any valid CSS-compatible color string, and the `fontSize` is a number that represents the size in pixels. You can configure font attributes in any object that includes text: titles, tick captions, legend labels, or tooltips, or you can set global defaults that will be inherited by text elements that don't explicitly set font attributes.

# Selecting standard fonts

The basic font properties are named `fontFamily`, `fontSize`, `fontStyle`, and `fontColor`. Some objects have prefixed versions of these same properties. These objects are listed as follows:

| Object containing text element | Description | Font properties |
|---|---|---|
| Chart.defaults.global | Global defaults | defaultFontFamily, defaultFontSize, defaultFontStyle, defaultFontColor |
| Chart.defaults.global.title | Chart title | fontFamily, fontSize, fontStyle, fontColor |
| Chart.defaults.scale.ticks | Axis label | |
| Chart.defaults.scale.ticks.minor | Minor tick label | |
| Chart.defaults.scale.ticks.major | Major tick label | |
| Chart.defaults.global.legend | Legend label | |
| Chart.defaults.global.tooltips | Tooltip header | titleFontFamily, titleFontSize, titleFontStyle, titleFontColor |
| Chart.defaults.global.tooltips | Tooltip body | bodyFontFamily, bodyFontSize, bodyFontStyle, bodyFontColor |
| Chart.defaults.global.tooltips | Tooltip footer | footerFontFamily, footerFontSize, footerFontStyle, footerFontColor |

Objects that have font configuration properties

Since it's usually good practice to avoid using more than one font family for the whole chart, global options are the best place to configure this property. You can also set other font defaults:

```
Chart.defaults.global.defaultFontFamily =
    'Courier, "Courier New", "Lucida Console",
monospace';Chart.defaults.global.defaultFontSize = 12;
Chart.defaults.global.defaultFontStyle= 'normal';
Chart.defaults.global.defaultFontColor = '#333';
```

You can always choose to override specific properties where appropriate, such as the font size of a chart title:

```
Chart.defaults.global.title.fontSize = 24;
```

And you can override it again, setting a different value in the chart instance, if necessary:

```
const chart = new Chart("my-chart", {type: 'line', data: {...},
    options: {
        title: {
            display: true,
            text: "Very large title that doesn't fit in the default space",
            fontSize: 20
        }
    }
});
```

# Using Web fonts

Chart.js can use any fonts that are available for your website. Besides the standard fonts supported by all browsers (*serif, sans-serif, monospace*), you can also use online fonts loaded by a style sheet.

In the following example, we are using a free web font (OFL license), called *Yanone Kaffeesatz*, obtained from Google Fonts. To install it, simply load the CSS by adding the following link to the <head> of your HTML page:

```
<link href="https://fonts.googleapis.com/css?family=Yanone+Kaffeesatz"
      rel="stylesheet">
```

Now you can use the Yanone Kaffeesatz font family in CSS and HTML. Canvas can set it as the context font, using the font property. The simplest way to use it in Chart.js is to declare it as the default global font. You can also configure any font styles if this feature is available:

```
Chart.defaults.global.defaultFontFamily = '"Yanone Kaffesatz", sans-serif';
```

In the following example, we changed several font properties (family, color, size, and style), using global options from one of the pie/doughnut charts that were created in the last chapter:

```
Chart.defaults.global.defaultFontColor = 'black';
Chart.defaults.global.defaultFontFamily =
      '"Yanone Kaffesatz", "Helvetica Narrow", "Arial Narrow", sans-serif';
Chart.defaults.global.defaultFontSize = 24;
Chart.defaults.global.defaultFontStyle = 'normal';
Chart.defaults.global.title.fontSize = 40;
Chart.defaults.global.title.fontColor = 'hsla(240,50%,70%,1)';
Chart.defaults.global.legend.labels.fontColor = 'hsla(120,20%,60%,1)';
```

The result is shown in the following diagram. The code is available in Fonts/fonts-1.html and requires the installing of the Yanone Kaffesatz font (or any other font, if you edit the code):

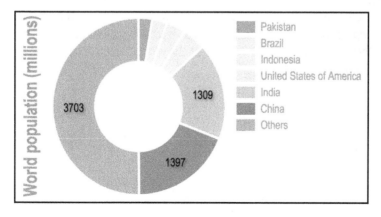

A doughnut chart using a web font for titles and labels. Code: *Fonts/fonts-1.html.*

# Colors, gradients, patterns, and shadows

Choosing an effective color scheme for data visualization is no easy task. Colors aren't simply used to make a chart look nicer. Besides distinguishing and suggesting associations between sets of data, they may also communicate information through aspects such as hue, contrast, saturation, or lightness. They can even influence the mood of the viewer. The choice of colors is never neutral. It may attract or repel the viewer from relevant information.

Other aspects may be important, depending on your audience. You may want to use gradients, bevels, and shadows for purely aesthetic reasons, but if your audience requires maximum accessibility, you may also need to consider the use of color-blind-safe palettes or patterns.

# Configuring colors

Chart.js supports standard HTML/CSS color names and codes (see `Chapter 2`, *Technology Fundamentals*), which are assigned to properties that control fonts, strokes (lines, and borders), and fills. You can select a color by its name (for example, red), hexadecimal code (`#f00`, `#ff0000`), or three-argument generator functions that receive RGB or HSL components (`rgb(255,0,0)`, or `hsl(0,100%,50%)`). CSS color generator functions also include a four-argument version that controls transparency with the alpha component (`'rgba(255,0,0,1)'`, or `'hsla(0,100%,50%,1)'`).

The `Chart.defaults.global.defaultColor` property sets a default color for all the chart components, but it is mostly overridden by the default configurations for fonts, scales, graphical elements, and charts that default to monochromatic tones. These properties occur in different chart elements. They have different names, but they all end with the `Color` suffix. The basic configuration properties (used in `Chart.defaults.global` or the `options` object) contain a single color, but they may also be an array of colors when applied to a single dataset.

# Color schemes and palettes

Chart.js does not include a native color palette generator. In our examples so far, we have either assigned explicit colors, created color palettes with no more than six colors, or used random color-generator functions. But colors are an important means of communicating information in a chart, and should be chosen carefully. If not used with care, your chart may suggest nonexistent relationships among data, deceiving the viewer. Colors that vary in lightness and saturation suggest a sequential relationship (stronger/weaker or hotter/colder). Opposing data can be better represented using divergent color palettes, where extremes are represented by complementary colors. If your data represents different categories, it will be better visualized with a qualitative color scheme. Depending on your audience and the purpose of your chart, you may also need to consider accessibility issues, such as color blindness or rendering in color-limited devices, when selecting colors. All these tasks are facilitated by the use of a specially-designed color palette or scheme.

A color palette is a fixed-size sequence of colors and is usually represented as an array in JavaScript. A **scheme** represents a collection of color palettes and is usually a function (or an object) in JavaScript. You can use a scheme to generate a palette containing an arbitrary sequence of colors.

You can write your own palettes, schemes, and color generators, but it's much easier to generate carefully-selected palettes and schemes using popular services and JavaScript libraries.

ColorBrewer, by Cynthia Brewer, is a website where you can generate an array string containing a palette of colors carefully designed to not only look nice on your page, but to also consider the type of data you are using (qualitative, diverging, and sequential) and its accessibility (color blindness, display/print, and grayscale). You can select and view the effects in real time, configure accessibility and data properties, and generate a color string in different formats (including JavaScript arrays and CSS):

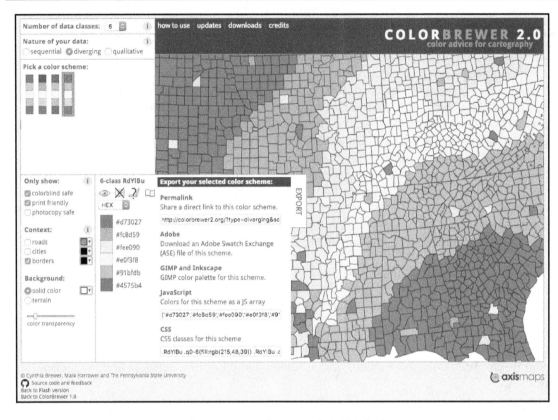

Using ColorBrewer to select and generate a small color-blind-safe palette

Let's try it out with a simple bar chart containing a single dataset listed in the code, as follows:

```
<body>
<canvas id="canvas" width="200" height="100"></canvas>
<script>
    const data = {
        labels: ["Mon", "Tue", "Wed", "Thu", "Fri", "Sat"],
        datasets: [
            {
                data: [10, 5, 2, 20, 30, 41],
            }
        ]
    };
    new Chart('canvas', { type: 'bar', data: data,
                        options: {legend: {display: false}} });
</script>
</body>
```

When you load the page, it should display a monochromatic bar chart, where all the bars share the same tone of gray.

Using the *ColorBrewer* site, choose a six-color palette, configure any properties you wish, and then copy the JavaScript array to your clipboard. Paste it as the `backGroundColor` property for the dataset:

```
datasets: [{
    data: [10, 5, 2, 20, 30, 41],
    backgroundColor:['#d73027','#fc8d59','#fee090','#e0f3f8','#91bfdb','#4575b4
    ']
}]
```

Then load your chart and see the result. It should be similar to the following bar chart. The full code is in `Colors/colors-1-brewer.html`:

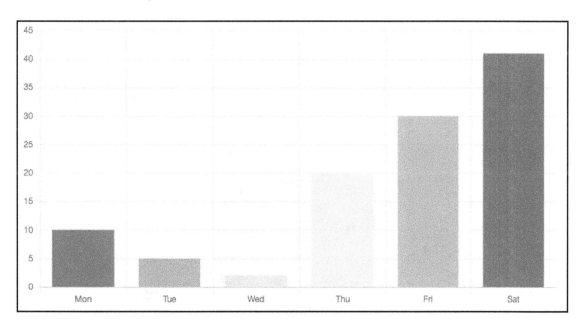

Chart using colors from a ColorBrewer six-color diverging palette. Code: *Colors/colors-1-brewer.html.*

The *ColorBrewer* palettes are limited to nine colors (or even fewer, depending on the settings you choose). If you need more colors, you can choose them from *Paul Tol's schemes page,* which is also very popular, or use other generators (there are many).

Another option is to use the Google `palette.js` library, which contains color palette-generating functions. It supports all schemes from ColorBrewer and *Paul Tol's color schemes page*, and includes additional generators for HSV, RGB, and Solarized schemes. To use it, you need to include the `palette.js` file on your page. You can download it from the GitHub site or use a CDN:

```
<script src="https://cdn.jsdelivr.net/npm/palette.min.js"></script>
```

Now you can generate palettes by calling one of the color scheme functions listed in the demo page located at `google.github.io/palette.js`, shown as follows:

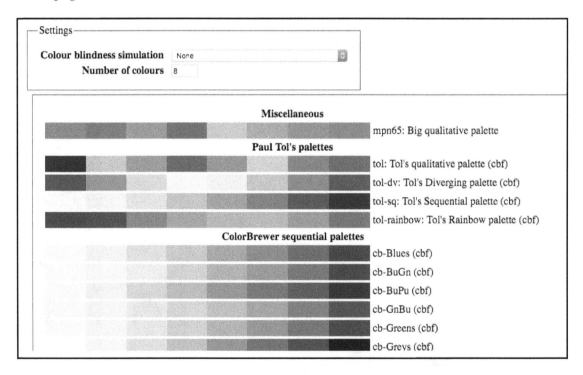

Page with a list of color schemes supported by the palette.js generator (see the full demo page at google.github.io/palette.js)

The demo page allows you to experiment with different schemes, check how many colors you can include in a palette, and simulate different levels of color blindness. The following code will generate a palette for our bar chart containing six colors from Paul Tol's qualitative color scheme:

```
const colorsArray = palette('tol', 6);
```

The colors array contains the hexadecimal codes of the colors, but Canvas (and Chart.js) will not show the colors unless there is a hash character before the number. The following code fixes this:

```
const colorsArray = palette('tol', 6).map(n=>'#'+n);
```

Now just set the `backgroundColor` property as the colors array:

```
backgroundColor: colorsArray
```

The result is shown as follows. The code is in `Colors/colors-2-palettejs.html`:

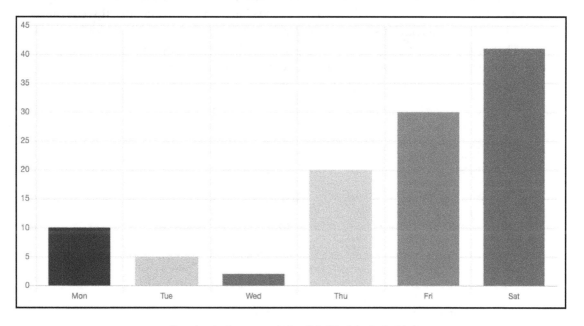

Chart using colors from a generated palette. Code: *Colors/colors-2-palettejs.html*

# Gradients

There is no native support in Chart.js for gradients, but they are fairly easy to generate with Canvas. The problem is that a gradient has an absolute position in a Canvas object, while your chart may be responsive. If the chart is resized, the gradient has to be recalculated and the chart updated.

One way to deal with this is to call a gradient function as soon as the chart is created and every time the window is resized, feeding the Canvas gradient function with the dimensions of the area where the gradient will be applied. We can do this with a callback and the Chart.js `update()` function.

A gradient in Canvas is created with the following function:

```
canvasContext.createLinearGradient(x0, y0, x1, y1);
```

The gradient contains the equation of a perpendicular line. To create a linear gradient that varies along the *y* axis, we need to draw the line from the bottom of the chart to the top. That means that x0 = x1 = 0, y1 is the bottom of the chart, and y0 is the top. If we write a function that receives a chart instance, we can retrieve that information from `scales["y-axis-0"].top` and `scales["y-axis-0"].bottom`. Here is a function for drawing gradients for the background colors and a line chart with two datasets (`Colors/colors-3-gradient.html`):

```
function drawGradient(chart) {
    const x0 = 0;
    const y0 = chart.scales["y-axis-0"].top;
    const x1 = 0;
    const y1 = chart.scales["y-axis-0"].bottom;

    const gradient1 = chart.ctx.createLinearGradient(x0, y0, x1, y1);
    gradient1.addColorStop(0, 'hsla(60,100%,70%,.4)');
    gradient1.addColorStop(1, 'hsla(0,100%,25%,.8)');

    const gradient2 = chart.ctx.createLinearGradient(x0, y0, x1, y1);
    gradient2.addColorStop(0, 'hsla(300,100%,70%,.4)');
    gradient2.addColorStop(1, 'hsla(240,100%,25%,.8)');

    chart.data.datasets[0].backgroundColor = gradient1;
    chart.data.datasets[1].backgroundColor = gradient2;
}
```

You have to call that function as soon as the chart is created and then invoke `update()` to redraw the chart. After each resize, call it again. This can be done automatically using the `onComplete()` animation callback, as shown in the following code:

```
const data = {
    labels: ["Sun", "Mon", "Tue", "Wed", "Thu", "Fri", "Sat"],
    datasets: [
        {
            label: 'Week 1',
            data: [2, 5, 2, 0, 20, 48, 51],
            borderColor: 'red'
        },{
            label: 'Week 2',
            data: [44, 36, 13, 40, 40, 9, 3],
            borderColor: 'blue'
        }
    ]
};

const chart = new Chart('canvas', {
    type: 'line',
    data: data,
    options: {
        animation: {
            onComplete: function(context) {
                drawGradient(context.chart);
            }
        }
    }
});
drawGradient(chart);
chart.update();
```

The final result is shown in the following screenshot:

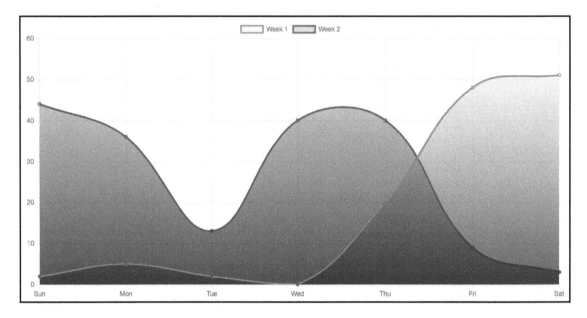

Line chart using gradients as backgroundColor for each dataset. Code: *Colors/colors-3-gradient.html.*

# Patterns

Patterns are a great way to create charts that don't depend on color-coding, and they can be used in color or monochromatic devices or print media. And they are, of course, color-blind safe. You can create patterns using HTML Canvas commands somewhat similar to the ones used for gradients, but it's much easier to use a plugin, such as the Patternomaly plugin, listed in the Chart.js official documentation.

You can obtain Patternomaly by downloading the JavaScript library from its GitHub repository (`github.com/ashiguruma/patternomaly`) or by using a CDN link:

```
<script
src="https://cdn.jsdelivr.net/npm/patternomaly@1.3.0/dist/patternomaly.min.
js">
</script>
```

To generate a pattern, all you have to do is choose a color and call `pattern.generate()`, which will randomly select 1 of the 21 patterns available:

```
pattern.generate('rgb(50%,20%,10%');
```

You can also choose a specific pattern as the first argument of `pattern.draw()`:

```
pattern.draw('triangle', 'lightblue');
```

A list of the supported patterns is shown as follows (`Colors/colors-4-patternomaly.html`):

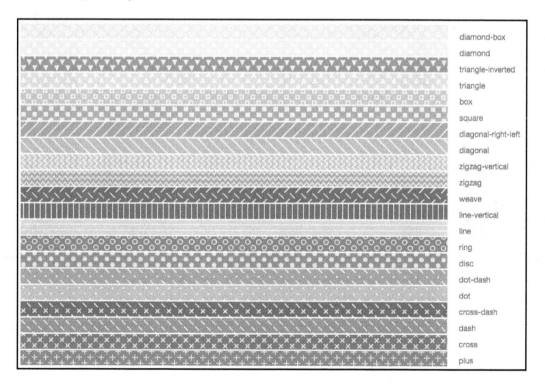

Patterns available in the patternomaly.js plugin. Code: *Colors/colors-4-patternomaly.html.*

The `generate()` function also accepts an array of colors as an argument. You can include the palette obtained for the Color Brewer example and generate patterns based on them:

```
let patternArray =
['#d73027','#fc8d59','#fee090','#e0f3f8','#91bfdb','#4575b4'];
pattern.generate(patternArray);
```

Let's use patterns to color our bar chart. For this example (`Colors/colors-5-pattern.html`), we will pass a call to the `pallete()` function from the `palette.js` library (which returns an array of colors) as the parameter for `generate()`, and assign it to the `backgroundColor` property for the bars:

```
backgroundColor: pattern.generate( palette('tol', 6).map(n=>'#'+n) ),
```

The result is shown as follows:

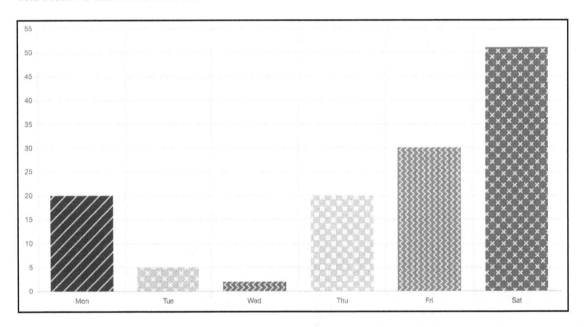

A color-blind-safe chart using generated patterns and colors. Code: *Colors/colors-5-pattern.html*.

# Shadows and bevels

There are several third-party plugins listed in the official Chart.js documentation, and one of them, called `chartjs-plugin-style`, adds a few styling options for charts; these options include bevels, shadows, and glows. To use it, you can install the plugin via npm or download the JavaScript file from `nagix.github.io/chartjs-plugin-style` that can be imported on to your page:

```
<script src="../JavaScript/chartjs-plugin-style.min.js"></script>
```

Now you can use new properties in your datasets to add bevels, shadows, and glows. The following example configures bevels and adds shadows to a simple bar chart. The names of the properties should be self-explanatory:

```
const data = {
    labels: ["Mon", "Tue", "Wed", "Thu", "Fri", "Sat"],
    datasets: [
        {
            label: 'Week 1',
            data: [20, 5, 2, 20, 30, 51],
            backgroundColor: ['yellow','red','blue','green','orange',
            'cyan'],
            bevelWidth: 3,
            bevelHighlightColor: 'rgba(255, 255, 255, 0.75)',
            bevelShadowColor: 'rgba(0, 0, 0, 0.5)',
            shadowOffsetX: 5,
            shadowOffsetY: 5,
            shadowBlur: 10,
            shadowColor: 'rgba(0, 0, 0, 0.5)',
        }
    ]
};

new Chart('canvas', { type: 'bar', data: data,
                      options: {legend: {display: false}} });
```

The final result is shown next. You can also mix it with generated colors, palette functions, and patterns. Try it out with different types of charts! The code is in `Colors/colors-6-shadows.html`:

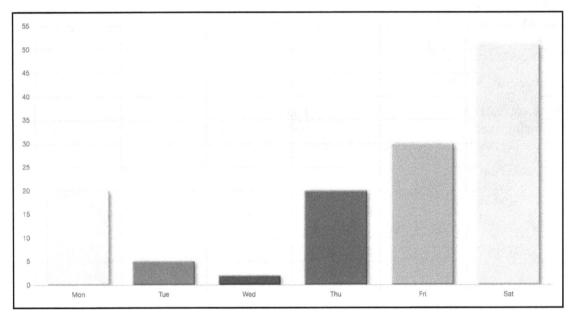

A bar chart enhanced with bevels and shadows. Code: *Colors/colors-6-shadows.html*.

# Adding text elements and labels

You can always add captions and titles outside your chart, using plain HTML or JavaScript. However, Chart.js also includes properties that draw and configure text elements inside the canvas as part of the chart. If the properties don't give you enough flexibility, you can use callbacks to filter or generate labels. If tooltips, titles, and legends aren't enough, you can also use plugins to add labels to bars, slices, and lines. You can even draw over the chart using plain HTML Canvas. This section will explore some of these techniques.

# Legends and labels

Legends are displayed by default in bar, line, pie and doughnut charts. They appear as a list of labeled, colored boxes that relate to the color of the lines, bars, or slices represented by a dataset, and they are rendered on the screen even when there is a single dataset. In such cases, you may wish to hide them. You can also tune several other properties and callbacks. The most important properties are listed as follows:

| Property | Value | Description |
|---|---|---|
| Display | true or false | Shows or hides the legend of the chart. The default is true. |
| Position | 'top', 'bottom', 'left', 'right' | Selects the position of the label in relation to the chart. The default is 'top'. |
| Reverse | true or false | Reverses the order of the labels in the legend. The default is false. |
| Labels | Object | Configures the text and the colored box for each label. |

Main properties of the legend object

There are also two callbacks you can attach to legends:

| Property | Parameters | Description |
|---|---|---|
| onClick | (event,label): the label.text property contains the text of the label; the label.datasetIndex contains the index of the array. | Reacts to a 'click' event. The default implementation toggles the label and associated dataset on and off. |
| onHover | (event,label): the label.text property contains the text of the label; the label.datasetIndex contains the index of the array. | Reacts to a 'hover' event. This callback is not implemented by default. |

Callbacks for the legends object

The following example contains a simple three-dataset line chart. Instead of hiding the dataset, the `onClick` callback for the legends was overridden to change the color of the selected dataset to gray. Note that the dataset index is obtained from the callback parameters, but the dataset properties are changed in the object tree for the current chart (`this.chart.data.datasets`):

```
const data = [[12,19,3,5,2,3],[6,5,33,2,7,11],[2,3,5,16,0,1]],
    strokes = ['rgba(54,162,235,1)','rgba(255,99,132,1)',
               'rgba(132,255,99,1)'],
    fills =
    ['rgba(54,162,235,.2)','rgba(255,99,132,.2)','rgba(132,200,99,.2)'];
const grayFill = 'rgb(0,0,0,.2)';
const grayStroke = 'rgb(0,0,0,.8)';

const datasets = [];
for(const i = 0; i < data.length; i++) {
    datasets.push({
        label: 'Dataset ' + (i+1),
        data: data[i],
        backgroundColor: fills[i],
        borderColor: strokes[i],
        borderWidth: 1
    });
}

const myChart = new Chart("myChart", {
    type: 'line',
    data: {
        labels: ['Day 1','Day 2','Day 3','Day 4','Day 5','Day 6'],
        datasets: datasets,
    },
    options: {
        legend: {
            position: 'left',
            reverse: true,
            onClick: function(event, label) {
                const index = label.datasetIndex;
                const dataset = this.chart.data.datasets[index];
                if(dataset.backgroundColor == fills[index]) {
                    dataset.backgroundColor = grayFill;
                    dataset.borderColor = grayStroke;
                } else {
                    dataset.backgroundColor = fills[index];
                    dataset.borderColor = strokes[index];
                }
                this.chart.update();
            }
```

```
            }
        }
    })
```

The following screenshots show the chart before and after clicking on a dataset. See the full code in `Text/text-1-legend-callback.html`:

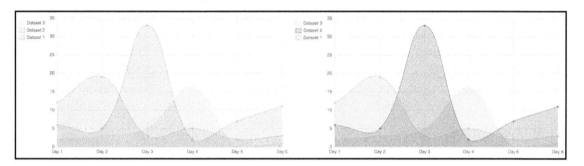

Implementing an onClick callback to change the color of a dataset. Code: *Text/text-1-legend-callback.html*.

The `legend.labels` property is used to configure the appearance of the individual legend labels. The following table shows the properties you are most likely to use:

| Property | Value | Description |
|---|---|---|
| fontSize, fontStyle, fontColor, fontFamily | Number and string | Font properties inherit global font. |
| boxWidth | Number | The width of the colored box. The default is 40. |
| Padding | Number | The padding between rows of colored boxes. |

Main properties of the legend.labels object

There is no property to set the color of the colored box. It will normally inherit from the global `defaultColor` if no colors are assigned to the datasets. You can change this behavior with the `generateLabels` callback property. You can also filter out unwanted labels by assigning a function to the filter `callback` property. These are listed as follows:

| Property | Parameters | Description |
|---|---|---|
| generateLabels | (chart): The current chart. This is the same as this.chart. | The default implementation returns the dataset label as text and a rectangular colored box that matches the dataset's colors. |
| filter | (label, item): label.text contains the text of the label; label.datasetIndex contains the index of the array; item.datasets contains the dataset array; and item.labels contains the *x* axis labels or pie slice labels. | This contains a filtering function that returns true for labels that should be displayed. The default implementation returns true. This property only filters out labels, not datasets (the lines or slices will still be displayed). |

Callback properties for the legend.labels object

Label styles can be configured inside the `options` object, in each chart instance, or for all charts using the `Global.defaults.legend` object, for example:

```
Chart.defaults.global.legend.labels.fontSize = 16;
Chart.defaults.global.legend.labels.boxWidth = 20;
```

The following filter configuration will only show the labels for datasets that have a maximum value below 20. All three datasets will be shown, but only two labels will be displayed (Text/text-2-legend-label.html):

```
labels: {
    filter: function(label, item) {
        return Math.max(...item.datasets[label.datasetIndex].data) <= 20;
    }
}
```

The `generateLabels` callback should only be implemented if you want to create your own legend. If you have a very complex legend, you can generate an HTML legend implementing a callback function for the `Chart.defaults.global.legendCallback` property or in each chart using the `legendCallback` property in options. This will be explored in Chapter 7, *Advanced Chart.js*.

# Titles

The default in Chart.js is to have the title turned off, since you can also create your title with greater flexibility in HTML. If you still want to have a title in your chart, you need to set at least set two properties: `display` (with the value `true`) and `text` (with the text of your title). Other properties you might want to configure are listed as follows:

| Property | Value | Description |
|---|---|---|
| display | true or false | Displays the title. The default is false. |
| text | String or String[] | A string containing the text of the title or an array of strings, for a multi-line title. |
| fontStyle, fontFamily, fontSize, fontColor | String and Number | Font attributes. The default fontStyle is bold, but the others are inherited. |
| lineHeight | Number | The default line height is 1.2. |
| padding | Number | The default padding is 10. |
| position | 'top', 'bottom', 'left' or 'right' | This is where the title should be placed. The default is 'top'. The titles' places on the sides will be rotated 90 degrees counterclockwise. |

Main properties of the options.title object

You can configure the title using `Chart.defaults.global.title` for all charts, or in the `options` object for a new chart instance. You can also change the title at any time after updating a chart or responding to events.

# Adding labels to lines, bars, and slices

In Chapter 4, *Creating Charts*, we used a simple plugin to add labels to pie slices. In this section, we will show you two others that allow a lot more customization. They are listed in the official documentation for Chart.js but are developed by third parties and should be installed or downloaded from their own repositories.

The `chart-plugin-datalabels` plugin offers the highly customizable labeling of values in all types of charts, with support for scripting and event handling. You can see several samples in `chartjs-plugin-datalabels.netlify.com/samples/`, where there is also a link to the documentation and the GitHub repository. The easiest way install it is with a CDN. Include the following code in your page:

```
<script src="https://cdn.jsdelivr.net/npm/chartjs-plugin-datalabels">
</script>
```

Configurations can be made per dataset, per chart, or globally, using one of the three contexts as follows:

- In datasets: `dataset.datalabels.*`
- In a chart instance: `options.plugins.datalabels.*`
- Globally, for all charts: `Chart.defaults.global.plugins.datalabels.*`

The local settings override the global ones. Details are beyond the scope of this chapter, but the plugin is very well documented. The following is a simple example, using the line chart we used in the previous sections. All the configuration was done in the `options.plugins.datalabels` object, which adds nice labels inside rounded rectangles over the data points (see `Text/text-4-datalabels.html`):

```
options: {
    plugins: {
        datalabels: {
            backgroundColor: function(context) {
                return context.dataset.borderColor;
            },
            borderRadius: 4,
            color: 'white',
            font: { weight: 'bold'},
            formatter: Math.round
        }
    },
}
```

The result is shown in the following screenshot:

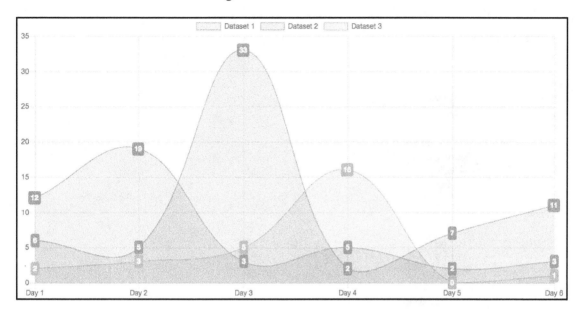

Using the chartjs-datalabels plugin to add value labeling to a line chart. Code: The code is in *Text/text-4-datalabels.html*.

There's a lot more that can be done with this plugin. Try it on other charts and check out the samples.

A second labeling plugin is `chart-plugin-outlabels`. It allows for better visualization of the data values in pie and doughnut charts, displaying the labels outside the slices. You can see a sample in `piechart-outlabels.netlify.com/sample/`, where you will also find a link to the documentation and the GitHub repository. To use it on your page, include the following:

```
<script src="https://cdn.jsdelivr.net/npm/chartjs-plugin-piechart-
outlabels"> </script>
```

As in many other plugins, configurations can be made per dataset, per chart, or globally, using one of the three contexts as follows:

- In datasets: `dataset.outlabels.*`
- In a chart instance: `options.plugins.outlabels.*`
- Globally, for all charts: `Chart.defaults.global.plugins.outlabels.*`

The plugin also introduces a new chart type: outlabeledPie. It can be used in place of pie or doughnut and is simpler to configure.

The following is a simple example of the doughnut chart we used in previous examples, using an outlabeledPie (see Text/text-5-outlabels.html for the full code):

```
const data = {
    labels: ["Mon", "Tue", "Wed", "Thu", "Fri", "Sat"],
    datasets: [
        {
            label: 'Week 1',
            data: [20, 5, 2, 20, 30, 51],
            backgroundColor: palette('tol', 6).map(n=>'#'+n),
        }
    ]
};

new Chart('canvas', {
    type: 'outlabeledPie',
    data: data,
    options: {
        zoomOutPercentage: 30,
        plugins: {
            legend: false,
            outlabels: {
                text: '%l %p',
                color: 'white',
                stretch: 45,
                font: {
                    resizable: true,
                    minSize: 12,
                    maxSize: 18
                }
            }
        }
    }
});
```

The result is shown in the following screenshot:

A pie chart with values labeled by the chartjs-outlabels plugin. Code: *Text/text-5-outlabels.html.*

Check the documentation for more options, and try to use this plugin in other charts.

# Interactions, data updates, and animations

Unless configuration options are changed, all charts come pre-configured with default behaviors and transitions, which are animated. Animations are triggered by events, such as window resizing, data updates, or user interaction. The default pre-configured chart interactions include hovering the mouse over or near value points (used to trigger the appearance of tooltips containing details) and clicking or touching legends. This provides basic interactivity with smooth data transitions, but you may still want to fine-tune it by writing callbacks for different events or animation stages, changing animation properties such as duration or ease algorithms, or even turn the animations off completely. If you need more control, you can extend much of this functionality using plugins or standard JavaScript.

# Data updates

An interactive chart may display data that is changing periodically. A web page might contain an algorithm that changes data automatically; it may download new data files with new data, or it may allow the user to enter or request changes in the source-data values. In any of these cases, as soon as the new data is available, the chart should be updated. Data updates can occur automatically inside callback functions or can be explicitly called using the update() command. To use it, you will need to save a variable handle to the chart object:

```
const chart = new Chart(...);
 // make changes
 chart.update();
```

When using callbacks, you can usually refer to the current instance of the chart, using the this keyword:

```
callback: function() {
     // make changes
     this.chart.update();
 }
```

Changes usually involve properties in datasets and options of a chart instance. Let's see an example. In the following code, the square() function will square all the data values in a chart and change the *x* axis to a *logarithmic* scale. The squareRoot() function does the opposite. After updating the grid (with the undocumented scaleMerge() function), the chart is updated:

```
function square(chart) {
    const datasets = chart.config.data.datasets;
    for(let i = 0; i < datasets.length; i++) {
        for(let j = 0; j < datasets[i].data.length; j++) {
            let value = datasets[i].data[j];
            datasets[i].data[j] = value * value;
        }
    }
    chart.options.scales.yAxes =
        Chart.helpers.scaleMerge(Chart.defaults.scale,
                            {yAxes: [{type: 'logarithmic'}]}).yAxes;
    chart.update();
}

function squareRoot(chart) {
    const datasets = chart.config.data.datasets;
    for(let i = 0; i < datasets.length; i++) {
        for(let j = 0; j < datasets[i].data.length; j++) {
```

```
            let value = datasets[i].data[j];
            datasets[i].data[j] = Math.sqrt(value);
        }
    }
    chart.options.scales.yAxes =
        Chart.helpers.scaleMerge(Chart.defaults.scale,
                                 {yAxes: [{type: 'linear'}]}).yAxes;
    chart.update();
}
```

The HTML button is registered as an event listener that calls one of the two functions, depending on the current *y* axis type, and updates the chart:

```
let button = document.getElementById("toggle");
button.addEventListener('click', function() {
    const type = myChart.options.scales.yAxes[0].type;
    if(type == 'linear') {
        square(myChart);
    } else {
        squareRoot(myChart);
    }
});
```

Try it out. The full code is in `Animation/animation-1-update.html`, and the following screenshots show the chart in the two different states:

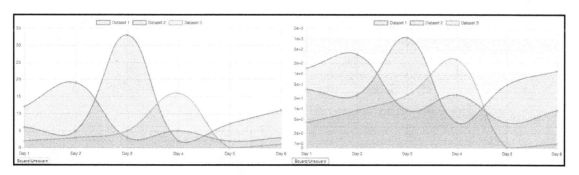

Updating a chart after changing values and scales. Code: *Animation/animation-1-update.html.*

# Events

You can select which events your chart will respond to by locally configuring the `options.events` property, or globally using `Chart.defaults.global.events`. The default configuration includes an array with six event names:

```
events: ["mousemove", "mouseout", "click", "touchstart", "touchmove",
"touchend"]
```

These are the events the browser will listen to when the cursor is within the canvas context. They control the behavior of clickable items such as legend labels and tooltips. If you are writing your own handlers, you may wish to turn off some events by redefining the property to include an array containing fewer events. For example, if you want to disable hovering and touch events in a chart, allowing only the `click` event, you can add the following to your options configuration:

```
options: {
    events: ['click']
}
```

# Configuring animations

You should have noted that when you click the button, the lines don't move to their new positions immediately. The chart transitions smoothly, and it takes about a second. Transitions triggered by calling `update()` will automatically use standard animation configurations.

There are two animation properties you can easily change. They are listed as follows:

| Property | Values | Description |
|----------|--------|-------------|
| Duration | Number | The duration of the animation in milliseconds. The default is 1,000 (one second). |

| Easing | 'linear', 'easeInQuad', 'easeOutQuad', 'easeInOutQuad', 'easeInCubic', 'easeOutCubic', 'easeInOutCubic', 'easeInQuart', 'easeOutQuart', 'easeInOutQuart', 'easeInQuint', 'easeOutQuint', 'easeInOutQuint', 'easeInSine', 'easeOutSine', 'easeInOutSine', 'easeInExpo', 'easeOutExpo', 'easeInOutExpo', 'easeInCirc', 'easeOutCirc', 'easeInOutCirc', 'easeInElastic', 'easeOutElastic', 'easeInOutElastic', 'easeInBack', 'easeOutBack', 'easeInOutBack', 'easeInBounce', 'easeOutBounce', 'easeInOutBounce' | The easing function to use for the animation. These are based on *Robert Penner's Easing Functions* (`robertpenner.com/easing`). They are easier to choose if you look at a graphical representation of each one, which is available at `http://easings.net`. |
|---|---|---|

Properties for the options.animation object

To make an instant transition to the new values (without any animations), you should include an object containing `duration:0`:

```
options: {
    animation: {
        duration: 0
    }
}
```

Now the change will happen instantly.

Properties can be configured per chart, in the options object, or globally in `Chart.defaults.global`.

There are two `callback` properties for configuring animations, listed as follows. One allows you to hook on to each step of the animation, and the other allows you to run code after the animation is complete:

| Property | Parameters | Description |
|---|---|---|
| onProgress | (animation): The main properties are animation.chart (the current chart), animation.currentStep, and animation.numSteps (currentStep/numSteps returns a percentage of the animation so far) | Called after each step of an animation. |
| onComplete | (animation): The main properties are animation.chart (the current chart), animation.currentStep, and animation.numSteps (currentStep/numSteps returns a percentage of the animation so far) | Called at the end of an animation. Any changes to be applied after the chart is rendered (such as a Canvas overlay) should be called in this context. |

Callback properties for options.animation

We added an HTML progress bar to the web page of the previous example and configured the line chart animation to last five seconds in the following code. At each step, the progress bar is updated by the `onProgress` callback function. Each callback also prints the current step to the JavaScript console each time it is called:

```
<body>
<canvas id="myChart" width="400" height="200"></canvas>
<form><button type="button" id="toggle">Square/Unsquare</button></form>
<progress id="progress" max="1" value="0"></progress>
<script>
    . . .
    const progress = document.getElementById("progress");
    . . .
    const myChart = new Chart("myChart", { type: 'line', data: {...},
        options: {
            animation: {
                duration: 5000,
                onProgress: function(animation) {
                    console.log(animation.currentStep /
                            animation.numSteps);
                    progress.value = animation.currentStep /
                            animation.numSteps;
            },
            onComplete: function(animation) {
```

```
                    console.log(animation.currentStep);
                }
            }
        }
    })
    let button = document.getElementById("toggle");
    button.addEventListener('click', function() {...});
</script>
```

The full code is in `Animation/animation-2.html`. Here is a screenshot showing the animation halfway through:

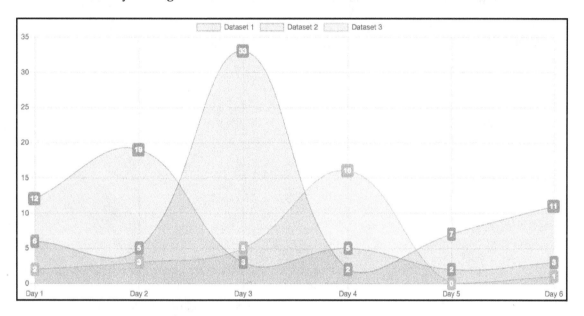

Using a progress bar during a five-second animation, after updating the chart. Code: *Animation/animation-2.html*.

In this example, the `onComplete` callback is simply printing to the console, but it is one of the most important callbacks if you need to update or change anything after the chart is rendered on the screen. If you draw something to a Canvas outside a callback, Chart.js will erase it. In `Chapter 4`, *Creating Charts*, we used it to draw text, using the Canvas API over a doughnut chart. In this chapter, we added a gradient color to the chart, after every resizing event.

# Summary

In this chapter, we explored several ways to configure the look and feel of interactive charts created with Chart.js, using native properties, as well as some extensions and plugins.

We first learned how to set global defaults, which can be inherited by multiple charts and used to set a consistent theme across different charts, sharing basic layout, fonts, and color schemes. We also explored some online services, tools, extensions, and plugins for styling charts and adding labels. Then we configured the behavior of a chart after updates and user interactions, tinkering with animation algorithms and callbacks.

You already know enough Chart.js to create any chart. In the next chapter, we will dive deeper into some of these topics, configure tooltips, learn how to program the Chart.js API, and you will learn how to create your own plugins.

# References

**Books and websites**:

- Chart.js official documentation and samples: `https://www.chartjs.org/docs/latest/`

**Data sources**:

- Volumes of the World's Oceans (based on ETOPO1): `Chapter03/Pages/BarChart1.html` **and others.** `https://www.ngdc.noaa.gov/mgg/global/etopo1_ocean_volumes.html`
- World population: `Chapter04/WPP2017_UN.csv`. *United Nations World Population Prospects 2017.* `https://www.un.org`

# 7
# Advanced Chart.js

When you create data visualizations with Chart.js, most of the work you will have involves preparing the data so that it can be loaded and used by a chart instance. You don't have to worry much about fonts, padding, axes, screen resizing, or responsiveness, since new charts are preconfigured with defaults intended for optimal presentation and interactivity. In the last chapter, we learned how to adjust colors, labels, animations, and other typical configurations in different types of charts. In this chapter, we will explore configuration topics that you won't use as frequently, and that may require additional coding, extensions, and integration with other libraries, such as tooltip behavior configuration, label generation, scripting, creating mixed charts, creating plugins, using the Chart.js API, and using HTML Canvas with Chart.js.

What you will learn in this chapter includes the following:

- Tooltip configuration
- Advanced legend configuration
- Displaying multiple charts
- Extending Chart.js

## Tooltip configuration

Tooltips are the main feature used by Chart.js to reveal quantitative details about data. While some context comes from the grid, the only way to natively display data right next to the data point is using a tooltip. Of course, you can label the value points as we saw in the previous chapter, but that requires extensions or plugins, and may clutter your chart if used in excess. Chart.js visualizations rely on interactivity to show details. In this section, we will learn how to configure the way these details are displayed.

Tooltips can be configured for each chart using the tooltips key in the `options` object. They can also be configured for all charts using `Chart.defaults.global.tooltips`. The properties of these objects that you can configure are listed in the following table:

| Object | Value | Description |
|---|---|---|
| titleSpacing | Number | Space before and after each *title* line. Default is 2. |
| bodySpacing | Number | Space before and after each *tooltip* item. Default is 2. |
| footerSpacing | Number | Space before and after each *footer* line. Default is 2. |
| titleMarginBottom | Number | Margin after the `title` in pixels. Default is 6. |
| footerMarginTop | Number | Margin before the `footer` in pixels. Default is 6. |
| xPadding | Number | Vertical padding in pixels. Default is 6. |
| yPadding | Number | Horizontal padding in pixels. Default is 6. |
| enabled | true or false | Turns tooltips on or off. Default is true. |
| intersect | true or false | If true, the tooltip interaction mode will only be applied when the cursor hovers exactly over the point (inside the pointHitRadius). If false, it will be applied at all times. Global default is true, but changes depending on the type of chart. |

| | | |
|---|---|---|
| mode | nearest, index, dataset, x, y. Deprecated values are label (same as index), and single (behaves like nearest when intersect: true). | Selects the tooltip interaction mode. nearest displays the value of the nearest point (includes one item per tooltip), index displays values of all the points with the same index (will include an item for each dataset in the same tooltip), dataset will display the entire dataset in a tooltip. Two other modes are available for cartesian scales only: x will include in the tooltip all items that share the same x coordinate value, and y will include all items that share the same y coordinate value. index mode, which in Cartesian scales defaults to the x indexes, can also be set for the y indexes by adding the property axis: y. The global default is nearest but it changes depending on the type of chart. |
| position | average, nearest, or a custom position | Defines where the tooltip is positioned in relation to the value point. The default is average. (You can define your own custom position creating an entry in the Chart.Tooltip.positioners map that returns an object with *x* and *y* coordinates.) |
| titleFontFamily, titleFontStyle, titleFontColor, titleFontSize | String and Number | Font attributes for title (which is configured using callbacks). |
| bodyFontFamily, bodyFontStyle, bodyFontColor, bodyFontSize | String and Number | Font attributes for body (which is configured using callbacks). |

| footerFontFamily, footerFontStyle, footerFontColor, footerFontSize | String and Number | Font attributes for footer (which is configured using callbacks). |
|---|---|---|
| caretSize | Number | Size in pixels of the tooltip arrow. Default is 5. |
| caretPadding | Number | Distance of the arrow tip from the tooltip position (example: the value point). Default is 2. |
| cornerRadius | Number | The radius of the rounded rectangle in pixels. Default is 6. |
| backgroundColor | CSS color | The background color of the tooltip. Default is rgba(0,0,0,0.8). |
| multiKeyBackground | CSS color | The background of the colored box (won't be visible if the dataset color is opaque). Default is #fff. |
| borderColor | CSS color | The border color of the tooltip. Default is rgba(0,0,0,0). |
| borderWidth | Number | The border width of the tooltip. Default is 0. |
| displayColors | true or false | If false, hides color boxes. Default is true. |
| callbacks | Object | An object containing several callback functions. See the *Tooltip callbacks* section on tooltip callbacks in this chapter. |

Static properties for tooltips (used in the *options.tooltips* key)

In the following example, several default style properties were changed for the tooltips of a chart instance. Each tooltip will have a gray background, a yellow 3-pixel border, a pink 16-pixel title, an italic body, and a 10-pixel arrow, distant 10 pixels from the data point:

```
const data = {
    labels: ["One", "Two", "Three", "Four"],
    datasets: [{label:'Dataset 1',... },{label:'Dataset 2',...},
    {label:'Dataset 3',...}]
};
new Chart('chart', {type: 'line', data: data,
    options: {
```

```
        legend: { display: false },
        tooltips: {
            mode: 'index',
            titleFontSize: 16,
            titleFontColor: 'pink',
            bodyFontStyle: 'italic',
            titleSpacing: 10,
            caretSize: 10,
            caretPadding: 10,
            backgroundColor: 'rgba(10,10,60,.5)',
            borderColor: 'yellow',
            borderWidth: 3,
        },
    }
});
```

The full code is in `Tooltips/tooltip-1.html`. **The result is as follows:**

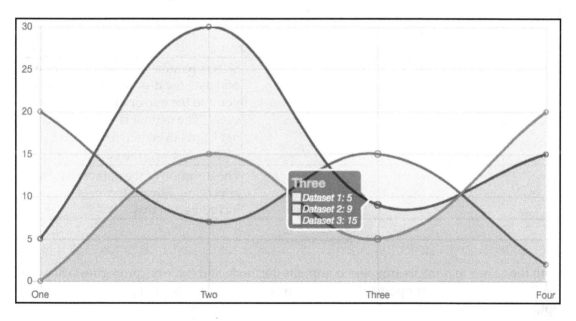

Tooltip with modified border color and width, background color, title font size and color, body font style,
caret arrow size, and padding (distance from value point). Code: *Tooltips/tooltip-1.html.*

# Hovering interactions

Tooltips respond to hover events. The next table lists properties of the hover object, which can be configured globally using `Chart.defaults.global.hover` or locally using `options.hover`:

| Object | Value | Description |
|--------|-------|-------------|
| intersect | true or false | Same behavior as `tooltip.intersect`. Tooltips can respond to different intersect states when hovering. |
| mode | nearest, index, dataset, x, y. Deprecated values are label (same as index), and single (behaves like nearest when intersect: true). | Same behavior as `tooltip.mode`. Tooltips can respond to a different mode when hovering. |
| axis | x, y, xy | Selects parameters that are used to calculate the distance from the value point to the cursor during a hover event. The default is x. Horizontal bar charts override this to y so that `mode:index` can select different bars. |
| animationDuration | Number | The duration of the animation. This affects any hovering events, including tooltips. |

Configuration options for the hover object

Both the hover and the tooltip objects support the mode and intersect properties. They are similar, but the hover property also applies to non-tooltip events (configured with the optional onHover callback).

If the intersect property is true, the event will only be fired if the mouse is directly over a bar or pie slice, or within a certain radius from the value point (for line, scatter, and bubble charts). If intersect is false, the event may be fired before the mouse is over the value point.

The `mode` property selects the data values related to the event. If `intersect` is `false`, and `mode` is `nearest`, it will select the nearest point.

When used in tooltips, the `mode` property also determines which items appear in a tooltip. If `nearest`, it will show the value that is nearest to the point where the mouse is (typical in scatter and bubble charts). The property can also have the following values:

- `point`, showing only items that actually intersect the point (typical inline charts)
- `index`, showing all the points at the same index (typical in a bar or pie chart)
- `dataset`, listing all points in the dataset

There are also two more modes that are exclusive to Cartesian scales: $x$ and $y$, which selects all points with the same values of $x$ and $y$, respectively.

Edit the `Tooltips/tooltip-3-modes.html` file and experiment with different modes. The following screenshots show some tooltip modes applied to a line chart with three datasets:

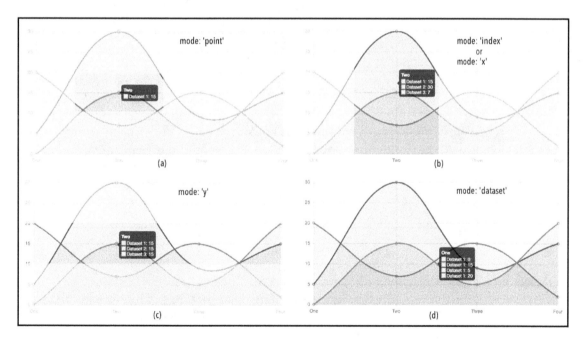

Tooltip interaction modes: (a) displays single value point; (b) displays items with same index (or x value in this case); (c) displays items with same y value; (d) displays all items in a dataset. Code: *Tooltips/tooltip-3-modes.html*.

# Scriptable properties

Tooltips have three properties that receive functions. One allows you to replace the Canvas-generated tooltips with your own custom HTML tooltips. The other two allow sorting of tooltip items (when several items appear in a single tooltip) and filtering. These properties are listed as follows:

| Object | Parameters | Description |
|---|---|---|
| custom | (tooltipModel) | Used to generate custom HTML tooltips. See the *Custom HTML tooltips* section on HTML tooltips in this chapter. |
| filter | (item, data); array of datasets in data.datasets; array of labels in data.labels; item.x and item.y contain coordinates of the value point, item.xLabel and item.yLabel the labels in each axis, item.index is the index of the item in the dataset, and item.datasetIndex is the index of its dataset. | A function that returns true or false and is called before rendering a tooltip item. If it returns false, the item will not be rendered. |
| itemSort | (item1, item2); each parameter is an item object with the following properties: x, y, xLabel, yLabel, index, dataSetIndex. | Sorts items (in tooltips that contain multiple items). The function returns a number. If item1 < item2 the function should return negative value, if item1 > item2 a positive value should be returned, and zero should be returned if they are equal. |

Scriptable properties for tooltips

Let's see some examples. In the following code (Tooltip/tooltip-4-script-filter.html), the filtering function ignores all items that contain *y* values greater than 20. Additionally, the events key was used to reduce the events the tooltips respond to. In this example, they are only activated with clicks:

```
const data = {
    labels: ["One", "Two", "Three", "Four"],
    datasets: [{label:'Dataset 1',... }, {label:'Dataset 2',...},
    {label:'Dataset 3',...}]
```

```
};
new Chart('chart', { type: 'line', data: data,
    options: {
        legend: { display: false },
        tooltips: {
            mode: 'index',
            intersect: false,
            filter: (item, data) => data.datasets[item.datasetIndex]
                                        .data[item.index] < 20
        },
        events: ['click']
    }
});
```

The following screenshot shows the result of clicking near the values points of `index` 1. Since one of the three points is greater than `20`, it doesn't show up in the tooltip:

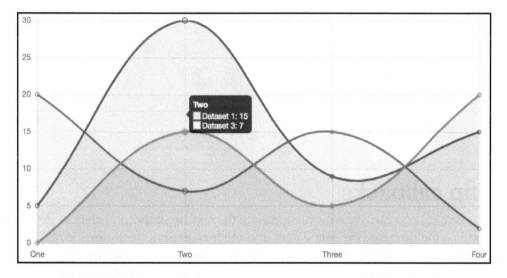

Tooltip with mode: index filtering only items that have a y value less than 20. Code: *Tooltip/tooltip-4-script-filter.html.*

This other example (`Tooltip/tooltip-5-script-sort.html`) configures item sorting in *ascending* order by the *y* value, in the same chart:

```
new Chart('chart', { type: 'line', data: data,
    options: {
        legend: { display: false },
        tooltips: {
            mode: 'index',
            intersect: false,
            itemSort: (a,b) => b.y - a.y
```

```
        },
        events: ['click']
    }
});
```

The result is as follows. Note that the tooltip items are ordered by their *y* value:

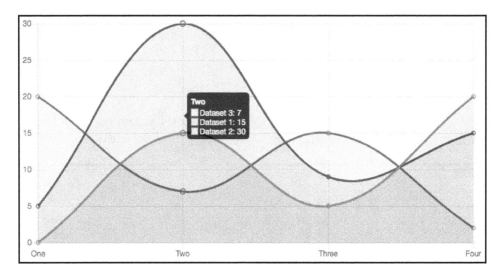

Tooltip with mode: 'index' sorting items by their *y* value. Code: *Tooltip/tooltip-5-script-sort.html.*

# Tooltip callbacks

With `callbacks`, you can dynamically generate the text contents and colors of the items displayed in a tooltip based on data values and other accessible attributes. The `Callbacks` are properties of the `tooltips.callbacks` object, which can be configured globally (`Chart.defaults.global.tooltips.callbacks`) or locally per chart instance (`options.tooltips.callbacks`). They are listed in the table as follows:

| Object | Parameters | Description |
|--------|-----------|-------------|
| `beforeTitle, title, afterTitle` | `(item[], data)`; array of datasets in `data.datasets`; array of labels in `data.labels`; each item element contains the following properties: `x`, `y`, `xLabel`, `yLabel`, `index`, `dataSetIndex`. | The `title` function returns the text for the tooltip title. You can also implement other functions to include text above or below it. |

| | | |
|---|---|---|
| `beforeBody, body, afterBody` | The `body` function returns the text for the tooltip body (including labels). You can also implement other functions to include text above or below it. | |
| `beforeFooter, footer, afterFooter` | The `footer` function returns the text for the tooltip footer. You can also implement other functions to include text before or after it. | |
| `beforeLabel, label, afterLabel` | `(item,data)`; array of datasets in `data.datasets`; array of labels in `data.labels`; `item.x` and `item.y` contain coordinates of the value point, `item.xLabel` and `item.yLabel` the labels in each axis, `item.index` is the index of the item in the dataset, `item.datasetIndex` is the index of its dataset. | The `label` function returns the text for this label. You can also implement other functions to include text above or below one or more labels. |
| `labelColor` | `(item, chart)` | The function returns the color of the text box of an individual item label |
| `labelTextColor` | `(item, chart)` | The function returns the color of the text for an individual item label |

Callbacks to create and change the text contents of tooltips

The following example (`Tooltips/tooltip-6-callback.html`) uses `callbacks` to add extra text to the title, insert separator characters above and below the item labels, and append a `footer` containing the average of all the value points:

```
new Chart('chart', { type: 'horizontalBar', data: data,
    options: {
        legend: { display: false },
        tooltips: {
            mode: 'index',
            callbacks: {
                footer: (items, data) => 'Average: ' + (data.datasets
                            .map(d=>d.data[items[0].index])
                            .reduce((a,b)=>a+b, 0) /
                            items.length)
                            .toFixed(2),
```

```
                    title: (items, data) => "Stage " + items[0].yLabel,
                    beforeBody: () => '=============',
                    afterBody: () => '--------------------',
                }
        },
        events: ['click']
    }
});
```

The result is as follows:

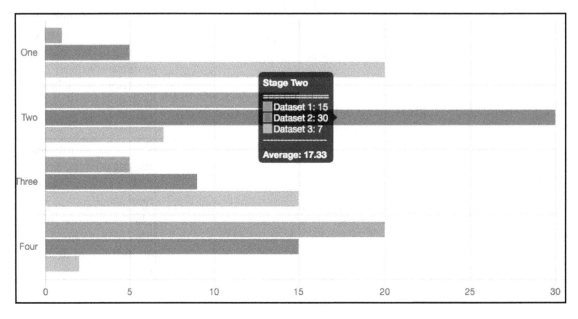

Tooltip with a footer, extra text in title, and separators before and after body created with callbacks. Code: *Tooltips/tooltip-6-callback.html.*

# Custom HTML tooltips

The `Chart.defaults.global.tooltips.custom` (or `options.tooltips.custom`) property receives a function that should build an HTML tooltip and connect it to a tooltip *model* object passed as a parameter. The tooltip model is a native object that responds to tooltip events and stores tooltip properties. Its properties can be copied and reused inside the HTML tooltip if desired.

The following example (`Tooltips/tooltip-7-custom.html`) shows how to create a simple custom HTML tooltip containing an image. The custom tooltip can be created using HTML as shown in the following snippet, or programmatically using DOM, and should initially be hidden (`opacity: 0`). When a `hover` event activates a tooltip, the model's opacity changes and the custom tooltip uses this state to make itself visible:

```
<html><head> ...
    <style>
        #tooltip {
            opacity: 0;
            position: absolute;
            margin: 5px;
        }
    </style>
</head><body>
<canvas id="chart" width="200" height="100"></canvas>
<div id="tooltip"></div>
<script>
    const data = {
        labels: ["jupiter", "saturn", "uranus", "neptune"],
        datasets: [{
            data: [142984,120536,51118,49528],
            backgroundColor: ['#d7191c','#fdae61','#abdda4','#2b83ba'],
        }]
    };
    new Chart('chart', { type: 'bar', data: data,
        options: {
            legend: { display: false },
            title: {
                display: true,
                text: 'Planetary diameters',
                fontSize: 24
            },
            tooltips: {
                mode: 'index',
                intersect: true,
                enabled: false, // turn off canvas tooltips
                custom: function(model) {
                    const tooltip = document.getElementById('tooltip');
                    if(model.opacity === 0) {
                        tooltip.style.opacity = 0;
                        return;                      }
                if(model.body) {
                    const value = model.body[0].lines[0];
                    tooltip.innerHTML = '<b>'+ value + " km<br/>"
                                        +'<img width="50"
                                        src="../Images/'
```

```
                                       +model.title[0] +'.jpg"
                                       </img>';
                        const pos =
                        this._chart.canvas.getBoundingClientRect();
                        tooltip.style.opacity = 1;
                        tooltip.style.left = pos.left + model.caretX +
                        'px';
                        tooltip.style.top  = -50 + pos.top +
                        model.caretY + 'px';
                }
            }
        }
    }
  });
</script>
</body></html>
```

The code extracts the title and filename from the tooltip model's `title`, and the value from the model's `body`. The custom tooltip also used the model's coordinates to decide where it would be placed. The result is as follows. If you hover over the labels in the *x*-axis or the bars, the HTML tooltip will be shown above each bar:

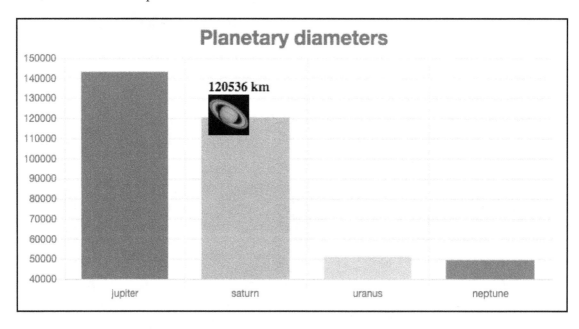

Bar chart with a custom HTML tooltip that appears when the mouse hovers over a bar or label. Code: *Tooltips/tooltip-7-custom.html*.

Positioning tooltips in pie charts is a bit more complex. For more examples on how to create custom HTML tooltips, check the samples page in the official documentation.

# Advanced legend configuration

Chart.js provides default presentation and behavior for legends and labels. In the previous chapter, we saw some examples of how to change the default behavior by programming the `onClick` event handler callback. In this section, we will see how to generate individual labels and, if you need even more control, how to create custom HTML legends.

# Generating labels

Labels can be generated with the `generateLabels` callback property. They should return an item object (the same object that is passed to an `onClick` function), which contains the properties listed as follows:

| Object | Value | Description |
|---|---|---|
| text | String | The text of the label |
| datasetIndex | Number | The index of the label |
| fillStyle, strokeStyle, lineCap, lineJoin, lineDash, lineWidth, lineDashOffset | The same values as the corresponding Canvas commands | Fill and stroke attributes for the legend box |
| pointStyle | circle, cross, crossRot, dash, line, rect, rectRounded, rectRot, star, triangle | If legend.labels.usePointStyle is true, the label will use the same point style as the chart. This allows you to set a different point style for the legend labels. |
| hidden | Boolean | If true, chart elements related to the dataset will not be rendered |

Properties of a legend label object (received by onClick and returned by generateLabels)

The following code shows configuration for legend labels (`Legend/legend-1-gen-labels.html`) using a `generateLabels` callback. The colored box is configured as a rotated rectangle with `pointStyle`. The label's `fontSize` controls the size of the font and point. The border color of each dataset is the fill for each label:

```
options: {
    legend: {
        labels: {
            usePointStyle: true,
            fontSize: 14,
            generateLabels: function(chart) {
                const items = [];
                chart.data.datasets.forEach((dataset, i) => {
                    items.push({
                        text: dataset.label,
                        datasetIndex: i,
                        fillStyle: dataset.borderColor,
                        lineWidth: 0,
                        pointStyle: 'rectRot',
                    });
                });
                return items;
            },
        },   ...
    }
}
```

The result is as follows:

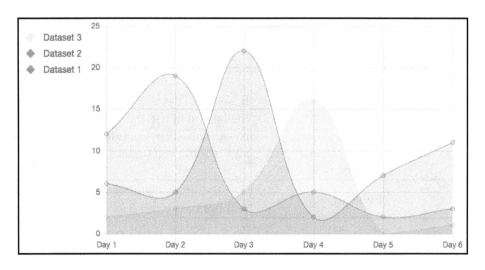

Generated labels with different symbols for legends. Code: *Legend/legend-1-gen-labels.html.*

# HTML legends

If you have a very complex legend or wish to display a legend outside the Canvas mixed with the HTML in your page, you can generate custom HTML legends. To create them, you need an empty `<div>` block:

```
<div id="chart-legends"></div>
```

So, the legend can be attached to the page's body. Then, you implement a `callback` function for the `Chart.defaults.global.legendCallback` property or `options.legendCallback` that returns the HTML for the legend. You can create the content dynamically and apply CSS styles with property values copied from the chart. The HTML is generated with `chart.generateLegend()`.

It's easier with an example. The following code implements a simple HTML legend from an HTML list. You can run the full code in `Legend/legend-2-html-callback.html`:

```
const myChart = new Chart("myChart", {
    type: 'line',
    data: {
        labels: ['Day 1','Day 2','Day 3','Day 4','Day 5','Day 6'],
        datasets: datasets,
    },
    options: {
        legendCallback: function(chart) {
            const labels = document.createElement("ul");
            labels.style.display = 'flex';
            labels.style.justifyContent = 'center';

            chart.data.datasets.forEach((dataset, i) => {
                const item = document.createElement("li");
                item.style.listStyle = 'none';
                item.style.display = 'inline';

                const icon = document.createElement("div");
                icon.style.width = icon.style.height = '15px';
                icon.style.display = 'inline-block';
                icon.style.margin = '0 6px';
                icon.style.backgroundColor = dataset.borderColor;

                item.appendChild(icon); // add colored square
                item.innerHTML += dataset.label; // add label text
                labels.appendChild(item);
            });
            return labels.outerHTML;
        },
```

```
        legend: { display: false, position: 'bottom' }
    }
});

const legend = document.getElementById('chart-legends');
legend.innerHTML = myChart.generateLegend(); // generates HTML
```

The new legend doesn't replace the default label. Unless you wish to display both legends, you should hide the default legend using `display: false`.

No behaviors are included in these HTML legends. You need to implement them yourself using JavaScript events. The following screenshot shows the result of the previous code:

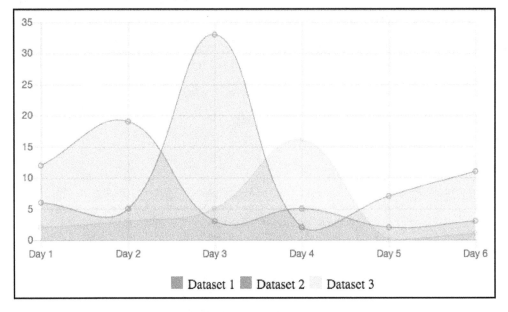

Legends created with HTML. Code: *Legend/legend-1-gen-labels.html.*

# Displaying multiple charts

Many times, you need to display more than one chart in a page to present different sets of data, or different views of the same data using different chart types. You may also wish to draw multiple charts over the same axes, so they can be compared. Another possibility is to use Canvas to draw over or under a chart and add context or additional data. All these scenarios are possible in Chart.js, but they require different strategies.

## Rendering many charts on one page

You can render several different charts on the same page by simply drawing a separate Canvas for each one.

The following example displays four charts on one page that share the same data. First, we need to set up the canvases using HTML and CSS:

```
<html lang="en">
<head>
    <script src=".../Chart.min.js"></script>
    <style>
        .container {
            width: 98%;
            height: 80vh;
            position: absolute;
        }
        .top {
            height:50%;
            position: relative;
        }
        .col {
            width: 50%;
            position: absolute;
        }
        .col:nth-child(2n-1) {
            left: 50%;
        }
        .footer {
            height: 50%;
            position: relative;
        }
    </style>
</head>
<body>
<div class="container">
    <div class="top" width="400" height="200">
```

```
        <div class="col"><canvas id="chart1"></canvas></div>
        <div class="col"><canvas id="chart2"></canvas></div>
    </div>
    <div class="top" width="400" height="200">
        <div class="col"><canvas id="chart3"></canvas></div>
        <div class="col"><canvas id="chart4"></canvas></div>
    </div>
    <div class="footer">
        <form>
          <button type="button" id="changeData">Get Data</button>
        </form>
    </div>
</div>
<script> ... </script>
</body>
</html>
```

The JavaScript code is shown in the following code. The chart initially loads some static data, but every time the button is pressed, the data changes and the charts are updated. The updateData() function was created to simulate new random data that is loaded into each chart every time the button is pressed:

```
function updateData() {
    charts.forEach(c => {
        let datasets = 3
        if(c.canvas.id == 'chart4') {
            datasets = 1;
        }
        for(let i = 0; i < datasets; i++) {
            for (let j = 0; j < 6; j++) {
                c.config.data.datasets[i].data[j] =
                Math.ceil(Math.random() * 25);
            }
        }
        c.update();
    });
}

Chart.defaults.global.legend.labels.boxWidth = 15;

const data = [[12, 19, 3, 5, 2, 3],[6, 5, 22, 2, 7, 11],[2, 3, 5, 16, 0, 1]],
        labels = ['Day 1','Day 2','Day 3','Day 4','Day 5','Day 6'],
        strokes =
        ['rgba(54,162,235,1)','rgba(255,99,132,1)','rgba(132,255,99,1)'],
        fills=
        ['rgba(54,162,235,.2)','rgba(255,99,132,.2)',
        'rgba(132,200,99,.2)'];
```

```
const datasets = [];
for(let i = 0; i < data.length; i++) {
    datasets.push({
        label: 'Dataset ' + (i+1),
        data: data[i],
        backgroundColor: fills[i],
        borderColor: strokes[i],
    });
}

const charts = [];

charts.push(new Chart("chart1", { type: 'line',
    data: { labels: labels, datasets: datasets }
}));

charts.push(new Chart("chart2", { type: 'bar',
    data: { labels: labels, datasets: datasets }
}));

charts.push(new Chart("chart3", { type: 'radar',
    data: { labels: labels, datasets: datasets },
    options: {legend: {display: false }}
}));

charts.push(new Chart("chart4", { type: 'doughnut',
    data: {
        labels: labels,
        datasets: [datasets[0]].map(d => ({
            data: d.data,
            backgroundColor: ['#d73027','#fc8d59','#fee090',
                              '#e0f3f8','#91bfdb','#4575b4'],
        })),
    },
    options: {legend: {position: 'left'}}
}));

document.getElementById("changeData")
        .addEventListener("click", updateData);
```

You can see the following result. Run the full code from `Multiple/ multiple-1-canvas.html`. Press the button and observe all the charts changing at once:

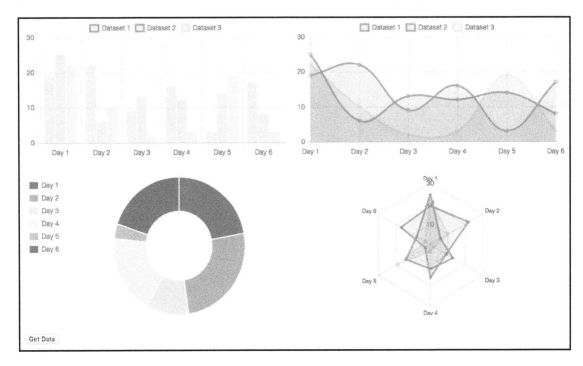

Displaying and updating multiple charts in one page. Code: *Multiple/multiple-1-canvas.html*.

# Mixed charts

Mixed charts are charts of different types that share the same axes. A typical example is to overlay a bar chart with one or more line charts. In Chart.js, this is achieved simply by adding a different `type` property in one or more datasets.

In the following example (`Multiple/ multiple-2-mixed.html`), a bar chart is used to display a set of values and a line chart is used to show the accumulated average:

```
const values = [12, 33, 42, 67, 90, 56, 51, 78, 95, 101, 120, 140];
const averages = [];
for(let i = 0; i < values.length; i++) {
    averages[i] = values.slice(0,i+1).reduce((a,b)=>a+b,0)/(i+1);
}
```

```
new Chart("myChart", {
    type: 'bar',
    data: {
        labels: ['Jan','Feb','Mar','Apr','May','Jun','Jul',
                 'Aug','Sep','Oct','Nov','Dec'],
        datasets: [{
            type: 'line',
            label: 'Line dataset (average)',
            data: averages,
            borderColor: 'red',
            fill: false
        },{
            label: 'Bar dataset (totals)',
            data: values,
            borderColor: 'blue',
            backgroundColor: 'rgba(0,0,120,.6)'
        }]
    }
})
```

Since bar is the default type, it doesn't need a type property. There could also be additional datasets for each type.

The result is as follows:

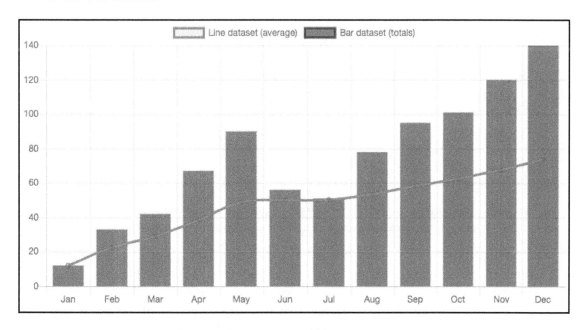

A mixed bar/line chart. Code: *Multiple/multiple-2-mixed.html.*

# Overlaying a canvas

One way to draw text and graphics on a chart is to draw on the same canvas *after* the chart is completely loaded. You can do that implementing your code in a function assigned to the `animation.onComplete` property. You can also write a simple plugin. Another way to draw over or under a chart is to draw on top of another canvas, and position it *exactly* over or under your chart canvas. This is easy to do if you won't be resizing your page. If you do any resizing, you will have to write additional scripts to scale your canvas content to keep it in sync with the chart (in this case, a plugin would be a better solution).

As an example, let's use the `GeoJSON` world map we loaded and rendered in `Chapter 2`, *Technology Fundamentals*, and place it under the bubble chart with the city populations we created in `Chapter 4`, *Creating Charts*. Since the map uses a simple cylindrical projection, we just have to make them both the same size, and use CSS absolute positioning to stack one over the other:

```html
<html lang="en">
  <head>
        <script src="../JavaScript/canvasmap.js" ></script>
        <script src=".../Chart.min.js"></script>
        <script src=".../papaparse.min.js"></script>
        <style>
            canvas {
                position: absolute;
                top:   0;
                left:  0;
            }
        </style>
  </head>
  <body>

<canvas id="map" width="1000" height="500"></canvas>
<canvas id="my-bubble-chart" width="1000" height="500"></canvas>
<script>...</script>
</body></html>
```

The drawings also have to start on the same point and use the same scales. The code uses four functions from `JavaScript/canvasmap.js`: a simple script that draws a map from GeoJSON data:

- `map.setCanvas(canvas)`: receives the background canvas where the map will be drawn
- `map.drawMap(geodata)`: receives an array of GeoJSON features and draws the map

- `map.scaleX(longitude)` and `map.scaleY(latitude)`: converts latitudes and longitudes into pixel coordinates

The following code obtains the `canvas` context for the map and sets its fill and stroke styles, loads and parses a GeoJSON file containing shapes for a world map, and a CSV containing city names, populations, latitudes, and longitudes. It then calls functions to draw the map and the chart:

```
const mapCanvas = document.getElementById("map");
const mapContext = mapCanvas.getContext("2d");

// Map ocean background
mapContext.fillStyle = 'rgb(200,200,255)';
mapContext.fillRect(0, 0, mapCanvas.width, mapCanvas.height);

// countries border and background
mapContext.lineWidth = .25;
mapContext.strokeStyle = 'white';
mapContext.fillStyle = 'rgb(50,50,160';

// setup map canvas
map.setCanvas(mapCanvas); // Function from JavaScript/canvasmap.js

// load files
const files = ['../Data/world.geojson', '../Data/cities15000.csv'];
const promises = files.map(file => fetch(file).then(resp =>
resp.text()));
Promise.all(promises).then(results => {

    // Draw the map
    const object = JSON.parse(results[0]);
    map.drawMap(object.features); // function from
    JavaScript/canvasmap.js

    // Draw the chart
    const data = Papa.parse(results[1], {header: true});
    drawChart(data.data);  // function described below
});
```

The radius of each bubble will be somewhat proportional to the population. This function will return a value that fits well in the map:

```
function scaleR(value) {
    const r = Math.floor(value / 100000);
    return r != 0 ? r/10 : .25;
}
```

The drawChart() function uses the parsed CSV datasets to generate an array of location objects, each containing *name* and the required bubble chart properties: *r* radius and *x, y* coordinates. The generated locations array is used as the dataset for the bubble chart:

```
function drawChart(datasets) {
    const locations = [];
    datasets.forEach(city => {
        const obj = {
            x: map.scaleX(+city.longitude), // From
            JavaScript/canvasmap.js
            y: map.scaleY(-city.latitude),  // From
            JavaScript/canvasmap.js
            r: scaleR(city.population),
            name: city.asciiname
        };
        locations.push(obj);
    });

    const dataObj = {
        datasets: [
            {   data: locations,
                backgroundColor: function(context) {...}
            }
        ]
    }
```

The options configuration object must configure scales so that there are no margins. Setting min and max properties for the ticks, removing legends and making responsive:false will guarantee this. Tooltips were also configured to show name and population (this is not shown here, but you can see the full code in Multiple/multiple-3-overlay.html):

```
const chartObj = {
    type: "bubble",
    data: dataObj,
    options: {
        scales: {
            xAxes: [{ display: false,
                ticks: {
                    min: map.scaleX(-180), // match map size
                    with
                    max: map.scaleX(180)   // canvas size
                }
            }
            ],
            yAxes: [{ display: false,
                ticks: {
```

```
                        min: map.scaleY(-90), // match map size
                        with
                        max: map.scaleY(90)   // canvas size
                }
            }
        ]
    },
    tooltips: {...}, // see full code
    animation: { duration: 0 },
    responsive: false,
    legend: { display: false }
    }
};
new Chart("my-bubble-chart", chartObj);
}
```

The final result is as follows. The chart is interactive; you can hover over a large city and get details:

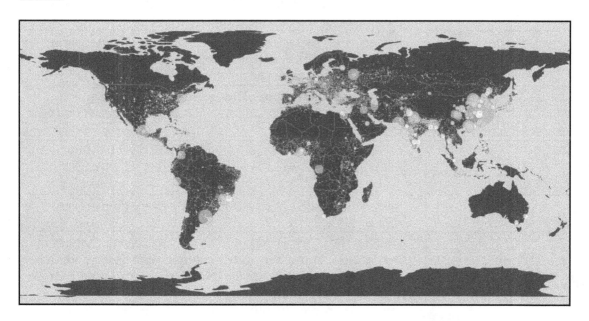

Two stacked HTML Canvases: one draws an SVG GeoJSON map, the other draws a bubble chart with Chart.js.
Code: *Multiple/multiple-3-overlay.html.*

Since we used very large files in this example, it takes a while to load the chart and the tooltips may run a bit slow on some systems. A quick way to optimize it is to reduce the data files previously before loading them. You can also filter and only use the large cities, drawing the small ones separately with Canvas.

# Extending Chart.js

There are several ways to extend Chart.js. You may use the prototype methods, callbacks, and event handlers and interact with the rendering process; you can create plugins, which have their own life cycle and are easier to reuse in other charts; and you can extend Chart.js from existing charts or even create new charts and scales.

# Prototype methods

Prototype methods are automatically called during rendering and updates. You can also call them directly if you need to interfere with the rendering process. They are listed in the following table:

| Method | Description |
|---|---|
| destroy() | Destroys a chart instance. This can be used if you wish to reuse the canvas, or remove the chart completely. |
| reset() | Restores the chart to its initial state (after layout and before its initial animation). A new animation can be triggered with render() or update(). |
| stop() | Stops an animation loop. This is usually called in an onProgress callback. Calling render() or update() will resume the animation. |
| clear() | Clears the chart canvas (effective after the chart has finished rendering). You can call render() or update() to draw it again. |
| resize() | Resizes the chart. Called automatically every time the canvas is resized. |
| update(config) | Updates the chart. This should be called after any changes in the datasets. You can include a configuration object with the following properties: *duration* (Number) to control the redraw animation duration, *lazy* (boolean) to decide if the animation can be interrupted by others, and *easing* (String), to select an easing function. |
| render(config) | Redraws all chart elements but does not update the chart elements for new data. |
| toBase64Image() | Generates the chart as a new base64-encoded PNG image. It can be displayed in an HTML page, or converted into a blob for download. |

| generateLegend() | Returns the contents of the options.legendCallback property (an HTML legend) when called. |
|---|---|
| getElementAtEvent(e) | Used in event handlers to obtain the element at an event. |
| getElementsAtEvent(e) | Used in event handlers to obtain all elements with the same data index at an event. |
| getDatasetAtEvent(e) | Used in event handlers to obtain an array of elements that belong to a dataset. |
| getDatasetMeta(index) | Returns the metadata for the dataset corresponding to the index. |

Chart.js prototype methods

Some of these methods are used to trigger the execution of life cycle callbacks in plugins. Many are already called automatically and may not be effective in all stages of an animation, since other stages may call methods that undo the desired effect.

In this chapter, we saw an example with generateLabels(), and in the previous chapter, we used update(). Event methods are common in event handlers, which receive a JavaScript event.

The toBase64Image() method generates a Base64 image string. Call it in animation.onComplete or in any callback function that is invoked only when the chart is fully drawn (otherwise it may generate a partially drawn or blank image). It returns a string that can be assigned to the src attribute of an HTML image for rendering on an HTML page:

```
<image id="image"></image>
...
<script>
new Chart("chart", { type: 'line', data: {...},
    options: {
        animation: {
            onComplete: function () {
                let image = document.getElementById('image');
                image.src = this.toBase64Image();
            }
        }
    }
});
</script>
```

You can also use it to create an image for download with a blob function. Use the `b64-to-blob` function available from `www.npmjs.com/package/b64-to-blob` or via CDN by adding the following line to your page:

```
<script src="https://unpkg.com/b64-to-blob"></script>
```

Add the following tag where you want the download link:

```
<a id='link' download='chart.png'></a>
```

Then, place this code in the `animation.onComplete` function:

```
const link = document.getElementById('link');
const blob = b64toBlob(image.src.split(',')[1], 'image/png');
link.href = URL.createObjectURL(blob);
```

After the chart loads, it will create a link that, when clicked, will download a PNG image of the chart. The full code is in `Extensions/ext-1-prototype.html`.

# Creating plugins

Plugins are the most efficient way to extend Chart.js. A plugin can insert code before and after different phases of the rendering cycle of a chart. At each phase, it can access the chart object and read configurable options. This can be used to change practically any property or behavior of the chart.

Plugins are designed to be reusable. During the previous chapters, we used several popular plugins to extend Chart.js in different ways. They are great to encapsulate complexity, but simple plugins can also be very useful.

In the last example, we created a download link for a PNG version of the chart. If you tried it, you may have noticed that the image has a transparent background. This is OK if your background is white, but if it isn't, the chart may be hard to read. A naïve approach to fixing the problem would be painting the canvas white using CSS or fill commands. But, it won't work because Chart.js redraws the canvas during its render cycle. You also need to deal with any animations, resizing, updates, and other events that might reset the background *after* you changed its color. This is a case for a plugin. With a plugin, you can insert code during the render cycle, draw the background after the canvas is initialized, and before the chart is drawn.

The render life cycle of Chart.js is illustrated as follows. When the chart is loaded for the first time, it performs the **init**, **update**, and **render** steps. Every time the page is resized, **update** and **render** are executed, and on **events**, the **render** step is performed:

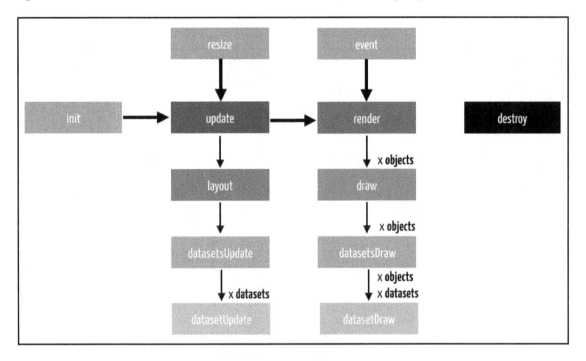

Chart.js life cycle. Each phase can be intercepted by plugin callbacks.

Depending on your plugin, you may need to intercept one or more of these steps. The following table lists the callbacks that are available for plugins. Each `callback` function contains at least two parameters: a reference to the chart instance and an `options` object (configured under a plugin ID key, in `options.plugins`). Some callbacks may have additional parameters:

| Method | Parameters | Description |
|---|---|---|
| beforeInit<br>afterInit | *(chart, options)* | Called before and after *new* `Chart()` is invoked |
| beforeUpdate<br>afterUpdate | *(chart, options)* | Called before and after the *update* stage |
| beforeLayout<br>afterLayout | *(chart, options)* | Called before and after the *layout* stage |
| beforeDatasetsUpdate<br>afterDatasetsUpdate | *(chart, options)* | Called before and after updating all datasets |
| beforeDatasetUpdate<br>afterDatasetUpdate | *(chart, dataset, options)* | Called before and after updating each dataset |
| beforeRender<br>afterRender | *(chart, options)* | Called before and after the *render* stage |
| beforeDraw<br>afterDraw | *(chart, easing, options)* | Called before and after the *draw* stage |
| beforeDatasetsDraw<br>afterDatasetsDraw | *(chart, easing, options)* | Called before and after drawing all datasets |
| beforeDatasetDraw<br>afterDatasetDraw | *(chart, dataset, options)* | Called before and after drawing each dataset |
| beforeEvent<br>afterEvent | *(chart, event, options)* | Called before and after *events* |
| resize | *(chart, dimensions, options)* | Called after resizing |
| destroy | *(chart, options)* | Called after `chart.destroy()` is called |

Life cycle callbacks that can be used in plugins

To see a demonstration of these methods, run the `Extensions/ext-2-plugin-lifecycle.html` file. It logs every life cycle event while a chart with three plugins is rendered and destroyed.

A plugin is a simple object. An `id` property is not necessary unless you plan to configure the plugin in the *options* object. You can include just the callback properties you need. The following code will create a simple configurable plugin that will draw a blue square in front of the chart, and a red one in front of the axes but behind the bars (`Extensions/ext-3-simple-plugin.html`):

```
const plugin = {
    id: 'p1',
    afterRender: function(chart, options) {
        chart.ctx.fillStyle = 'blue';
        chart.ctx.fillRect(60,60,100,100);
    },
    beforeDatasetsDraw: function(chart, percent, options) {
        chart.ctx.fillStyle = 'red';
        chart.ctx.fillRect(200,60,100,100);
    },
};
```

This effect is shown here:

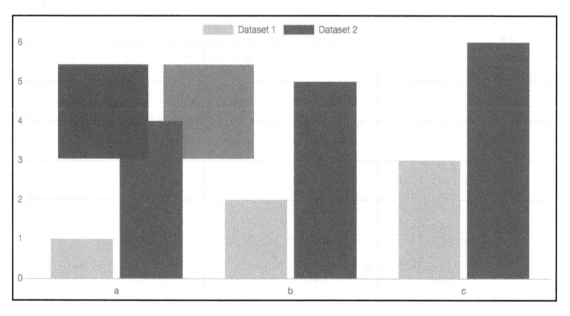

The blue and red squares were drawn in the chart using simple plugins. Code: *Extensions/ext-3-simple-plugin.html*.

If you are writing a plugin locally and have multiple charts, you can include a list of plugins to add to each chart using the *plugins* key in the Chart() constructor. It takes an array:

```
new Chart("chart", {
    type: 'bar',
    data: {...},
    options: {...},
    plugins: [plugin1]
});
```

Plugins should be reusable whenever possible. Reusable plugins are normally created in separate .js files and made automatically available to all charts. In this case, they should be registered globally with the following:

```
Chart.plugins.register(plugin);
```

Let's create a plugin for the last example so that the image and the chart have an opaque background. Plugins should have configurable options. There are greater chances you will reuse this plugin if you can configure the background color for each chart. We could also add the possibility of drawing a background image. The plugin will be stored in a separate JavaScript file, JavaScript/chartback.js, which creates the plugin object and registers it globally. The id is necessary so that a chart can identify the plugin and configure its options.

Since the image needs to be redrawn every time the chart is resized or updated, the best place to draw it is in the beforeDraw callback. This code will also place the image behind the axes:

```
const bgPlugin = { id: 'chartback',
    beforeDraw: function(chart, steps, options) {
        let ctx = chart.ctx;
        if(options.backgroundColor) {
            ctx.fillStyle = options.backgroundColor;
            ctx.fillRect(0, 0, chart.width, chart.height);
        }
        if(options.backgroundImage) {
            let image = new Image(chart.width, chart.height);
            image.src = options.backgroundImage;
            ctx.drawImage(image, 0,0,chart.width, chart.height);
        }
    }
}
Chart.plugins.register(bgPlugin);
```

To use the plugin, import it into the HTML file where the chart will be created:

```
<script src="../JavaScript/chartback.js"></script>
```

This plugin's configuration options can be set in the `options.plugins.chartback` key (`chartback` is the plugin's ID). This code is in `Extensions/ext-4-chartback.html`:

```
new Chart("chart", { type: 'bar', data: {...},
    options: {
        animation: {...},
        plugins: {
            chartback: {
                backgroundColor: 'white',
                backgroundImage: '../Images/mars.jpg'
            }
        }
    },
});
```

The chart will be drawn with an image behind. If you don't want the image, you can just set the `backgroundColor` and have a chart with an opaque background. The following screenshot shows a web page with the chart and the `.png` file loaded by an image viewer application:

Using a plugin that places a background image behind the chart. Code: *Extensions/ext-4-chartback.html*.

# Chart.js extensions

Besides plugins, Chart.js also includes an advanced extensions API where you can extend charts and axes. With this API, you can derive from existing chart types or create entirely new chart types by implementing the provided interfaces. This topic is beyond the scope of this book, but you can try out the examples provided in the official documentation or perhaps use some of the many popular extensions already available. A selection is listed in the official documentation.

# Summary

In this chapter, we explored several advanced Chart.js topics that you may rarely need, but give you more control over the look and feel of your charts, allowing a high degree of customization and the possibility of integrating it with standard web technologies and frameworks.

We learned how to configure tooltip and legend presentation and behavior using native Canvas options and custom HTML extensions, and how to create pages with multiple charts, mixed charts, and overlaying charts with other graphics using Canvas. We also wrote extensions for Chart.js using its programming API to generate a PNG version of a chart, and to create a simple plugin that adds a background image to a chart.

# References

**Books and websites**:

- Chart.js official documentation and samples: `https://www.chartjs.org/docs/latest/`
- Palette.js Color schemes: `http://google.github.io/palette.js/`
- Color brewer 2.0 by Cynthia Brewer: `http://colorbrewer2.org/`
- Patternomaly plugin: `https://github.com/ashiguruma/patternomaly`
- Datalabels plugin: `https://github.com/chartjs/chartjs-plugin-datalabels`
- Outlabels plugin: `https://github.com/Neckster/chartjs-plugin-piechart-outlabels`

**Data sources:**

- Volumes of the World's Oceans (based on ETOPO1):
  `Chapter03/Pages/BarChart1.html` **and others.** `https://www.ngdc.noaa.gov/mgg/global/etopo1_ocean_volumes.html`
- Geographical database: `Chapter02/Data/cities1000.csv`. GeoNames geographical database: `www.geonames.org`
- GeoJSON map of the world: `Chapter02/Data/world.geojson`. Simplified version adapted from `https://www.naturalearthdata.com`

# Other Books You May Enjoy

If you enjoyed this book, you may be interested in these other books by Packt:

**D3.js Quick Start Guide**
Matthew Huntington

ISBN: 9781789342383

- Build a scatter plot
- Build a bar graph
- Build a pie chart
- Build a force-directed graph
- Build a map
- Build interactivity into your graphs

**Mastering The Faster Web with PHP, MySQL, and JavaScript**
Andrew Caya

ISBN: 9781788392211

- Install, configure, and use profiling and benchmarking testing tools
- Understand how to recognize optimizable data structures and functions to effectively optimize a PHP7 application
- Diagnose bad SQL query performance and discover ways to optimize it
- Grasp modern SQL techniques to optimize complex SQL queries
- Identify and simplify overly complex JavaScript code
- Explore and implement UI design principles that effectively enhance the performance
- Combine web technologies to boost web server performance

# Leave a review - let other readers know what you think

Please share your thoughts on this book with others by leaving a review on the site that you bought it from. If you purchased the book from Amazon, please leave us an honest review on this book's Amazon page. This is vital so that other potential readers can see and use your unbiased opinion to make purchasing decisions, we can understand what our customers think about our products, and our authors can see your feedback on the title that they have worked with Packt to create. It will only take a few minutes of your time, but is valuable to other potential customers, our authors, and Packt. Thank you!

# Index

## A

animations
  about 219
  configuring 222, 225
area charts 87

## B

bar charts
  colors, configuring 66
  creating 61, 63, 65
  dataset configuration 66, 68
  fonts, configuring 66
  graphics context, setting up 61, 63
  responsiveness, configuring 66
bars
  stacking 83, 84
bevels 209, 210
bubble charts 130, 139, 141, 142

## C

callbacks
  configuring 184
Cartesian axes
  about 148, 149
  configuring 182, 183, 184
Cartesian grid lines 148, 149
Cartesian ticks 148, 149
Cartesian
  configuration options 146, 147
Cascading Style Sheets (CSS) 33, 35
category scales
  about 162
  axes, configuring 162, 164, 166
  grid lines, configuring 167
  ticks, configuring 166
chart defaults 193, 194

Chart.js
  about 58
  extending 254
  extensions 262
  installing 58, 60
  prototype methods 254, 256
  setting up 58, 60
charts
  selecting 7, 9, 10
  types 7
  updating 73, 75
  updating, with tooltips configuration 75
circumference
  modifying, in doughnut charts 123
  modifying, in pie charts 123
color palette generator 199, 201, 203
color schemes 199, 201, 203
colors
  about 198
  configuring 198
  configuring, for bar charts 66
configuration options
  for Cartesian 146, 147
  for pie charts 116
Content Delivery Network (CDN) 58
CSV
  about 42
  parsing 48
custom HTML tooltips
  about 238, 240
  advanced legend configuration 241
  labels, generating 241

## D

data formats
  about 42
  CSV 42

eXtensible Markup Language (XML) 43
  JSON 43, 44
data updates 219, 220, 221
data visualization library
  using 11
data visualization
  about 6
  chart, types 6
  creating, for Web 11, 13, 15
  creating, with Chart.js 15
data
  extracting 51
  extracting, with online tools 51, 52
  extracting, with XPath 52, 55
  loading 76, 79
  transforming 51
  transforming, with online tools 51, 52
dataset configuration
  for bar charts 66, 68
  for line charts 89, 91, 94
dataset properties
  for pie charts 115
default configuration
  about 187, 188
  chart defaults 193, 194
  global defaults 189, 191
  graphical elements 192, 193
  scale defaults 191, 192
delimiter-separated value (DSV) 42
Document Object Model (DOM) 13, 62
doughnut charts
  about 113
  circumference, changing 123
  data, preparing for 118, 121, 122
  with multiple datasets 125, 127

E

events
  about 222
  animations, configuring 222, 225
eXtensible Markup Language (XML) 43
external data files
  loading 44
  loading, with Fetch API 47
  loading, with JavaScript 45

loading, with JQuery 46
loading, with Web server 45
parsing 44
parsing, with Web server 45

F

Fetch API
  used, for loading external data files 47
fonts
  about 195
  configuring, for bar charts 66
  standard fonts, selecting 195, 196
  Web fonts, using 196

G

global default configurations 72
global defaults 189, 191
Goddard Institute for Space Studies (GISS)
  about 99
  reference 99
gradients 198, 203, 206
graphical elements 192, 193

H

horizontal bar chart
  about 79
  extra datasets, adding 80, 83
hovering interactions 232, 233
HTML DOM 30, 32
HTML legends 243, 244
HTML5 Canvas 37, 39, 40, 41

I

interactions 73, 219

J

JavaScript, for Chart.js
  about 20
  arrays 22, 24
  browser tools 20, 21
  data structures, used in charts 22
  functions 27
  objects 28, 29
  strings 25

types 21
variables 21
JavaScript
used, for loading external data files 45
JQuery
fundamentals 36, 37
used, for loading external data files 46
JSON 43, 44
JSON file
parsing 47

# L

labels
adding 210, 211, 213, 214
larger datasets
working with 76
legend configuration 241
legend labels
generating 241
legends 211, 214
line charts
about 87
creating 88
data, loading from external files 99, 100, 102
dataset configuration 89, 91, 94
options configuration 95, 96
with more than one dataset 96, 98

# M

map
displaying 49, 50
mixed charts
about 248
canvas, overlaying 250, 251, 253
multiple charts
displaying 245
rendering, on one page 245, 248
multiple datasets
working with 76
multiple files
loading 48

# N

numeric Cartesian scales
about 149

axis titles, configuring 153
grid lines, configuring 158, 160, 161
linear scales 150, 151
logarithmic scales 151, 152
ticks, configuring 154, 156, 157

# O

options configuration
about 68, 70
fonts, configuring 70, 71
for line charts 95, 96
text, configuring 70, 71

# P

patterns 206, 208
pie charts
about 113
circumference, changing 123
configuration options 116
creating 113
data, preparing for 118, 121, 122
dataset properties 115
values, showing in slices 116, 118
with multiple datasets 125, 127
plugins
creating 256, 259, 261
polar area charts 127, 129

# R

radar charts 108, 109, 111, 112
radial scales
about 175
angle lines, configuring 180, 181
grids lines, configuring 180, 181
point labels, configuring 176, 177
ticks, configuring 177, 179
responsiveness colors
configuring, for bar charts 66

# S

scale defaults 191, 192
scale service
configuring 185
scales

configuring 145, 181
scatter charts
  about 130
  creating 130, 133
  used, for revealing correlations 133, 135, 136
  with large quantities of data 137, 138
scheme 199
scriptable properties
  about 234, 235
  tooltip callbacks 236, 237
shadows 198, 209, 210
stacked area charts 104, 106, 107

## T

text elements
  adding 210
time scales
  about 168, 169
  axes, configuring 172
  grid lines, configuring 175
  ticks, configuring 173, 175
  time format, configuring 170, 171
titles

  about 215
  labels, adding to bars 215, 218
  labels, adding to lines 215, 218
  labels, adding to slices 215, 218
tooltip callbacks 236, 237
tooltip configuration 227, 230, 231
tooltips 73
transition
  about 73
  duration 73

## W

Web fonts
  using 196
Web server
  used, for loading external data files 45
  used, for parsing external data files 45
web-based visualizations 11

## X

XPath
  used, for extracting data 52, 55